D0982640

WITHDRAWN

By the Author

The Mythology of Imperialism

OUT
OF THE

WHALE

Growing Up in the American Left

AN AUTOBIOGRAPHY BY
JONAH RASKIN

NEW YORK   links   LONDON

Standard Book Number: 0-8256-3039-8
Library of Congress Catalog Card Number: 74-78870

Distributed by Quick Fox, Inc.
33 West 60 Street, New York 10023

Book and cover design by Sun-Up Studio

This book
is for
the
Raskins.

I would like to thank the 89th Street and UR families, especially Stew and Robert, and also the Geismars, Marge Piercy, Doris Lessing, Dana Biberman, Eric Foner, Marcia Peterson, the men's group and Danny Moses.

CONTENTS

A section of photographs follows page 138.

Some names and dates have been changed.

INTRODUCTION

JONAH
AND THE
WHALE

Jonah is walking alone by the Red Sea. His back is bent, his white robes are blown by the wind and he squints his eyes to keep out the dust. His bare feet are burned by the hot sand.

God is in Heaven. He looks down to earth, sees Jonah, cups his hands around his mouth and gives him the Word. He tells Jonah, his prophet, that he must go to Nineveh, the evil city. His mission is to tell the people of Nineveh that destruction is coming, the last judgment, the end of the world.

Jonah is afraid; he doesn't want to go, even though it's his destiny to go. The people of Nineveh aren't his people. They are, in fact, his enemies, and the enemies of his people, the Hebrews. "Why should I preach to them? What about my own safety?" he asks. Jonah runs away from Nineveh, violates the law, flees from authority and becomes a fugitive from God. He steals aboard a ship and hides in the darkness.

But he can't hide from the Lord. A storm breaks out. The thunder, lightning and the angry sea terrify the sailors. Water pours over the sides, the ship is nearly destroyed. Jonah crouches in the dark hold of the ship. He has brought the sailors bad luck, and he knows that he's at fault, that he's done wrong. He deliberates carefully, decides he must make amends, climbs onto the deck, and tells the sailors he's responsible for the storm. They cast him into the sea. The waves subside, the storm ends, the sailors are saved, and peace is restored. By surrendering himself to the angry waters he calms the waters. By submitting himself to the destructive element he saves himself, the ship, and the sailors.

Now Jonah is in the ocean, carried by the swift current. In the distance, on the curve of the horizon, he sees a small black dot. It comes closer and closer, growing larger and larger. It's a monster. Leviathan opens his mouth wide and swallows Jonah. For three days and three nights he's a prisoner inside the cage of the whale. Old Jonah dies and is reborn.

Then the whale spits him up; he's resurrected. Jonah emerges from the whale's dark belly onto the shores of light, ready to descend on evil Nineveh. Jonah is now one with the whale, the sea, the universe. He freely accepts his own destiny.

He walks day and night to reach the city. When he arrives at the gate a soldier holds up a torch to see the face of this stranger and admits him to Nineveh. The next day, in the marketplace, Jonah brings them the Word of God. Unless there's a reformation and a new city, he says, the old, corrupt city will be destroyed. Jonah terrifies the Ninevites. They abandon their wicked ways, reject violence, dismantle their empire and reform. God spares them. The city is saved and given new life.

Having completed his mission Jonah leaves Nineveh. He has received no thanks and no reward. He is tired and sits down outside the walls of the city under the hot sun. He squints his eyes to keep out the dust. God, in Heaven, looks down at Jonah and sees that he's uncomfortable. He takes pity on Jonah and grows a gourd to give him shade. And for a brief while Jonah is comfortable. He falls asleep and wakes refreshed. But God reaches down from Heaven and plants a worm in the gourd. The worm eats the gourd, the gourd withers, dies, and again Jonah bakes in the hot sun. Now Jonah is angry with God. But God tells him he has no reason to be enraged. He's God, all time and space, the universe itself. He can threaten the destruction of Nineveh, and he can spare Nineveh. He can grow a gourd and destroy the gourd. And that's the way of the universe. Jonah nods his head. He understands that freedom is the recognition of necessity.

My name is Jonah too. This is a book about me. It's Jonah's book. It's about prophets, fugitives, prisoners, the law, the city, the storm, and peace. It's about Leviathan, and the Ninevehs we inhabit with our friends and lovers. It's my testament.

CHAPTER
ONE
NAMES

"We're going to take a new name," my father said. "It's just for the summer. When we return home we'll be the Raskins again as always. It should be easy for you to remember our new last name because it's like my first name. For the next month we're going to be the Samuels. Think you can remember?"

My father was sitting behind the steering wheel of our car, talking as he drove, peering out at the highway, and then turning around to look at us in the back seat.

"Sure," my brother Dan said.

"Yes, but what's it for? Is it a game?" I asked, leaning over my father's shoulder so that I was almost talking directly into his right ear.

"Well, no, it's not exactly a game," he said. "The place we're going to is a resort for progressive people like us. The government doesn't like us because of our ideas. If they knew we were there they'd probably see to it that I couldn't earn a living. I might even have to go to jail. You wouldn't want that would you?" Sam turned his head to the right so that he could gauge my response.

"No." I shook my head from side to side.

"That's why we're going to be the Samuels. It's for our own protection. Government men go to the resort, look at the names in the book, and then visit the people at their homes. They ask them questions about their friends, their beliefs, their money, and sometimes when they don't answer the questions they put them in jail. By taking the name Samuels we'll be making it a bit harder for them to find us."

"Could I have a new first name too?" I asked. Names were very important to me because ours were so unusual. My parents were not religious but they thumbed carefully through the Bible and named me Jonah, and my brothers Daniel and Adam. The Old Testament was the first real book in our lives because it contained the story of the prophet Jonah, the Book of Daniel, and Genesis. Adam and Eve had been expelled from the Garden of Eden, brave Daniel had trusted in the Lord in the Lion's Den, and Jonah tried to escape the Lord and the Lord made a giant fish to swallow him. My name conjured up images of Nineveh, the evil city, the Leviathan (which I confused with the whale that swallowed Pinocchio), the ship, the crew, the storm, the gourd and the worm, the eye of God. Raskin too was a potent name. Sam told us that it was a derivation from Raz Khan, a central Asian word which meant a relative of the king. My royal ancestors, I imagined, had looted and burned their way westward into Europe along with Genghis Khan and his hordes.

A new name was important; it meant becoming a new person.

"Do you have a new name in mind?" Sam asked.

"I was thinking about Edgar," I said.

"Why Edgar?" my mother asked.

"You know the man on television who makes Charlie McCarthy, the puppet, talk."

"You mean Edgar Bergen, the ventriloquist?"

"Yes. I'm going to learn to keep my lips sealed, throw my voice, and impersonate other people. My voice will seem like it's coming from under beds, inside closets, and from behind doors."

"That's a stupid idea. I don't like it," Dan said, rolling up the window so that the wind wouldn't blow his hair about.

"You're just jealous," I said. "I'll know how to throw my voice, and you won't."

"No. It's not that. It's the name Edgar."

"What's wrong with Edgar?" I glared at Dan.

"Didn't you ever hear of J. Edgar Hoover, dummy!"

"He's not a dummy. He just forgot," Millie said, as she turned around in the front seat. "Now, just sit back and relax because we're almost at the resort."

"I think that you'd better forget about a new first name. Jonah Samuels is just fine," my father said.

"I forgot about J. Edgar Hoover. Honest I did. But someday I do want a new first name too." I looked at Millie for sympathy and forgiveness.

"How about Zeke?" my father said.

"Now you're making fun of me. That's not fair."

"Zeke, Zeke, Zeke," Dan shouted. "I see a Zeke." Then Sam and Dan started laughing and the back seat of the car shook so much it felt as if we were going over a bumpy road. I was angry at them, but I also felt silly for introducing *Edgar* to everyone in the first place. But it *had* seemed like a good idea. Edgar Bergen wasn't like Edgar Hoover. And it wasn't as odd a name as Jonah. Jonah made me feel like I was wearing a bright orange hat in the school playground, surrounded by kids wearing gray hats. I wanted to try on a gray hat, to see if it would make a difference.

We were driving on Route Six in our new Dodge station wagon, approaching Monticello, New York. The Dodge was the most expensive car my parents had ever bought. It was big and sturdy and made me feel that it belonged to an embassy; it gave a feeling of security on dangerous hills and sharp curves.

It was August of 1952. Our vacation was half over. July had been a disaster. We were on our way in the safe Dodge to a resort for radicals, known officially as "The Fur and Leather Workers Union Resort" (the Furriers, for short) but usually referred to as "White Lake Lodge." The Resort was on White Lake—a short distance from Woodstock, N.Y.—and the name White Lake Lodge sounded innocuous and innocent. Which name you used depended on whom you were talking to.

We had been driving for weeks all over New York State—starting from home, Huntington, Long Island, and going to the far western tip of the state, near Jamestown. We visited with relatives in Binghamton who owned a shoe store, saw the Baseball Hall of Fame at Cooperstown, slept in motels, ate at diners, and stopped at gas stations to pee. We were vagabonds, nomads. We lugged our belongings in and out of the Dodge and in and out of mildewed rooms, washed our clothes in coin-operated laundries, collected soap bars and matchbooks from the restaurants and motels on the road, and for fun kept a record of the license plates we noticed from far-off states like Wyoming and Arizona.

For weeks it seemed like we had no resting place, no calm, no time to unpack suitcases, or explore neighborhoods. Sam had driven every mile of the journey, without an accident, flat tire or motor trouble. The Dodge performed wonderfully. Millie read the maps, gave directions, got us lost and was abused, put us back on the road and received no thanks.

Sam was forty-two years old, a young-looking, stocky and powerful man; his physical force made me think of a sledgehammer. There were deep lines on his cheeks, scars on his forehead and on his nose because he had been in a bad bicycle

3

accident. He had been in the hospital for several days; when he came home his face was scraped and bloodied and I hardly recognized him. The story of his life was written on his granite-like complexion. Millie was thirty-six years old. She had green cat eyes and a shiny face which looked like a pinkish bar of soap lying on the ledge of a porcelain tub. She was nervous, usually quiet, and when she spoke it was to caution Sam to be careful, to drive slowly. Dan was two years younger than me; he was more relaxed and more graceful. His face was fuller, his eyes less narrow. We often fought each other with our fists, and sometimes with knives, broken soda bottles or rocks. It was difficult to sit together side by side in the back seat. Adam, the youngest, the baby, was two years old, the center of attention and everyone's favorite. I was ten and a half years old. I looked into the rear-view mirror. I saw my short black hair, big nose, the cleft in my chin, slanty, Oriental-looking eyes, and floppy ears.

We were on our way to White Lake Lodge, to the Furriers. But that wasn't our original destination. We had changed our plans. At the start of July we had intended to spend the summer on a farm in western New York. Sam and Millie had responded to an advertisement in *The New York Times* which promised an exciting summer for the whole family, living with a farmer, his wife and kids. We arrived at the farm after ten days of hard traveling. There were pigs in the front yard and cornhusks in the mud. The farmer's wife met us on the front porch and introduced herself.

"And you must be the Raskins," she said smiling. Sam and Millie introduced themselves. The woman invited us in. We walked up the wooden steps. She showed us the dining room, where we would all eat together, and the kitchen where fat flies stuck to the brown flypaper, and then led the way, talking all the time, up a long carpeted staircase, the longest staircase I'd ever seen. I held on to the rail. It was steep and dangerous. There was a funny smell of wet and dirt, of rooms with windows which had never been opened. It smelled bad. It was the smell of something rotting, I thought, or maybe dead. It was the smell of poverty, and I was smelling it for the first time. At the top of the flight of stairs the woman opened a door.

"This will be the young man's room, I expect," she said, looking down at me, and then into Millie's sunlit face.

"I was expecting something else," my mother said, rubbing her fingers over a dusty chest of drawers. The window shades were stained yellow; there was a cobweb in one corner, and the room was dominated by a large four-posted bed covered with a white bedspread. On the wall was a framed needlepoint sampler that read "God Bless This Home."

"Isn't it nice?" the woman asked me. But I heard my mother say, "Come along Jonah." She was already half-way down the stairs, before I was even aware that she had left the room. I followed after her, nearly tripping on the way down, but reached the ground floor safely. The sun was setting. I could see it through the gauze curtains in the living room. The TV set was on, but black and white lines crisscrossed and marred the picture. It was difficult to see the images. The man and his son were sitting catty-corner on an old, dusty easy chair staring at the TV. So far they had not said one word, and they had not moved.

"I'll be putting up a new aerial to improve the reception." Those were the man's first words. He apologized for the poor picture. "Right now we only get two channels, but you'll be able to see all the programs from the city soon as I get to work on the roof."

"Is that Hopalong Cassidy?" I asked, squinting my eyes, edging toward the TV and looking for a place to sit.

"Sure is. Plenty exciting too."

"Jonah." My mother called out to me. "Don't sit down just yet, dear. Come out to the car for a moment." She was standing next to the woman who was resting her hands on her hips, looking down at the floor, and pointing the toes of her right foot like a ballet dancer. They had been talking but I was so absorbed in Hopalong Cassidy that I heard nothing of their conversation. Millie took my hand. We walked out the front door, down the steps, past the pigs and corncobs.

"How come Dad's in the car?" I asked.

"We're not going to stay here. Your father thinks we won't have a good time. There's no lake or pond and you know how much you like to swim."

"Yes. But I'm so tired. Can't we stop some place and rest for a while?" She opened the back door of the car and I got in. I didn't want to crawl back into the Dodge as I had done so many times before. The woman had showed me *my* room. It smelled funny, but still I saw myself living and sleeping there. In the house I could unpack, stretch out, unwind, and watch TV. I didn't quite understand why we were leaving, why the farm was unacceptable, why we had come so far only to go back.

My father turned the key in the ignition. The motor started. The car lurched ahead. I looked out the back window at the farmhouse. It grew smaller and smaller in the evening dusk. I was sad, but somehow I trusted that my parents were right. They knew what was best. I wouldn't have been happy there, I told myself, but I wanted a farmhouse where I could have a perfect summer.

At first we had no alternative destination. Our summer plans collapsed. So that night and for the next few nights we rented a cabin in a state park. The wood fire in the living room made it cozy and warm. And the cedar paneling smelled good. During the day we swam in a lake and explored the woods, and along the riverbed we discovered fossils of plants and insects which had been alive millions of years ago. I gathered them up and felt that they were as precious as diamonds or sapphires. The ferns of long ago looked like the green ferns on the riverbed. The imprint was delicate, and the little lines were perfectly preserved. And the buzzing, darting dragonfly overhead looked like the imprint of the ancient insect preserved in the cold, frozen slime.

"This is evidence. It's clear proof," Sam said, "that this whole area was very different from what it is now." He was teaching us again, giving us a lecture—though we didn't know the word and didn't resent his "talks." "Much of this area was submerged under water. The climate was subtropical. Then the Ice Age came; great glaciers from the North Pole pushed millions of tons of earth, like giant bulldozers, and created mountains, rivers, valleys. The ice fields got about this far south, and then they melted. The mountains all around us are the mounds of earth the glaciers deposited here."

"How old are they?" I asked.

"I don't know for sure, but these mountains are among the oldest in North America. See how flat they are. They weren't always like that. Once they were tall and pointy, but the wind, rain and snow worked away at the face of those mountains for millions of years until they became rough and craggy, and today they have no sharp peaks at all."

All around it was green and warm. There were bright birds in the trees. I put the fossils in my pockets, and we walked along the old riverbed back to the cabin.

Then my parents decided to go to White Lake Lodge. We left the park early one morning, drove for two more days along narrow roads overlooking deep gorges, descending into valleys, climbing mountains. Finally, we reached the Catskills. We were approaching the Fur Workers Resort. I wanted it to be our final resting place, but I didn't want to be disappointed again. Maybe my parents wouldn't like it. I pretended that I wasn't interested or curious. As we got closer and closer to the resort Millie became more and more nervous. She fidgeted with the dial on the radio, picked up the newspaper, glanced over it, and put it down again. Several times she reminded us that our last name was Samuels. We assured her we wouldn't forget. Then, suddenly, just as I was about to doze off in the back seat she shouted, "Here it is." My father immediately turned the car off the highway to the left and passed through two stone turrets on either side of an asphalt road. He had done it swiftly and smoothly as if we were the good guys in a movie, escaping from the villains.

I didn't fully understand what was happening. But I was apprehensive. I didn't want to be caught, exposed, punished. I wanted us to escape. I wanted to be safe, but I knew that what we were doing was unusual and unconventional.

"I don't think anyone saw us," my mother said. She was more relaxed now.

"There was no car parked at the entrance, but we don't know for sure they aren't here. Sometimes they hide in the woods," Sam said.

"Who's hiding?" Dan asked.

"The FBI. Like you and Jonah they take down the license plate numbers of cars. But for them it's not a game. They trace the license plate, find out who owns the car and investigate them. Even if they don't see our faces; even if they don't know our name, if they get the license plate they'll find out who we are."

"Couldn't we cover the license plate?" I asked.

"That's illegal," Sam said. "If a cop saw us driving on the highway without a license plate, or if the license plate was covered, he'd stop us, question me, and at the very least he'd give me a ticket for violating the law. If you don't have a license plate

7

you arouse suspicions. That's just what we don't want to do."

"Couldn't we have a license plate for home and on the road and take it off only when we come here?" Dan asked.

"No. We can't really do that," Sam said. "But in a way we're doing something like that by taking a new name. At home and on the road we're the Raskins; but when we're at White Lake Lodge we're the Samuels."

"I understand."

Sam lifted his foot off the accelerator. The car slowed down. It was quiet. There were deep woods on both sides of the road.

"Do you think they got our number?" Dan asked.

"Probably not," Millie said.

The car came to a stop in the parking lot, between two white lines. Sam took the key out of the ignition. The vibrations ceased. The roar of the road stopped—though there was a faint echo of tires pounding the pavement—and it was still.

"I'll go over to the office and register," Sam said to Millie. She was slightly groggy. The weeks on the road showed on her soft skin. Then she sat up and snapped out of her daze. Adam was asleep on her shoulder.

"I don't want to wake him just yet," she whispered. "He hasn't slept much recently."

"Can I go with you?" I asked.

"Come on," Sam said. We walked across a well-manicured lawn. Vacationers were sitting in folding chairs. We opened the screen door and entered the office. It was big, modern, clean. There was linoleum tile, a large fan, new easy chairs, spotless windows. It seemed fresh. It was my first big hotel and I liked it; it was superior to the old, musty-smelling farm.

"Hello. I'm Mr. Samuels. I phoned and made a reservation. We're five."

"I'll see what I have for you," the man behind the desk said, taking a cigar from his mouth. He wasn't as nice as the woman on the farm. She had wanted to please. And he didn't, it seemed. But he gave us two rooms with a bath.

Sam picked up the fountain pen on the desk, turned the book around and signed his name. I stepped up close and watched. There in black ink on white paper was written Sam Samuels. The man behind the desk didn't ask for identification papers or a driver's license. He assumed that

Sam Samuels was really standing before him.

"This your boy, Mr. Samuels?"

"Yes. This is my oldest son, Jonah."

"Your car out back?"

"It's the Dodge station wagon."

"I'll send the porter for your luggage. You're in 2-A." He handed Sam the keys. "Now, if you'll pay in advance for the first week. Cash or check?"

"Cash."

Outside the office I poked Sam in the ribs with my finger.

"That was neat," I said.

"It was necessary," he said. "It wasn't hard. You could do it if you had to."

"I'm not sure I could," I said. "I'd be afraid."

A month later we left. It was a wonderful summer. We ate our meals in a restaurant three times a day. There were waiters. We played baseball and went swimming in White Lake. Once Sam and Millie took me to see the entertainment in the evening. There were singers who stood in a spotlight on the stage, a pianist and a comedian. The people in the audience applauded. Then just before we went back to our room we all stood up and sang together. The spotlight was on the audience, on us. Everyone sang the last song. It was the most moving. Hundreds of people sang together, with expressions of both courage and fear on their faces:

> And before I'd be a slave
> I'd be buried in my grave
> And go home to my Lord
> And be free.

It made me think. These people said that they would rather be dead than be in chains. Did they really mean it? Who was the Lord they would go to? Was he the Lord of Daniel and Jonah? How could they be free if they were dead and buried?

Once at the dinner table I had forgotten to say Samuels and instead said the forbidden word—Raskin. My brother Dan heard me, but no one else noticed. The word didn't register on their minds. Dan didn't yell at me, and he didn't say anything to Sam. He just looked at me, nodded his head and smiled. I don't think it did any harm.

Besides the fossils I had gathered, I took back with me to Huntington books and records about Negroes, Russia, prehistoric times, Abe Lincoln, baseball. But the ride home was sad. I was taking new things to Huntington, but I felt that I was leaving more behind. We were going back to Huntington, but it didn't seem like home. I had mixed feelings about going back to school and becoming Jonah Raskin again. At one point—I don't remember exactly where it was on the road from the resort to Huntington—Sam became very serious. For most of the summer he had been relaxed. But now his voice changed. It sounded urgent and tense.

"I don't think that you boys should tell your school friends about White Lake Lodge since it's run by the Fur Workers Union. Some people who want to destroy unions and hurt working people and progressives say it's run by Communists. Your school friends won't know anything about the Fur Workers Union. But their parents might, and if they do they'd make life unpleasant for you. They probably won't let you play with their kids. I think it's best if you say you were at an ordinary hotel in the Catskills—like the Concord, or Grossinger's."

"I understand," Dan said.

I felt that the summer was covered over. It sank beneath the surface. No one would be able to see where we had been or what we had done. It was a secret. It was hidden, but at the same time it was alive inside me.

"Can we go back one day?" I asked. I didn't want the wave of normality and conformity to keep it buried forever.

"Some day. Yes. Some day we'll come again. But you shouldn't think about that now. School starts in a week, and that'll be exciting too."

CHAPTER
TWO
HAPPY FAMILIES

I. EXCAVATING

The fossils of ferns and insects radiated mystery. They were my prize possessions, a link between me and the origin of things, and far, far more significant than bubblegum baseball trading cards. They were labeled and on display in the living room, our home museum, along with arrowheads, Indian pots and Mexican statues. I collected the fossils in July and August, during summer vacations when my father and I, two hot scavengers, walked together along dry riverbeds in upstate New York or along the coast of New England. We were detectives overturning sweaty stones, digging in the clay, excavating prehistoric life. Nothing was more exciting than trekking for fossils—except perhaps peering through a telescope at the night sky. Fossils beneath the earth's surface were evidence of vanished species—one layer beneath another, life piled upon life. The sky held the promise of new life in space, one universe behind another. I'd dream about the solar system, the planets spinning in darkness, the loneliness of the little earth in the infinite galaxy, and hope that there were friends on other worlds.

What had lived was dead. What had been visible was invisible. What was free was trapped, but through no fault of its own. The species were not to blame. The earth itself was guilty, for it changed, the climate altered, plants, animals, insects died, fell into the hot mud, were compressed, and now millions of years later only their imprint was recorded in cold stone. I spent long afternoons in the Museum of Natural History circling round and round the reconstructed skeletons of dinosaurs, giant creatures who had once wandered the earth freely.

On winter days I stretched out on the living room floor, thumbed through books about prehistoric man, fixated on one illustration—a mastodon frozen solid, preserved perfectly for thousands of years in a Siberian ice field. The dead came back to

11

life; warmth, the thaw, unlocking the past, conveying frozen creatures into the present.

Growing up in the 1950's felt like living in a New Ice Age; McCarthyism wasn't simply a new "ism," a political idea, a committee, it was a geological era—the age of the Cold War. The climate of the 1930's, which had allowed radicals to grow, teach, write, organize, be fruitful and multiply, had vanished. The polar regions were everywhere. The terrain had changed. It was no longer the America of *Grapes of Wrath,* of dust bowl refugees, of sit-in strikes at Ford plants in Dearborn, Michigan. Main Street looked different; highways replaced dirt roads, suburban developments were built where forests and meadows had been. The old inhabitants fled and lurked in dark places. They departed from sunny Hollywood and went abroad to find a better climate in Paris and London.

Like the mastodon, Reds were becoming extinct. Some had adapted to the new conditions and only slightly resembled their old selves. They developed armor or tried to fly. Others burrowed deep down to hide. Some, the informers, looked like mutants, deformed men and women. Maybe one day Reds—creatures from a bygone geological era—would be preserved in a museum. Visitors would look at them in a glass case, the way they looked at stuffed animals or Iroquois Indians in the glass cases in the Museum of Natural History. Scenes of Richard Nixon interrogating Alger Hiss would be presented in a waxwork museum.

From Washington the ice flowed, drove Reds into hiding, into jails, and into the grave. The ice men in Washington sought the extermination of a species; riverbeds dried up, crops failed, deserts covered the land. Extinct volcanoes erupted, continents drifted apart, oceans covered dry land. East and West were driven apart; Reds in government and universities departed, leaving wastelands, and earth creatures were submerged under water. It was the hour of the mole.

II. ROSENBERGS AND RASKINS

Julius and Ethel Rosenberg, creatures from the 1930's and 1940's, were rendered extinct in 1953 in the electric chair. They were burned. When ice couldn't freeze them, when floods wouldn't wash them away, fire destroyed them. They were a strange white species, bound to a red hot chair. The species

12

watched and was terrified, stampeded in fright. I was hysterical, and I was only eleven years old. I didn't know Julius and Ethel or their two sons Michael and Robert, but the electric current passed through my cells too.

The Raskins were like the Rosenbergs, except that Julius and Ethel were dead and my parents were alive. The trial and the execution of the Rosenbergs was the first public, historic event which I felt wasn't distant or external—a headline in *The New York Times*—but which transformed my own feelings, jarred my metabolism, threw me off balance. I experienced it biologically and chemically. I was threatened by the case. I felt vulnerable. I was terrorized by both the state, which had murdered, and by the Rosenbergs, because they had established a code of behavior beyond anyone's reach. They had chosen to remain silent, proclaim their innocence and die, rather than give names, confess their guilt, and live. Their behavior was inexplicable, unfathomable. They were middle-class fanatics. They were unhysterical, and their failure to become hysterical made me even more hysterical. An unheroic, ordinary couple had acted heroically. Julius was no Humphrey Bogart, Ethel was no Lauren Bacall, but they acted as bravely as stars in a Hollywood movie. Only the audience didn't know the most wonderful truth about America. Our real heroes and heroines weren't on the movie screen, but on death row in Sing Sing. To my high school teachers and friends Julius and Ethel were villains. "I hope they fry those Jew Commies," a classmate had said, "and teach those reds a lesson." I listened calmly, tried to show no emotion, to remain cool, but inside hysteria exploded. To act as Julius and Ethel had acted brought no applause, no stardom, no compassion, but only hatred, anger, denunciations. They died alone, with integrity, billed by the state as despicable spies. Heroism in the 1950's was silent and secret.

The choices they faced were painful. I discovered that choices weren't simple. Life and the truth, death and falsehood were inextricably connected in the moral melodrama of Julius and Ethel Rosenberg. They had chosen the truth, and truth meant death. I imagined myself in similar circumstances in a prison cell, facing a wall, offered a choice. If I chose falsehood I'd live, but I'd have a death in life, I'd live with remorse and guilt. The Rosenbergs focused the painful choices.

Even at eleven, I believed that Julius and Ethel were innocent,

13

that they were framed, that they had not stolen the secret of the A-bomb, had not given it to the Russians. In a country preoccupied with secrets and secrecy, I was in possession of a secret truth, and that truth was that there was no A-bomb secret. Daydreaming in my room in the hot summer of 1953 I'd recreate the trial—*The People* vs. *The Rosenbergs* in the Court of Jonah. I sat impassively behind a desk, dressed in black robes, holding a gavel, listening to the arguments of the defense and the prosecution. I deliberated carefully, pounded the gavel and ruled "not guilty."

When I asked my father why the Rosenbergs were tried and executed, he said that during the Korean War it was necessary to whip up anti-Communist hysteria, to make the American people fear and hate the Reds, and accept the necessity of witch-hunts, purges, investigations at home, and a war in Asia thousands of miles away. The government wanted the people to believe that there was a fifth column inside the U.S., an army of traitors, sapping the vital strength of the nation, and syphoning it off to Russia. To stop the flow of atom secrets the pushers had to be killed. In Russia they tried, banished, and executed people who were against the state, so my teachers said. But to my way of thinking they did the same in America.

"Russians gather secretly at night in cold basements," my social studies teacher said, "and listen to messages of hope broadcast on Radio Free Europe. It's the only voice of freedom in their lives. If they're caught, they're sent to Siberia." In Huntington reading radical books and listening to left-wing records I felt like the dissident Russians in Moscow and Kiev. If we were caught we'd be sent away.

I asked my father, "Why isn't my teacher outraged about the fact that we have to listen secretly to 'subversive' records about Joseph McCarthy? Why doesn't he worry about us here instead of Russians halfway around the world?"

"They're like the monarchs of Europe before Columbus sailed to America," my father said. "They've created a mythological earth where there's no freedom in Russia and total freedom in America. They live in a flat world. We need a new voyage of discovery."

If innocent people like the Rosenbergs could be found guilty and executed, then my parents too could be found guilty and executed. But who was guilty and who was innocent? What was guilt and what was innocence? My parents weren't Russian spies, but they were sympathetic to Russia, and in the eyes of America that was guilt. Besides my grandparents were Russian. I had Russian blood in me. I was guilty. When I was ten, my father gave me a book with a red cover, imprinted with a hammer and sickle, entitled *Russia*. He bought the book from a radical bookseller in the city. On the last page there was a map of Asia and North America, which showed how close Russian Siberia was to Alaska. When the Bering Straits froze you could walk across a bridge of ice, from America to Asia, as the Eskimo fishermen in fact did. At the bottom of the page there was a drawing of an American boy about my age wearing a white T-shirt and sneakers, his arm around a little Russian girl wearing a peasant dress and boots and holding flowers in her hands. It was one of my favorite books and I brought it to school to show to my favorite teacher. He wasn't a radical, but I wanted to share my deepest feelings with him. I also wanted to be his prize pupil, his pet. Each week I tried to impress him with tales about my extraordinary feats of daring. I began to make up stories. I lied to him because my real life wasn't exciting enough. My final feat was to show him a book I knew no other student in the class would ever bring him; it was a rare treasure. I knew I was taking a risk, for my possession of the book would make me suspect. Perhaps I wasn't a loyal, patriotic American; perhaps possession of the book was proof that I was a Red spy. But I decided to take the risk. It was painful to go to class everyday, to have a close relationship with my teacher, and yet to hide so much from him.

Mr. Lee had photographs on the bulletin board which showed American nuclear tests in the South Pacific, "the mushroom cloud," as he called it, rising into the tropical sky. He was a patriotic American, a veteran of World War II, with a scar on his neck, where a Nazi bullet had struck his vocal cord, and a speech defect because of the wound. One day after class I handed him the book. Almost as I did it I wanted to take it back, because it was handing over evidence. My fingerprints were on the red book with a hammer and a sickle on the cover. Of course, Mr. Lee found the book fascinating. There was no other book like it, and he regarded me in a new light. But when he asked me where I had gotten the book I knew that I couldn't tell the truth, that I had to lie. "My father bought it at Macy's for Christmas," I said, placing the guilt on my father.

"Then why," Mr. Lee asked, turning the book to the back inside cover, "does it say 'The Progressive Book Store, New York City'?"

"I don't know," I said, trying desperately to look innocent but knowing that he knew I was lying. "I've never heard of the Progressive Book Store." He handed me the book but didn't ask me any more questions. I was in a perilous situation; Mr. Lee could label me a Red before the rest of the class, then everyone would hate me.

Those were my worst fears. Fortunately they never came true, and Mr. Lee never again mentioned the book, or the *progressive* book store. And yet I was not at ease in his class. I didn't forget that Mr. Lee had evidence and if he wanted to he could use it against me. But I guess he wasn't a mean man; he didn't bring the inquisition to his classroom and didn't set up a mini-committee, and didn't become a grade school Joe McCarthy. I guess he was like a lot of ordinary Americans who didn't like the Reds but didn't go along with investigators either. I assumed that Mr. Lee knew my secret identity and that he knew that I knew that he knew. It was an unspoken but fundamental assumption in our sixth-grade relationship. The next year, my first year of junior high, I went to another school, left Mr. Lee behind and started again with a new teacher and a clean slate.

I grew up knowing that it was often necessary to lie, but it was difficult to lie; one was punished for lying, and parents and teachers stressed the necessity of honesty. Even when my mother answered the telephone and said that my father, who was sitting beside her, wasn't home, it hurt. But when my father lied I knew that it was for survival. When we spent the summer of 1952 at the Fur Workers Resort we took the name Samuels. My brother Daniel and I were afraid, but we assumed that Sam was right. We were taking the name Samuels as a shield. There was nothing criminal about vacationing in the Catskills, but to the FBI it *was* criminal, and our names would be added to their files. When we left White Lake Lodge, Sam told us not to say anything to our school friends or their parents. "If you do," he said, "you'll probably lose their friendship, and we'll be isolated and harassed." We knew that his prognosis wasn't fanciful because

16

someone had set a fire in our back yard the previous fall, the leaves had burned, the porch had caught fire, and the firemen, in putting the blaze out had hacked and chopped away at the house, leaving a gaping hole. Someone had thrown a rock into the window with a note attached. "Get out Jews. Go back to Russia!" A conservative lawyer in the neighborhood and a business rival of my father's had investigated his ties to the American Labor Party and Henry A. Wallace, the Progressive Party candidate for president in 1948. My father was called a Red. Sam was well known in town; he was born in Huntington and people had known him since he was a kid, so they didn't think of him as a dangerous Red, but still he was afraid of being disbarred and not being able to make a living. So we were cautious. Whenever we needed to be secret, we became the Samuels.

I believed the Rosenbergs, like us, were not guilty as Red spies, but I believed they, like us, were guilty for being radicals. They insisted that they were not on trial for their political beliefs, that Communism wasn't the real issue, and yet to me it was. They were simultaneously guilty and innocent, as we were simultaneously guilty and innocent. The Rosenbergs denied that they were Communists, and yet they were executed as Communists.

Whatever secrets we had, and whatever lies we made up to tell school friends, teachers and neighbors, they were insignificant when compared with the lies and deceptions the U.S. government offered about the Rosenbergs. To charge them with stealing A-bomb secrets was a cosmic lie. The notion that American citizens, an ordinary couple from the Lower East Side, would work for the Soviet Union was a cruel joke on the universe of nuclear particles.

But the Rosenbergs were tried, not for specific acts—the government's case was as flimsy as a jello box top—but for their beliefs. And our beliefs were like their beliefs. The Raskins were almost a mirror image of the Rosenbergs. Like them we sang Leadbelly's and Pete Seeger's songs, like "The Peat Bog Soldiers," which was written in Germany by Jewish radicals like us whom the Nazis wanted to exterminate. We protested the lynching of Negroes like Willie McGee in the South. Like the Rosenbergs we rooted for the Brooklyn Dodgers, and our favorite player was Jackie Robinson. Like the Rosenbergs we read the Declaration of Independence on July 4th and posted it on the wall. It was our revolutionary manifesto. Like Julius, Sam spoke of the progressive tradition in American history. Sam, like Julius, said he was loyal to America. My father, like Michael Rosenberg's father, had protested the treatment of the Scottsboro Boys. Both were students in New York in the 1930's and had lived on Campbell's pork and beans in the Depression. They had listened to soap box speakers, gone to rallies. Sam, like Julius, spoke of the Jewish history of resistance and rebellion: the release from bondage in Egypt, the long march from captivity and slavery to freedom in Israel. Sam and Julius sprang from a decade when emotions and passions were not locked inside, when feelings were openly expressed. In the 1930's when Sam and Julius went to the theater to see Clifford Odets's play *Waiting for Lefty* they jumped out of their seats and shouted "Strike! Strike! Strike!" They weren't embarrassed, and no one thought it was in poor taste. The entire audience had risen and was on its feet. But in the 1950's, everyone was cool. No Public Display of Emotion was the rule. In the 1950's when I went to the theater the audience sat quietly and applauded politely, but no one was aroused.

Like the Rosenbergs, the Raskins said that Communism was not the issue. The Rosenbergs' motto was "courage, confidence, and perspective." Sam Raskin said that it wasn't important whether or not we were Communists, for the crucial point was that we believed in human dignity and self-respect.

Raskins and Rosenbergs were members of the same family. Except that the Rosenbergs were poor city relatives from the Lower East Side. We lived in suburbia; we were middle class. My father was a lawyer. Money saved us. Our concern with community affairs saved us. The shingle outside my father's office, the diplomas on his wall kept him out of prison. I was glad that Sam made money, that we lived in a big comfortable house, had two cars, could afford vacations. We didn't look like Reds; we looked exactly like our next-door neighbors. But we paid a price for having money, too. It made me feel guilty, made me feel uncomfortable when my school friends, working class Italians and Jews, came to our house. They stole cigarettes and money from my mother, but I didn't stop them. *It was right to steal from the rich, right to take if you didn't have, that's what Sam said. My friends were Robin Hoods; unfortunately we were the feudal lords.* I felt it was morally superior to be poor; we were middle class and so I felt morally inferior. The only thing to do was to let my poorer friends steal from my parents. After all, revolutions were made by the poor and oppressed. That's what Sam said. And yet not one of them was radical. It was confusing to a twelve-year-old; we were middle class and radical, we believed in revolution. My friends were poor and reactionary and were opposed to revolution. The perfect combination of forces seemed impossible to attain—to be poor and radical and to want a revolution. Under these imperfect circumstances I chose to be a radical, or was I choosing to be middle class rather than poor?

I experienced McCarthyism as an attack on the family, as an attempt to separate parents from their children, to force brothers to betray their sisters, to make orphans of sons. In the late 1960's when friends talked about the family as an oppressive institution which ought to be abolished I reacted in alarm and defended it. Family unity was essential in the Ice Age. I knew that there were good families and bad families, happy families and unhappy families, equal and unequal relationships between husbands and wives, parents and children, but fundamentally there was the enemy—the state, on one hand, and us, the Raskin family, on the other. Our family offered a barrier against Joe McCarthy, the ice man. But the family wasn't *the* answer to the inquisition. I knew that sons had testified against their fathers, that David Greenglass, Ethel's brother, had cooperated with the government and had testified against her, against his own sister and brother-in-law. Enemies, spies, betrayers lurked even within the inner family circle.

My mother's sisters, my aunts (they dominated my uncles), lived in Brooklyn, were working class Jews and secret radicals, atheists who spoke Yiddish. They were terrified of McCarthyism, afraid they'd lose their jobs as civil servants in the city. They were pathological because of the Cold War. Like my grandfather who had fled from Russia in 1905 to escape the czar's army, and like my grandmother who hid in a basement for two weeks while Jews were rounded up and shot in Rumania's worst pogrom, their children, my aunts and uncles, were fugitives too, in flight from America, from crude American values, the ugliness of the street, from anti-Semitism and anti-Communism. They were not wanted by the police, they were not hunted down by the FBI, but they acted as if this was the case. The name on the bell downstairs, and on the mailbox on King's Highway in Brooklyn, the house built by my grandfather Aaron, a bricklayer, and the name in the telephone directory was and still is Quitkin. Aaron Quitkin died in 1949, but his name has not been removed from the mailbox or from the telephone directory, not out of laziness, or forgetfulness, but as a willful attempt to remain anonymous and hidden. My Aunt Iris has been married for the past twenty-five years. She took her husband's name when she married, but her phone and the name on the buzzer is still listed under her father's name.

My Aunt Iris and Aunt Sarah were once investigated, but they overreacted to the harassment. My Aunt Sarah, a grade school teacher in the Bronx, was investigated and threatened with the loss of her job because she signed a petition for Benjamin Davis, a Communist Party candidate for Manhattan City Council in the 1930's and because her car was seen parked outside a hall where the Communist Party was meeting. Sam defended her, won the case, and she retained her job. I don't know if she was innocent or guilty; I almost don't know what the words mean in regard to her. She was charged with being a Communist, denied it, and got off. My father argued that her husband, my Uncle Joshua, who *had* been a Communist, and was dead, told her what to think, who to vote for, what petitions to sign. Since he was a Red, and she didn't argue with him because he was her husband, Sarah had signed the petition, my father argued, because Joshua stuck it in her face and handed her a pen. What else could she do? She wanted to be a good wife, maintain matrimonial harmony. She signed. By accident her car was parked outside a building where the Communist Party was meeting. She had gone to the Barrymore Theatre to see Tennessee Williams's play *Cat on a Hot Tin Roof,* couldn't find a parking place near the theater, and by coincidence parked outside the Palm Gardens Hotel where the party was deliberating. When the FBI combed the area, jotting down license plate numbers, they recorded hers too and it went into a big file in Washington.

"It was an indiscriminate listing of numbers," my father argued.

Aunt Sarah won her case because she played dumb. The committee members were all men who easily believed that this timid woman with her white gloves and silly hat, who continually dropped her pocketbook, had no political ideas, had no ideas at all, in fact, because she loved her husband, as all women loved their husbands. She did as she was told. That it was her own idea, and not my father's to take this tack, to play this role, made it seem no less excusable in 1969, fifteen years later, when my brothers and I, my wife, and our friends criticized Sam and the old left for its male chauvinism.

"Your goal," my wife said, "was to get off, maintain your jobs and security at all costs, even if it meant compromising your politics." After her investigation Aunt Sarah taught for fifteen more years in the New York City school system and retired with a pension. By 1969 she was a Zionist, a friend of Albert Shanker and opposed to community control of schools in New York City. "It would have been better for all concerned," Sheila said, "if she had been fired. She wouldn't have become so conservative. She'd have maintained her dignity and self-respect, and she'd still be a lefty."

My Aunt Iris maintained her radicalism through the 1950's and 1960's, but it was hidden, camouflaged, for she never went on a demonstration, never signed a petition, and forbade me to send her radical publications through the mail. The execution of Julius and Ethel Rosenberg terrified her, made her reluctant to go to meetings or share her political views except with my mother and father. But I trusted her, trusted my mother's relatives. They were so afraid that they would be utterly silent; they'd vanish, go abroad, or underground, take on different identities, work as garbage men or maids in strange cities. But they wouldn't rat on us.

As a family we weren't religious and didn't go to a synagogue; I had never learned to read Hebrew, wasn't bar mitzvahed, and it wasn't until I was twenty that I knew why Jews celebrated Yom Kippur. None of my grandparents tried to teach me about Judaism and none of them encouraged me to go to a synagogue.

I was embarrassed about being a Jew. I was uncomfortable when my school friends or their parents asked me questions about the Jewish religion, because I was unable to give them the answers. I said I was Jewish because I didn't want to confess that I was an atheist. By allowing them to perceive me as a Jew and not an atheist I protected myself. I was less of an enemy. For as bad as Jews were in the eyes of my school friends, and many of them were openly anti-Semitic, being an atheist was worse. But

21

taking on the name Jew as a shield against atheism didn't give me much comfort. It wasn't much of a disguise, for it didn't really hide me. Jews were foreigners, subversives, un-Americans. There were only three other Jews in my class. In the Rosenberg trial, the judge, the prosecutor, the defendants and their lawyers were Jewish. Therefore, the prosecution could claim that anti-Semitism wasn't an issue. But I believed that to most Americans a Jew was a spy Rosenberg, not a Judge Kaufman or an investigator Cohn; a Jew was evil, not good, a sinner, not a saint, a subversive, not a patriot.

My father's family was upper middle class, suburban Jewish. They belonged to country clubs, drove Cadillacs, went to Miami Beach in January. The women played Mah-jongg, the men played bridge. They went to a reform temple, went nightclubbing, supported the Korean War, and raised the American flag behind their swimming pool in the back yard. My mother's family belonged in the pages of Chekhov or Dostoevsky, my father's family in Philip Roth. My father talked politics with his sisters and brothers-in-law. He terrified me because I thought he was exposing himself, confessing to his enemies. I believed that they might charge him with being a Russian spy, because he defended the Soviet Union, the Russian Revolution, blamed the U.S. for starting and perpetuating the Cold War, dredged up the Sacco and Vanzetti and Scottsboro cases to demonstrate the absence of civil rights and civil liberties in the U.S.A. On one hand I was proud of him, because he was courageous; he said what he believed and he didn't hide his politics. He wasn't cowed or intimidated. He attacked the Jewish investigators and ice men—Roy Cohn, David Greenglass, Irving Kaufman, Saypol. But I also felt that he was reckless, that he endangered not only himself but my mother and my brothers. If he was arrested and sent to jail, I didn't think we could survive. We'd be desolate. We'd have no money; we'd be alone. My father sensed what I never could as a kid in the 1950's—that there was room to maneuver, some things you could say or do and not be sent to jail and other things which were dangerous and could result in arrest. He knew how much and how little to say, where and when to say it. I always assumed that the slightest statement, even the public confession of a preference for the color red or the Cincinnati Reds (who changed their name to the "Red Legs" to make it clear, in case anyone wondered, that they weren't Commies), was grounds for an investigation. I would sit silently and listen nervously to my father's attacks on HUAC, Roy Cohn, on Jews who were *shanda for the goyem*—all this to his brothers and sisters-in-law who were *shanda for the goyem* in the local business world. I wished that he would stop, before the tension became too great, before the roof caved in. The arguments were never resolved. No one won, and I wanted a winner, a resolution, an answer. I wanted my father to be at peace with his family and friends. He assumed that because they were his brothers, his cousins, or because they were his old friends, former radicals from the 1930's, he could trust them, prod them, arouse their indignation about lynching in the South, the Army-McCarthy hearings, but I didn't feel the strength, the integrity of *that* family tie. Julius's family had supported him; Ethel's family had betrayed her. A similar fate might befall us.

Neither the Jewishness of my mother's family nor the Jewishness of my father's family was appealing, because the world of Brooklyn Jews was alien, poor, old. It was neurotic in its preoccupation with the past, sickness, disease; each of my aunts and uncles collected something—rare China, newspaper clippings of nuclear tests, nuts and bolts, empty coffee cans. They were neurotically paranoid in their fears of seen and unseen FBI agents. The world of suburban Jews was callous, greedy, crass, loud, and flashy. Golf clubs, martinis, Bert Parks on TV, long, painted fingernails and dancing troupes. The Brooklyn Jews were puritanical and sexless, the Long Island Jews were vulgar and pornographic.

I didn't want to become an orphan like Michael Rosenberg, with adopted parents, a stepmother and a stepfather, living in a strange house. In 1955 I met Michael Rosenberg, known as Michael Meeropol. He too, was a fugitive, was in hiding, using a name to protect himself, a cover, a disguise, like my Aunt Iris. As we too disguised ourselves and became the Samuels. I wondered whether he would ever come out, acknowledge his parents, seize the name Rosenberg again and proudly say he was the eldest son of Julius and Ethel. Or would he always remain Michael Meeropol?

By what names would we call ourselves, I wondered? I met Michael at a friend's unorthodox cultural bar mitzvah. There were Jewish folk dances and tales from Sholem Aleichem. Michael played the guitar and sang. I expected him to speak in radiant phrases, to exhibit extraordinary physical prowess, to dominate the air, things and people. But he was lackadaisical, gentle, shy. I wanted to touch him, embrace him, but I found myself walking around him as if he were a radioactive particle, a neutron or a proton in a high-speed reactor, and I was afraid of colliding with him and exploding.

The orphan adopted by another family, did he dream about Julius and Ethel? Was he in pain? Would he scream? Would tears roll down his cheeks? Would he take revenge on America? Would he vindicate his parents? I would join with him, seal a pact in blood, plot secretly under the dark stairs and render justice to an unjust land. I'd carry the secret scrolls to Nineveh and proclaim the truth:

The A-bomb was no American Secret
In Underground Labs Red Scientists
Discovered the Secret of the Atom.

The Rosenbergs were innocent.
Jonah the prophet spoke:

America your streets will be buried under the bones of your sons, drowned in the blood of your fathers, and the tears of your mothers. America we will haunt you until you release the ghosts of the Rosenbergs from the electric chair. Exonerate us or you will be cursed to eternity.

My mother's strategy was different from my father's. She had strong views, but she rarely articulated them. My father was the voice. My mother hid her political ideas or diluted them. She didn't want to offend people. My parents were close friends with Louis and Carla Silvers; he was Jewish, a radical in the 1930's, and a real estate and insurance agent in the 1950's. Carla was an Italian, a housewife; she was terrified when Louis's old left friends, usually frail as chalk, white haired, and soft spoken, came to visit. Once she was on the verge of calling the FBI, but my mother, using the argument that one ought to be polite to guests, convinced her not to call. Sam had a never-ending political debate with Louis, a disenchanted ex-party member concerned with slave labor camps in Siberia. They argued between themselves and never involved their wives. My mother talked to Carla only about food, children and the weather.

I was secure with my mother because I knew she wouldn't jeopardize the safety of the family as my father would. She'd be silent. She wouldn't broadcast her opinions or look for arguments. The fact that she always wanted to protect us, to fortify the family, was vital to my sense of safety, as a kid. Like Ethel Rosenberg she would hover over her sons and ward off hostile intruders. Millie and Ethel were like mother wolves protecting their young. I believed that the family was politically and emotionally the most important thing to preserve. It was the unit of human existence, a capsule of love in hostile America. In the family context we could be what we couldn't be outside in schools. We didn't have to pretend we were religious or Jewish or patriotic.

The Rosenbergs were a couple. Julius and Ethel were happily married, bound to one another, neither one willing to betray one for the other. I envisioned my parents as an inseparable eternal couple, too. The thought of their separation plunged me into the deepest despair. On two occasions as a kid I thought that they were going to get a divorce. I couldn't sleep or eat. One afternoon when I was nine, I overheard my mother call my father a "Bastard." It was so extraordinary because no one ever cursed in our house and because my mother and father never yelled at one another. He had gone off for the day and hadn't told her where he was going. Several months later I was awakened late one night to hear my mother and father arguing in the living room. My father was worried, couldn't sleep and was smoking a cigar in his easy chair.

"What's bothering you?" my mother asked, but he refused to say. He maintained utter silence. *What could have required such secrecy? What had he done?* I suspected two things: one, that he had undertaken a dangerous mission which would jeopardize our security; two, that he had refused a dangerous mission and felt guilty. For three days I worried that my parents would separate. Then I broke down.

"Ma, are you and daddy going to get a divorce?"

She laughed. "No of course not." She hugged me and I was relieved.

The outside world seemed so threatening, so unstable, so full of enemies, that I demanded a

25

stable home, loving parents, security.

My father believed in equality between the sexes, and he felt that his relationship with my mother was equal. But the differences between the two of them were immediately apparent. Sam went to his law office to work, my mother shopped, cooked, bought our clothes, kept the house clean, tucked us in bed at night. She was tender, emotional, considerate. My father was hard, aggressive, violent. When I misbehaved my mother always tried to control me with the threat of my father's strong right arm.

My parents had a set conversation piece. I heard it at least once a year in the 1950's. When my mother was angry at my father she said, "I don't know why I married you, left New York, and moved to the country." That had happened in 1938, four years before I was born.

"You were pining away on Kings Highway," my father said. "You can go back if you want."

One night before going to sleep he talked to my brother and me about Nazi concentration camps, the extermination of the Jews, the gas ovens. I wanted him to stop because it was late and I didn't want to have nightmares. My mother suggested that he tell the story in the morning, but he persisted and showed us photographs of Dachau and Buchenwald. I looked at the wall. There was an old oil painting in my bedroom of Hansel and Gretel, the gingerbread woman, and her oven. She was a Nazi; her gas oven would exterminate children. When my father finished his concentration camp bedtime story my mother tucked me into bed, stroked my hair and told me not to worry.

My father was dominant and aggressive. He had recognition from the outside world. My mother was passive. I spoke to her when I was sad or frightened. I sympathized with her, but, since she was the weaker one, since she existed in the home and not outside, I didn't want to identify with her. I forced myself to identify with my father because he could cope with teachers, policemen, judges, clients, with the FBI. As I grew older I grew further and further apart from my mother. My father could withstand the pressure of a McCarthy or a Roy Cohn, but my mother would fold. I believed that the Cold War dictated the necessity for a hierarchical family, a supreme authority, my father in command.

The Ice Age was our environment. To survive, one needed an ice pick. My mother's warmth would only dwindle and eventually freeze. A match couldn't defeat a glacier. Only ice could break ice. That's how I felt in the fifties.

The Raskin family survived the decade intact. There were no divorces, separations, widows, orphans, severe illness or death, no loss of job, poverty, prison terms, or exile. There was fear, caution, silence, anonymity. We endured.

In the twenties my father was the jazz age son of a successful Jewish immigrant businessman, in the thirties a Communist, a student, a union organizer, in the forties a husband, father, and an antifascist, in the fifties a prosperous real estate lawyer and a progressive in hiding. Only in the sixties, when his sons grew up, did he become an open, committed radical again, as he had been in the thirties. He came full circle. And by that time, in the late sixties, we had a very different perspective on the early fifties. We looked back into another geological era. A whole new and unusual species had appeared: Panthers, Yippies, Weathermen.

III. PANTHERS AND ROSENBERGS

No one in the new left talked about the Rosenbergs. They were rather drab, undramatic people, a married couple, with kids, an engineer and a housewife. John Brown was our hero, an American guerrilla warrior from bloody Kansas, a madman in the eyes of America, who had taken up arms to free slaves. He was a white man willing to sacrifice his own life to liberate black men.

A measure of the distance we traveled from 1950 to 1970 is indicated by the fate of Bobby Seale and Ericka Huggins. These two members of the Black Panther Party talked openly about armed struggle, picking up the gun, and socialism. The State of Connecticut wanted to send them to the electric chair but they were found not guilty, were acquitted and released from prison. Moreover, two years later, Seale ran, though unsuccessfully, for mayor of Oakland, California.

The Panther posters in New Haven in 1970 showed Bobby Seale strapped into a grotesque electric chair; I couldn't help but be reminded of Julius and Ethel in the electric chair. The response of the Panther Party in 1970 was different from the Communist Party in 1950. There were large demonstrations, and

Panther speakers threatened "If they give Bobby Seale the electric chair, there'll be no light for days." The threat of darkness and chaos in the land had never been made by the defenders of Julius and Ethel. *After all, they were peaceful, law abiding, and humane.* Many CP members didn't want to touch the Rosenbergs. The state used overkill against the Rosenbergs. Perhaps if they blame you for the Korean War, for Russian atomic power, the only proper response is to be outrageous—to respond in kind with the threat of ultimate doom. The sky will darken, there will be no light for days, blood will flow and evil Nineveh will be destroyed. The end is coming.

CHAPTER
THREE
LEVIATHAN AND SON

My father sat in an armchair, wearing his house robe, reading a book. There was a circle of light on the page. His lips moved, his head moved back and forth like a typewriter going line by line down the page. His whole body moved when he read. He paused, leaned his head back and reflected. His eyes closed. My mother sat on the orange sofa, watching him, knitting and dozing, knitting and dozing. Her legs were stretched out. The green ball of yarn was on the floor. The needles moved quickly in a circle then paused and the hands rested. Watching, knitting, dozing.

I watched them from outside. Their silhouettes were clear against the light in the living room. I didn't want them to catch me sneaking back into the house. I tiptoed carefully, turned the knob slowly, and opened the door. They didn't hear me enter. I got undressed in the dark and crawled into bed.

My parents were angry with me. "You've neglected your studies," my father said. "Football has become an obsession with you. You ought to study and develop your intellect." I had been elected captain of the high school football team and chosen for the County All-Star Team. Why wasn't he satisfied? Dino's father would have been. My mother was annoyed that I was going out with non-Jewish girls.

"What do you see in them?" she asked.

"They're sexy. Jewish girls are sexless."

"Don't be rude. I'll tell your father."

I was returning from a Saturday night party. The girls were OK. I had danced close with a redhead; her boyfriend was also on the football team, a second-string guard pushing hard to make the first team. Five days a week she wore a blue and white blazer embroidered with the cross of Saint Catherine and on weekends she wore tight sweaters and skirts to parties and the movies.

"She'll let you feel her up," the quarterback said. "She puts out." She put her arms around me, moved her thighs back and forth. And her boyfriend, the second-string guard pushing hard, was watching us.

Dee Dee, the Catholic school girl, always argued with April, my girlfriend, about Pat Boone and Elvis Presley; they fought for control of the turntable, for the power to decide what records were played. April was tall, blond, blue-eyed. I met her before the kickoff the first game of the season. She was standing on the sidelines in her cheerleader's skirt, sweater, and sneakers.

"If you make enough noise we'll win," I said. "See ya after the game." We won, and April and I went out for an ice-cream soda. Then I took her home. Her mother looked familiar.

"Do I know you?" I asked.

"I knocked at your front door last week to collect money for cerebral palsy," she said.

"This is my father," April said.

"Hello." He didn't answer. April's father was a Princeton graduate, a doctor, a heavy drinker. Dr. Kennedy didn't like me.

"That scar on your nose makes you look like a gangster," he said. "Raskin, Raskin, where have I seen that name? Is your grandfather Benjamin Raskin?"

"Yes."

"He was a smart Jew, had a good location, must have made a pile of dough. One rainy afternoon I bought a pair of galoshes at Raskin's to keep my feet dry. They lasted for years."

"Daddy what *are* you saying?" April whined.

"He was a good merchant, daughter; his grandmother had forearms like a Polack."

I wanted to forget my white-haired, thin grandfather, my short, stocky grandmother, and the little department store on New York Avenue where the poor Italian, Irish, and black families bought their clothing. I took a circuitous route and avoided it on my way to school. The floors sagged, it was dark and the counters were piled high with old-fashioned shirts and trousers.

April was my first serious non-Jewish girlfriend. My mother was worried I'd marry her. I was sixteen years old. My sex life was rudimentary. I made out with April and felt up Dee Dee when her boyfriend wasn't looking. I had my first girlfriend in 1954 when I was twelve. Puberty was swift and sudden. In a night the geography of my body changed: muscles bulged, glands secreted, fluids oozed, hair protruded. Blackheads and pimples surfaced on my nose and cheeks, made me feel self-conscious of my appearance, of ugliness, beauty, good looks, good grooming, underarm deodorants, hair creams, jock straps, combs, and lotions.

Pimples and erections betrayed me to teachers, girlfriends, my parents. Informers were inside and outside. My own body would rat on me. I couldn't trust it with a secret or a dangerous mission, for it would act independently, without consulting my mind. Suddenly, I discovered that there was a rebel force within, that there was a conflict between my head and my hands. Puberty was a frightening sexual rebellion. I wanted to be like the adolescent boys who had no visible signs of the biological changes beneath the surface, the boys who did not have bulges in their trousers or acne. I was self-conscious; everyone was watching me. In seventh grade a black friend nicknamed me "Boner" and from that year on, throughout high school, I was called "Jonah the Boner."

In July and August of 1954 I had received a sexual education from my camp counselor. He was a tall, blond nineteen-year-old lifeguard who stood on the raft silhouetted against the trees in a tight, black swimming suit. That winter my parents had lectured me about sex, but I resented their honesty and openness because I wanted to mask my own sexuality. I wanted to think of my parents as sexless; when my sexuality developed, theirs emerged simultaneously. I was shocked. Adolescence changed my relationship to my parents. I shared less of my life with them and more of it with my peers. They exposed what I wanted to conceal. I was ashamed. My parents offered diagrams of the male and the female reproductive organs. Everything was labeled: ovaries, testes, sperm, semen, eggs, the fetus. It was abstract and scientific, a specimen under the microscope, and not my body or my sexual imagination.

Billy, the counselor, told us stories in the bunk at night about his real and imaginary sexual encounters. The lights were out. His voice was erotic, enveloping, seductive. The camp was hushed; only the muffled beating of a bat's wings interrupted him.

"Redheaded Thelma and I," Billy said, "went to the pictures on Forty-second Street. We sat in the blue velvet seats in the last row of the balcony. She was a Queen. She unzipped my fly, and reached for my quivering cock. Her skin was flawless; she wore silk panties, and she was wet. She raised her skirt above her waist, pushed her underpants down to her ankles, and sat on my lap. It was the classic fuck. Last summer in Maine I was paddling alone in a canoe on a lake like glass. The sun set, the sky darkened, the lake narrowed, the woods approached the shore. There was no exit, and I was afraid that the canoe would be smashed against the rocks. Suddenly there was an opening, a narrow canal leading to a lake. A naked woman was bathing alone. Spontaneously we made love again and again. The next day I said goodbye and paddled home. Again and again I tried, but I never discovered the entrance to the lake." Billy's sex was more like an older brother's and more appealing than a father's.

The last weekend in July, Billy took us to the Amish County Fair in Kutztown. The main attraction was an auction, the Pennsylvania Dutch farmers bid for cows, pigs, workhorses, bulls. We sat in the bleachers. My hands rested on Joanna, a dark-haired girl sitting below me. The hands stroked her neck, shoulders, touched her breasts. The hands moved as Billy's hands would have moved. The hands felt the softness and warmth and conveyed it to the loins. The hands moved, the eyes watched the auctioneer, the ears listened to the bidding. Horses brayed, bulls bellowed. Our eyes didn't meet. Hands touched breasts. She didn't giggle or twitch. The hands were satisfied, the body was warm, electric, wet. The next morning, the middle-aged, paternal camp director woke me early. He wanted to speak to me about "a serious matter." I followed him down the dirt road to the baseball diamond. He lit his pipe, adjusted his horn-rimmed glasses. We sat in the newly cut hay; dragonflies darted overhead.

"Getting hot in the pants is disgusting," he said.

"What's that?"

"Don't play innocent. Look at me."

"I don't know."

"You had an erection. You were hot in the pants. You were petting Joanna."

"It was fun."

"It was disgraceful. You don't respect Joanna. I'm going to tell your parents." *My worst fears had come true. My body had betrayed me. My hands had gotten me into trouble. My parents would interrogate me, investigate me, ask me to confess. I would deny everything.* When they visited on parents' day, my parents didn't punish or scold me; they said nothing at all. But I was sure that they knew, and suspected that they'd blackmail me one day in the future.

Jonah and Joanna—we were a couple in summer camp. She was from Queens, my age, Jewish, from an old left family. She was sexually aggressive. I didn't demand or force; she initiated. Our relationship was secret. We went away from the bunkhouse and into the woods.

At the beginning of September I went home to Rogues Path, and she went home to Queens. The first week we talked on the phone, the second week we wrote letters. Then at the end of September she invited me to spend the weekend at her mother's apartment. Mrs. Levine was out of town. Everything was set. I hadn't yet used the twenty-five-cent prophylactic, bought in a slot machine in the men's room at a gas station, kept in my wallet. Every time I took out my wallet I saw the outline of the Trojan. Now I was ready. On Friday night I took the train to Queens. She met me at the station; we took the bus to her mother's, sat silently looking out the window.

"When are you going to get a car?" she asked. "All the guys in Van Buren High have hot rods." My hopes disintegrated. *She probably has a boyfriend, probably fucks in the back seat of the hot rod. My life was over.* I had imagined passionate lovemaking in the afternoon, a supreme romance, then a sad parting. We would kiss. I would step into the train at the last minute, wave goodbye and watch the tears on her face.

"It was a summer romance," she said. "Don't make it more than that."

"But it *was* more," I said.

I left her mother's apartment, took the bus to the Long Island Railway station, bought a ticket to Huntington and walked up the long, dim stairway. On the gray concrete platform I waited for the locomotive. It was dark and chilly; brown rats scurried across the tracks. Then the white light advanced in the darkness: the train crept closer, then slowly came to a halt. I sat alone in the last car and looked through the mud-streaked windows.

"Tickets, please." I was crying. "Son, don't take it so bad," the conductor said punching the ticket. Tears streamed down my face, and the old railroad car bounced along the dark tracks toward my father waiting at the Huntington Station.

I was a junior high school student and my parents encouraged me to make friends, go to dances, succeed, get A's, be like "them." My mother sent me to a dancing school, an orthodontist, a dermatologist. I hated dancing lessons and the doctors who twisted and squeezed my body. I was angry at my parents for insisting I go out into the world.

"I wish they'd leave me alone," I said to myself. They had been protectors; now they jeopardized me. I also had ambiguous feelings about my school pals. I fought them about stolen bases, third strikes, the rules of the game, fought them because they were little Joe McCarthys. When I invited them home my mother disapproved. She wanted me to have friends but disapproved of the friends I had.

One afternoon I told my father that I was going to see James Mason as General Rommel in *The Desert Fox*.

"You'll have to decide for yourself," he said, "but I don't think you should see a film which glorifies a Nazi. I didn't spend my life fighting fascism for nothing." I didn't go to the film and my friends didn't invite me to the movies again. Whenever I liked things American my parents disapproved. They didn't want me to eat pizza, drink Coca Cola, go to 3-D movies, hang out with "juvenile delinquents." But I liked the juvenile delinquents because, like me, they were outcasts and rebels. I was angry at my parents when they acted like cold, superior intellectuals. They talked about the people, but they didn't know anything about the fans in the stands at stock-car races (I went secretly with my juvenile delinquent friends), the soda jerk at the ice-cream fountain, the gas station attendant.

"How can I have friends," I asked, "if you won't let me go to the movies or stock-car races? They'll think I'm odd. They won't like me."

"Then find new friends," my father said.

My father wanted me to be the class valedictorian. "Being a radical," he said, "is no excuse for getting C's. You have to do better than them at their own game." His own strategy was to be the best lawyer in town, in business and in ethics. "If I'm a good lawyer," he said, "then I can have a political impact. If I'm sloppy in my legal work, no one will respect me politically." When I was a kid I took him literally. I decided it was best to act like a loyal, patriotic American, join the Elks, the Democratic Party, talk, act like them, become president. I'd pretend to be mild-mannered, patient, calm—like Clark Kent—but I'd really be a Red Superman. Inside the White House I'd discard my suit and tie, and hoist the red flag. My father deflated my dreams. "A lot of my old friends," he said, "got jobs in government and publishing houses and claimed that they were infiltrating the establishment. 'When we're in positions of power,' they said, 'then we'll do radical things.' Most of them forgot their radical intentions and just made money."

In high school I knew I couldn't get A's in history because my view of the past was in opposition to the teacher's view. My father taught me history at home. I accepted his version. If I expressed it in class I'd get a C or an F. My social studies teachers insisted that Russian foreign policy was motivated by the search for more warm-water ports. Hot and cold, summer and winter explained both Russian and Soviet life. The snow and ice defeated Napoleon and Hitler; Russian ports were frozen in winter so the Reds wanted warm waters. "Russians are all children," the teacher said. "They need strong father figures. That's what the czar was. That's what Stalin is." To argue with the teachers would be to question authority, and to question authority was to invite punishment and a poor grade. To get an A I'd have to be silent.

I discovered that I often didn't have to lie to be liked. I could simply not speak. Teachers and schoolmates assumed that I loved America, hated Russia, hated black people, and loved Nixon and Eisenhower. I was free to define myself, create my own character and personality. If I was silent about my real self I could build a fictional self, and they wouldn't know the difference.

I didn't confront teachers about politics, but throughout junior high school I was a practical joker, mocking teachers and watching the class laugh at them. Then they discovered I was the ringleader. The guidance counselor said to my mother: "He's a discipline problem and a latent juvenile delinquent, guilty of anti-social behavior." My mother told me to behave and study. She cooperated with the school authorities, but I became openly rebellious. I shouted, laughed, disrupted classes by sneezing, coughing, dropping books on the floor. I expressed my disdain for their ideas and values by all means except by direct political argument.

My mother wanted me to date "nice" girls; she didn't like the

Catholic school uniforms or the cheerleader smiles. My mother wanted me to go out with the Jewish daughters of her old left friends from New York. They weren't sexually attractive. No girl my mother wanted me to date could be sexy. If my mother liked her she must be sexless. I wasn't interested. Since my mother wasn't friendly with the mothers of the non-Jewish girls she had no way of arranging my social life with them. I went out with April and Dee Dee because I could shape my own relationships independently of my parents, especially my mother. I didn't want the world of my mother and the world of sex to touch. Going out with non-Jewish girls was also a way of infiltrating the WASP world. If I was seen with non-Jewish girls, maybe they'd assume I wasn't Jewish. Maybe they'd assume my parents weren't Jews either. I also had different feelings about non-Jewish girls. I didn't allow myself to be in love with them. I had been hurt by Joanna, I didn't want to be hurt again, and I thought that the real social barriers between me and the non-Jewish girls would prevent me from falling in love with them. If they rejected me I could say to myself that it was because I was Jewish and they weren't Jewish. Tragically, love was doomed because of our social differences.

Becoming captain of the high school football team was a subversive act, a rebellion against my parents. I established my own authority. It also satisfied my own needs for acceptance with integrity. My mind, my ideas weren't involved. I didn't feel I was suppressing my values or remaining silent. On the football field my body talked. At fifteen my skin was soft, my muscles taut. I stood before the mirror in my bedroom and flexed. I was agile and fast and I liked physical contact. On the football field I could express the violence I felt toward America—fathers, mothers, teachers, counselors, cops. The pent-up hostility exploded on the gridiron. I could see the stadium with my eyes closed; the goalposts, the midfield stripes, the ten-yard markers, the green turf. I knew the feel of a charging line, the snap of the ball from center, the broken field run, the touchdown, the bone-cracking tackle, the taste of dust, the smell of a recovered fumble.

We, the Blue Devils, beat Amityville, the Crimson Tide, for the championship. Four years earlier I was an awkward outsider, but now I was silhouetted against the sky in my football jersey, my American uniform, looking just like "them."

The football coach, Mr. Frankenberg, a Jew who had

converted to Catholicism, let me help plan all the games. I was his assistant coach as well as captain. Football was better than studying or going to class, and I lived in the gym and the locker room. Football was a group effort.

In football you drove them back, conquered territory, opened holes, blocked, tackled, red dogged, double teamed. The captain was a general, and his teammates were his comrades. There were Black, Irish, Italian, and French Canadian boys on the team—we were an international brigade.

As captain of the football team I became another Jonah— cheerleaders couldn't see who I really was. I hoped they would fall in love with the uniform, the image, the power, not the Jewish son with Red parents. The uniform would make up for the acne, and my beautiful body would make up for my social awkwardness.

The whole team went to a party at Tom's house. Tom was a reporter, a Catholic, and he went to mass every morning. Dino, the second-string guard and Dee Dee's boyfriend, crashed the party. He was bigger than me, wanted to crush me, but he was clumsy and slow. When I was a sophomore, I hated the first-string guard and wanted to hurt him. Now that I was captain, Dino wanted to "get me." He liked to be mean.

"Do you know what I'm going to do when I grow up?" he said. "I'm going to suck farts out of bus seats, smell the seats of girls' bikes." One summer Dino smashed his father's car drag racing. In his junior year he was expelled from school. The cops caught him sawing down the flagpole. He had asked me to join him. I refused and he called me a chicken. After he was expelled and couldn't play football, he hated me.

Dino's father was a salesman for Montgomery Ward. On Saturday nights he'd sit in the kitchen with Dee Dee's father, drink martinis and play poker.

"Don't you think my boy Dino will play pro ball for the Giants?" he asked.

"Yes, Mr. Forbes, he'll be a star."

"Why don't you give him a chance? You're the captain."

"Everyone's got to prove themselves."

"Your Dad's a Jew, isn't he? I never heard of a Jew captain before."

"No sir, I'm the first one."

"That's what I thought."

Tom's girlfriend, Sandy, came from Port Washington for the party. She was wealthy. Her father had a seat on the New York Stock Exchange, and a chauffeur drove him to work in a Rolls-Royce. Their house overlooked Long Island Sound. We'd stretch out on the purple sofas in the living room—it was the only house where the parents didn't send us to the basement. Tom put on Sandy's clothing, her slips, bras, and makeup and Sandy wore Tom's trousers, shirt, and tie.

"I'm Sandy," he said. "Look at my tits. She's Tom."

Tom had a crew cut and a purple birthmark under his right eye. He was a stylish dresser, carried a silver cigarette case. He was the best-read student in high school and was writing his own version of *Peyton Place*. Tom didn't care about Pat Boone or Elvis Presley; he collected records of Billie Holiday, Benny Goodman, Glenn Miller, Edith Piaf. On weekends we often took the Long Island Railroad to New York, wandered on Bleecker and MacDougal Streets, gaped at the women wearing peasant blouses in Figaro's. Mostly we browsed in a book store on Sheridan Square. Tom bought a thin volume entitled *Howl*. We were intrigued by the peculiar size and title of the book and the name of the publishing company, City Lights. The idea of buying poetry in the Village was exciting. *Howl* fit into Tom's back pocket and he carried it everywhere.

"What do you think of Allen Ginsberg being a homosexual?" he asked.

"I guess it's all right," I said.

"All the great writers were homosexuals—like Oscar Wilde," Tom said.

"Do you have to be a homosexual to be a writer?" I asked.

"No, but it helps."

Going home on the Long Island Railroad Tom read out loud from *Howl*. He thought it was the funniest book he'd ever seen. The commuters were annoyed, but he wasn't inhibited. For a mild-mannered reporter who didn't play sports, he was brave. For years I felt that my problems were unique, but Tom allowed me to see that other people had secrets, and submerged feelings too. He camouflaged his life from his parents. Who he believed he was, who he pretended to be, the roles he chose for himself, helped me to see my own images of myself.

The party was a disaster. Tom wanted it to be decadent, but it was just boring. April gossiped with Dee Dee about the senior boys who dated freshman girls. Dino was angry at Dee Dee for flirting; he went upstairs to talk to Tom's dad about football. I was restless. Dee Dee looked sexy. "Too bad she's not in her Catholic school uniform." I thought. "I'd like to feel her tits under the Cross of Saint Catherine." I sat down beside her, looked to see if anyone was watching, lifted her dress above her waist and touched her white underpants. Dee Dee smiled.

"Naughty boy," she said. "You'd better watch out, Dino is aching for a fight." I walked toward April, took her hand, and went into the furnace room. I spread an army blanket on the floor and we lay down side by side. We kissed. I got on top of April, but she pushed me away. I put my hands on her breasts but she lifted them and dropped them down. She had silky blond hair, white skin, blue eyes, and looked as if she was possessed of the secret of sex. She'd surrender it if the right man enacted the right ritual. But it wasn't I. We went back to the party. Everyone was dancing to a Chuck Berry record. It was chilly, noisy, frenetic. Dino thrust his body back and forth, Dee Dee lunged at him. Tom stuck out his tongue. Faces were frozen in distorted gestures. It was grotesque. The song ended. The pile of forty-fives was so deep that the record player wouldn't revolve at the proper speed. Chuck Berry's voice was distorted. The needle ground to a halt. Everyone stared at us.

"You little bitch," Dee Dee yelled. "Did you put out?"

April ran upstairs, and I stood alone facing Dee Dee.

"Did you fuck April?" she asked. I opened my mouth to speak. No words came, but the air parted. There was a sudden scream. I looked down, and saw Dee Dee shrieking on the floor. Tom laughed hysterically. Dino bound my arms and held me back.

"She didn't know what she was saying." Sandy said.

"What happened?" I asked.

"You knocked her down," Dino said. "This isn't a football game."

"Let me go," I shouted.

Dino stepped back. My arms were free. I paused, took a deep breath, darted up the stairs, kicked open the back door and started to gallop. I panicked. I had hit a girl. "Why had it gotten so confused? Why couldn't I attack the right people—the real enemy?" I couldn't control myself, my anger, my hands. I ran across vacant lots, cleared of woods, readied for housing developments. I ran past the silent, cold bulldozers, through the mud, over rocks, breathing heavily, my breath turning to thick fog. I crossed New York Avenue, ran past the darkened high school, past my grandfather's department store, past my father's law office, across the railway tracks, the baseball diamond, running and thinking of football games, of the touchdowns I had scored, pursued by enemy tacklers, running and thinking of Tom's basement, of Dee Dee on the floor, Dino binding me. I ran till I came to Rogues Path, opened the door and immediately turned on the television set. In the Katherine Hepburn-Spencer Tracy movie, I tried to forget, lose myself, hide.

For years I was afraid I would be betrayed by my Jewishness, my Redness, the life of my parents. But my own hands had betrayed me; my body, not my mind, was criminal.

The next day I told my father the truth. I couldn't lie. He listened, didn't judge or punish me and told me not to feel guilty. He had criticized me for playing football, neglecting my studies, but he didn't criticize this act of violence. My father seemed to understand and accept it, and I couldn't understand why. *Wasn't striking a girl the worst thing I could do?* Shouldn't I control myself; be rational? Didn't my father know that a *poison from my bloodstream had taken possession of me?* I didn't know my own passions, strengths, hates, desires. What could I do with my energy? What could I do with my power? I joined the wrestling team, disciplined my body, drilled, learned perfect control of my arms, legs, stomach, fingertips and ruled my limbs with an iron will. Wrestling was different from football. It was one against one. It was combat between two men; bodies were wrapped around one another, opponents practically embraced. Dino was also a wrestler, determined to supplant me from the first team. Every day I had to wrestle him on the mat. I joined the team, ran, sweated, exercised, lost twenty-five pounds in two weeks, ate raw eggs, wheat germ, blackstrap molasses.

Dee Dee's and Dino's mothers agreed that I should not be allowed to see their children. I was ostracized, exiled. I was barred from basement parties. Dee Dee thought that I should be committed to a mental institution. But Tom came to Rogues Path and lent me his copy of Kerouac's *On the Road*. April violated her mother's injunction and met me at Tom's. She wrote letters and called late at night. April's mother discovered we were meeting, but allowed us to see each other twice a week. She disliked Dee Dee's mother, a wealthy Catholic, and now Mrs. Kennedy could snub them. April's mother invited me to church as a way of saying she approved of me. I was feeling alone and unwanted, so I accepted her invitation. I thought that I could sit quietly in church, that no one would bother me, and that if I went to church April would accept me, love me, want me.

"Church is an important part of my life," April said. "My mother will think better of you."

"But my parents will think worse of me," I said to myself. I'd exchange one set of parents for another.

For a month of Sundays I went to church with April and her mother and father. The more often I went to church, the more sex I had with April. And the more sex I had the more willing I was to go to church. She rewarded me with sex, and I rewarded her by going to church. I got up early (I couldn't set the alarm because I didn't want my parents to hear it, but I woke up to my own internal alarm clock). I put on a white shirt, a blue tie, a suit, escaped by the back door, and walked to the Kennedys'. We drove to the First Presbyterian Church on Main Street in Huntington. To the right of the church was the library, a fort during the American Revolution. To the left of the church was the Bank of Suffolk County. A church had been built on the same site in 1653, the year the town was settled. It was burned by Indians in 1770, rebuilt on the same location in 1800, and renovated in 1890. There was a colonial graveyard (two Indians were buried there too) in the back. The wooden church was painted white; a beautiful steeple pointed up into the sky. The imported Swiss clock had gold roman numerals on its black face, but it worked imperfectly, and the bells had a dissonant quality. We sat in the Kennedys' pew. The carpet was scarlet, the seats were hard, the organ music was beautiful. When the choirboys passed the shiny copper coffers I looked into their hard faces and deposited a quarter.

"Please feel at home in Our Father's house," the minister said. "You must learn to confide in Him." He had a skin disease and wore gloves when he read the Bible.

In December I went with the Kennedys to the annual Christmas pageant. April played Mary Magdalen. Mrs. Kennedy invited me for Christmas dinner. Mr. Kennedy talked about Princeton in the 1930's.

"I had a Jewish squash partner," he said. "He was a Choate boy." On Christmas Eve Tom, Sandy, April and I went caroling. Tom and Sandy talked about getting engaged.

"You can have a seat on the New York Stock Exchange," Sandy's father said, "and an apartment on Park Avenue."

"I'm considering the spiritual life," Tom said. "I may join the Franciscan brotherhood."

One morning I spoke at the Sunday School about "Football and Belief." By using religious metaphors and talking about the *faith* that the quarterback had to have in his receivers, I convinced the congregation that I was religious, and that Our Father who art in Heaven played on the side of Huntington High School.

I had thought I'd only have to play the football captain on Saturday afternoon but discovered that I had to play the role all the time, especially on Sundays. The only place I didn't have to play football captain was at home, so I started to stay home more, to read, and study. It had become awkward and cumbersome to carry myself everyday as if I were wearing a jock strap, a helmet, cleats, shoulder pads, a uniform.

One Sunday my father saw me in my suit as I was coming home.

"Where've you been?"

"To church."

"So you're in love with Jesus Christ? Does the divine spirit move you my son?" He was angrier at me for going to church than for hitting Dee Dee. I knew he'd be watching me next Sunday morning. I wanted to evade his eyes, but that was difficult. He could sit upstairs in his chair, hear every sound and see me leave the house by the front or the back door. The last week in January I got up at 6:30 AM and went to the Kennedys'. Mr. Kennedy bought us coffee and doughnuts, and April and I discussed plans to go away for a weekend. The church was crowded. An old farmer, his clothes smelling of the earth and Long Island potatoes told me, "Your father is the most honest man in Huntington."

42

"Thank you, sir." I sat down with the Kennedys. The minister, wearing his black robes, walked up the carpeted steps.

"Today my text is Jonah's mission to Nineveh," he said. I turned aside from his gaze and saw that the entire congregation was looking at me. They looked like children who were at the theater for the first time in their lives. They had been given their cue. Everything had been rehearsed; this was the opening performance. But they didn't know what to expect. Then they faced the altar. The minister cleared his throat, adjusted the gloves on his hands, lifted the Bible, and read:

> Jonah prayed to the Lord his God from the belly of the Fish. I called the Lord in my distress, and he answered me.

> Men who worship false gods may abandon their loyalty, but I will offer thee sacrifice with words of praise: I will pay my vows: victory is the Lord's.

"Father, forgive us," Mrs. Kennedy whispered. I wanted to put my fingers in my ears and block out the sermon. I wanted to stand up and shout:

"I'm an atheist. God is dead."

But I remained silent. The church was macabre. The people looked like a seventeenth-century congregation of Puritans prepared to burn witches at the stake. They wanted me to kneel down. I was a prisoner inside the monster with scarlet carpets, hard pews, a medieval organ with beautiful music. I wanted to escape but it would be impolite, too dramatic to leave while the sermon was in progress. I controlled my impulse to scream, strike, run. I thought of my father's law office. I touched the scar on my nose. I waited till the end, then walked slowly and deliberately to the sidewalk on Main Street. I was outside the whale, away from the minister's eyes, away from the eyes peering from behind black veils. I was free. I was in daylight. April followed me and took my hand.

"What's the matter, love?" she asked.

"I won't be your Jonah, Goddamn it!"

"Don't take the name of the Lord in vain."

"Goddamn it!"

I turned away and walked home to Rogues Path. In the living room I pulled off my tie, unbuttoned my collar, and sat down on the sofa. My father was making a fire. "Don't you have one ounce of self-respect?" he asked.

"No, I don't and I don't care," I said. *I won't give him the satisfaction.*

"I hope your love affair with Jesus Christ is over," he said. *I won't say. I won't make him feel good or righteous. I want to be angry at him and at Leviathan. I want to escape from both.*

April wrote me a letter, but I never answered. In March I wrestled in the championship tournament. Dino came in first. He beat me. Tom decided to enter a Franciscan monastery and join the brotherhood after high school graduation. We worked together on his novel about the Peyton Place of Huntington. It was about parents and children and most of the characters were based on real people. There were two heroes, a young, handsome Roman Catholic priest and an old, bearded poet. They were close friends. But the novel was never finished. During Easter vacation, Dino was killed in a car crash. Tom and I went to the funeral; Dee Dee went with the captain of the baseball team. After the death we couldn't go on writing. Crocuses were blooming in the cemetery. Spring was on its way. Track season was ahead.

I wanted to train hard, discipline myself, control my body and my emotions. I set myself a goal—to run fast, to break the state record for the 440-yard dash. It would be a personal exercise. Whether I'd achieve the goal or not wasn't the most important thing. Success would be mastery of myself through meditation and action.

CHAPTER
FOUR
PEOPLE GOTTA WALK

I. MANHOLE COVER

Littered Thirty-fourth Street. Mounted policemen. Horseshit on the pavement. Late March, cold Saturday afternoon. Shadows growing. Bustling shoppers. Enticing Macy's mannequins. Hostile looks. Barriers. White faces. Black faces. Curses and chants. "Go back to Russia," "Nigger Lover," "Jim Crow must go," "Don't buy, pass 'em by."

The campaign against Woolworth's segregated lunch counters. On Saturday afternoons we marched, chanted, clapped hands, sang spirituals, drank steaming hot coffee, and ate doughnuts. The store manager pressed his nose against the plate-glass window and followed our movements with alarm. Shoppers expressed bewilderment and hostility, but most of them didn't cross our picket line. Woolworth's was empty.

The picket lines were integrated, and white people were welcome, but the young blacks coined the slogans, kept up the beat, and raised high our energy when it sagged to the sidewalk. The main fight against segregation was in the South; the Thirty-fourth Street picket line was a long way from the front but we sensed an intimate connection with the black men and women in Alabama and Mississippi who sat in, were arrested, carted off to jail, tried, jailed, released, and went back to Woolworth's to sit in again. Picketing on Thirty-fourth Street made me feel that New York wasn't an alien skyscraper giant. I was under the shadow of the Empire State Building, but one hundred black and white demonstrators with signs, chants, love, joy, and anger created a community in the chasms of cold steel and glass. I was naive. I thought that there was no danger from the courteous policemen, the gentle white citizens, the smiling Jewish merchants. This was the enlightened North; everyone was liberal.

The Ice Age was ending. March and April 1960 was the thaw after the long winter of the 1950's. Politics pushed upward through the cracks in the sidewalk. A new geological era was beginning, a new climate in the making.

Monday through Friday we went to lectures at Columbia College. Contemporary Civilization (Aristotle and Plato), Humanities (Homer and Aeschylus); groups and sets in Math; irregular verbs in French; grammar and composition in English. There were exams, papers to write, competition in the reading rooms of Butler Library, rivalry in the claustrophobic classrooms, prep school snobs, upper classmen who insisted we wear freshman beanies, and the dormitories (at least one student a year committed suicide by jumping from his cubicle in John Jay Hall).

The campus was a self-contained world. Students with bowed heads followed the patterned brick walks from dorms to lecture halls, to cafeteria, to library—and never ventured to the cement sidewalks of New York. At first the college was my cocoon, too, but then I made forays to Broadway and 116th Street, to Salter's for books, to Prexy's for a hamburger, french fries, and a coke, to Nat and Phil's for pipe tobacco. Then finally to Thirty-fourth Street, a distant territory in the South.

My best friends and I lived together in Livingston Hall. We ate, studied, traveled, went to class together. We were fused together because our parents were 1930's people, because we had all lived two lives in the 1950's. We had straight lives and underground lives. We had all succeeded in high school society, but simultaneously we felt that we didn't belong, that we were outsiders. One friend was the valedictorian, another a first-string basketball player, a third the editor of the school newspaper, a fourth was on the debating team, but all of us had a father, a mother, an aunt, or an uncle who was investigated, fired from a job, was in prison, deported, or who fled the country and lived in exile in Mexico, France, or Russia. Furthermore we met other Columbia College freshmen whose parents were liberals, or Roosevelt Democrats, and they too grew up in the 1950's feeling uncomfortable, paranoid, guilty.

In the 1950's we had known loneliness. We felt simultaneously like foreign agents and patriotic citizens. We were hybrids— Russian-Americans, American-Russians, half-red, half-white, living in a no-man's-land between here and there. None of us wanted to live in this mythical land—there were two languages, Russian and English, two capitals, Washington and Moscow, and two founding fathers—George Washington and V.I. Lenin. When people shouted

46

"Go back to Russia" it hurt because our grandparents had in fact come to America from Russia. We all had relatives in the Soviet Union. We were given two choices by America; we could be either un-Americans or All-Americans. We chose the latter. We assimilated, infiltrated, wore disguises, buried the un-American activities deep beneath the surface, and engaged in everyday espionage. We spied on normal Americans, observed their customs and imitated them.

Picketing Woolworth's meant removing the manhole cover, reaching down with both hands and pulling the subterranean world, the alien existence, into the open on the sidewalks of Midtown Manhattan. But not all of us surfaced. Several friends of mine were still cautious and afraid to express their beliefs, except in intimate old left circles. Their parents had warned them against revealing their un-American lives and instructed them to project the All-American image. As freshmen at Columbia we were fugitives from our parents for the first time in our lives; we had a new angle of vision to appraise our fathers and our mothers, and for the first time we saw flaws.

Our parents supported us, but they didn't help us lift the subterranean world to the surface. And we weren't the first to demonstrate. It wasn't until Negro-Americans, Afro-Americans, surfaced that we Russian-Americans, we un-American All-Americans also surfaced. Blacks lifted the manhole cover first, threw Uncle Tom's clothing into the underworld, and then we followed their example, discarded our football uniforms, graduation gowns, mortarboards, school medals.

When blacks surfaced we realized that a nation within a nation had existed underground in the Ice Age. We were all frozen. The country was inhabited by fugitives running from the past, their ancestors, parents, religion, bodies and minds. Now, the fugitives were coming home. The exiles were returning. Still, we weren't willing to surface everywhere. Sometimes we still tried to infiltrate; we wore our disguises, and looked normal.

The week after our first picket line I went to the "Jefferson," a radical book store to buy *The Daily Worker*. An FBI camera photographed everyone going in and out of the store, so I buried my face in the pages of *The New York Times*. Inside I bought a copy of the *Worker* and *The Essential Works of Joseph Stalin*. When the man at the cash register asked: "Would you like this covered in a brown wrapper?" I said "Yes." I didn't want passengers on the IRT to see my book and newspaper. Only in the secrecy of my dorm room, with the door locked, did I open the parcel and look at *The Daily Worker*. There was a photograph of my friend Peter Gordon and me on the front page. But this publicity, this exposure, was welcome, for we had made the headlines, had broken into history. We were news. We were celebrities. I phoned Peter at his parents' home in Great Neck.

"Your picture's on the front page of the *Worker,*" I told him.

"I can't talk now," he said and slammed down the receiver. The next day in the dorm he explained, "We can't talk about politics on the phone because it's tapped. My father said to me: 'Joe McCarthy is dead but don't let that fool you; his friends are still around. Don't expose yourselves too much. One day soon you may want anonymity again.'"

When I showed my Aunt Iris the *Worker,* she said, "My friends in the 1930's left school and work to join the revolution. Then it didn't come and they were persecuted victims. Don't overextend. Don't take unnecessary risks."

Having bought and read *The Daily Worker* I now had to dispose of it. To have it in the dorm room was incriminating. We discussed ways of getting rid of it. If we burned it we might start a fire. The smoke would attract attention. If we threw it in the garbage a maid might find it. If we walked to the 116th Street subway stop and left it on a bench for someone to read a policeman might see us. Finally we decided to cut it into shreds and throw it down the toilet. But the shredded *Worker* clogged the pipes, the toilet backed up, and the plumber had to fish it out with a long wire. Then he disposed of the waterlogged *Worker.*

II. DUST, OR THE FREE MARKETPLACE OF IDEAS

Peter Gordon was a year younger than me. He had freckles, and big feet, he was tall and thin. His father, Doug, and his uncle Chris both taught American history at City College in the 1930's, and both lost their jobs in the 1940's, following the investigation of "subversive" teachers. They never told him about the past. Peter found out by reading old newspaper files in Butler Library. He "investigated" his father and his uncle at the same time he did research for his term papers, and discovered the past they didn't want him to know. Doug and Chris were victims of McCarthyism

48

long before the word was coined, before the junior senator from Wisconsin had assembled legal vigilantes for his witch hunts. From the start, but increasingly after World War II, and especially during the Korean War, no one in the academic world would touch these red lepers for fear of contracting a contagious disease.

Chris started a publishing house. The books about black history gathered dust in warehouses, but the books about flying saucers and ESP were best sellers in drugstores and bus stations. He became well-off, cranked out a book a year on Nat Turner, John Brown, Upton Sinclair, the CIO, Thomas Jefferson, the New Deal; he was a Marxist intellectual respected in Warsaw, Moscow and Prague but an unknown in New York and San Francisco. He—the great scholar and teacher—had been wounded and rejected by America; now it was his day in the Communist spotlight. He let us know that he was the world's living authority on American history. We had better sit up and listen.

Chris and Doug were unequal twin brothers; Chris dominated Doug, and Doug accepted his subordinate position. When Chris was fired he lost his self-confidence. But then he became bombastic and belligerent. He had to prove he was good. He had to publish and publish fast. Some of his books were original, brilliant, carefully documented, lyrically written. Others were assembled quickly and carelessly. He plagiarized. He published these books not to make money but to best his academic rivals. They, of course, only reviewed his sloppy works and used his carelessness as grounds to denounce all Marxist scholarship.

Since Chris was always under attack by his former City College colleagues, Doug didn't want to trouble or disturb him. He rarely questioned or criticized his brother. When Chris was attacked in the *Times,* Doug wrote letters to the editor and signed them under a variety of assumed names. He indulged Chris's egotism and tantrums.

Doug's reaction to the investigation and his dismissal was very different. He withdrew, retreated. He felt increasingly insecure, developed a defeatist attitude, and didn't want to prove himself. Doug deferred to his brother and to the world. Doug became Chris's secretary, did his shopping, baby-sat for his kids, took books out of the library for him, brought his clothes to the dry cleaners. "He's been so persecuted," Doug said of his brother, "that he needs to be indulged."

Doug had two sons: Peter, his older son, was brilliant and was groomed to become a historian; his younger son was diffident and was abandoned to his own devices. He was neglected. Chris had two daughters: the older daughter resented her father's over-bearing personality and his politics, and she became a slick writer for a women's fashion magazine; the younger daughter was brilliant and was also groomed to become a historian. Chris compared the progress of his younger daughter with the progress of his older nephew. Doug evaluated the progress of his older son and younger niece. They competed through their children, for their children were a reflection of themselves. Each of them neglected one child—Doug his younger son, and Chris his elder daughter. They gave them up for lost. And the children were also tools for revenge against the world. If the younger daughter and the older son succeeded as historians, the fathers would be vindicated.

Doug was less successful than Chris. He hadn't received his Ph.D., hadn't published, hadn't gone on speaking tours, and he wasn't a *cause célèbre* when they both got fired from City College. Doug became a part-time teacher and itinerant lecturer and gave informal talks several times a week in the comfortable homes of affluent old lefties who sent their sons to Princeton and Columbia, traveled in Italy and Yugoslavia in the summer, vacationed in Miami Beach for ten days in January, and wanted to be well-informed about world events. Doug had to be careful in what he said, especially about the Middle East, because his old friends bought Israel bonds and didn't want to hear a critique of Zionism. But Doug was unwilling to compromise his political views; he spoke in Aesopian language. The moral was always at the end and everyone could interpret it in the light of his or her own experience.

Doug was respected by his contemporaries because he had integrity, courage, lived simply, and continued his political work. But they also treated him with condescension. Unlike them, he had not gone into business, had not turned his energy—which in the 1930's and 1940's had been harnessed for rallies and strikes, fund-raising drives for miners, circulation drives for the *Worker*—to the making, saving, and investing of money. Doug's friends laughed at him. He was a *schlemiel.* He read turgid political and economic studies and missed his appointments, and the janitor kicked him out of the library at ten PM. His jackets had missing buttons, threadbare elbows; his shoes had holes in the soles, and he drove a Nash with a broken muffler. But he could tell you the history of South Yemen, rice production statistics in Chinese communes before and after the Great Leap Forward, Patrice Lumumba's life story.

The parents of my friend Alan Singer paid Douglas to distill and serve the news to them and their friends as they lounged on Swedish sofas, drank demitasse, and munched on Danish pastry from Zabar's. Alan Singer's mother Nickola was aggressive, gossipy, determined to make her son a doctor so that he would not have to stand as her husband stood, behind a cash register. Short, stocky, high-strung Alan was a pre-med, and resented studying physics, chemistry, resented spending long hours in the labs experimenting with B. F. Skinner's rats. He vented his anger on the rats, prodding and poking them, and on Peter and me, because we studied art, history, and literature and didn't have to memorize boring formulas, diagrams, and charts. Mrs. Singer applied constant pressure. Alan dangled bright objects before Skinner's rats, and she dangled before him bright images of heroic, wealthy doctors who save humanity from deadly plagues and live in comfortable Mamaroneck.

Alan's mother taught grade school in an old Jewish neighborhood and watched with alarm as the color on the faces of the students changed from white to black. She wanted to teach *them,* push *them* out of the ghetto, toward the towers of City College, along the route of the chosen Jews. She was patient and long suffering, as her bridge partner knew, but she decided after one day of aggravation that they couldn't be taught, coming as they did from broken homes and brutal blocks. Her Marxism, which she dimly recollected, came to her aid: the social conditions prevented them from learning; her efforts were meaningless until the slums were eliminated by the socialist revolution she still hoped for. Educating the *schwartzes* now wasn't in the cards.

Alan Singer's father was a butcher in the Bank Street Market, and on Saturday we helped him sell chickens (he plucked them, gutted them, cleaned them himself on the worn chopping block he scrubbed every night with a steel brush, hot water, and soap), to Puerto Ricans, blacks, and poor whites. The market was much more exciting than Hamilton Hall at Columbia, for we could

51

study the faces, the lives of numbers men, pimps, prostitutes, Baptists, dignified old black women in white robes, cops in blue, wizened Italian women poking in the garbage for food scraps, the stinking fish merchants, the fortune tellers, and the man with a cap pulled over his face, who sold *The Daily Worker* to Mr. Singer. The poor shoppers robbed what they could from him and he in turn cheated them.

On Saturday night after work Alan went to see his girlfriend. She lived on Sutton Place South and went to the Dalton School. Her father was an industrialist and an art collector, and there were two Picasso's hanging in the living room. "She has a nice body," Alan told us the night he met her at a college mixer. He liked the idea of a wealthy girlfriend, and she was attracted to him because he was a Columbia College freshman and she was only a high school junior.

"Have you fucked Sutton Place yet?" asked Steve Raab, a fat, awkward Brooklyn kid.

"No," Alan said. "She's not a pig."

"But you only describe her body. Does she also have a mind?" Steve asked.

"You have a shitty relationship," Alan replied.

"At least it's intellectual," Steve shouted.

"It's a Nazi relationship. You order her to fuck, and you order her to worship your brain. One day she'll tell you to fuck off." Alan was angry.

Steve Raab's girlfriend lived on the Grand Concourse in the Bronx and went to City College. Her father was a garment worker, a trade union leader and lower middle class. Steve thought that he was doing her a favor by going out with her. He was lifting her socially and intellectually.

"She'll never tell me to fuck off," he said, "because she knows she'll never find another Marxist as good as me. She wants a husband who's a radical like her father. So I teach her Marxism and she lets me fuck her. You ought to date political women, especially since you're not fucking Sutton Place."

"Show me one," Alan said, walking back and forth nervously.

"At the next mixer talk politics," Steve suggested. On Saturday Alan went to the Columbia-Barnard tea and asked a freshman:

"Are you in favor of admitting Red China to the UN?"

"Are you crazy?" she said, turning her back on him. He asked another woman: "Are you in favor of unilateral disarmament?"

"Are you trying to seduce me?" the woman asked.

"Oh, no," Alan said. "It's a survey for the school paper."

"I feel like a fool," he told Steve later that evening. "I'm going back to Sutton Place to drop my load. At least she'll jerk me off."

"You're so horny you'd fuck anyone," Steve said.

"I wouldn't fuck a fascist," Alan said indignantly. Steve started to tease him.

"But you'd fuck a social democrat or a liberal wouldn't you?"

"Yes, that's different."

"I'd fuck a fascist," Steve said escalating his joke.

"That's disgusting!" Alan shouted, his nerves on edge.

"But I'd come right away and pull out, I'd be satisfied and she'd be unsatisfied. That way I'd have fucked fascism. An anti-fascist fuck." Steve beamed.

"Very funny," Alan said, irritated that he'd been made a fool.

I suggested that Alan come to the Thirty-fourth Street Woolworth's picket line. He hadn't picketed yet but I enticed him, I suppose unethically, with stories of the women I had met there. One Saturday he went with Peter and me but soon disappeared from the picket line. We saw him later in the dorm.

"I fell in love," he said.

"Is she beautiful?" Steve asked, teasing again, as usual. Alan nodded. "I'm glad she's not ugly," Steve said. "I wouldn't want you to marry an ugly woman. Is she a radical?"

"Her father knows my father from the party. He was the Moscow correspondent for *The Daily Worker.*"

"When are you getting married?"

"I don't know."

"Why not?"

"She's black."

"What difference does that make? You're progressive," Steve said.

Every Saturday she and Alan met at the picket line. He stopped working at the market. His father got angry at him but Alan said he had to study. She was a Hunter College freshman and lived in an apartment on St. Nicholas Avenue in Harlem. For the first time in his life Alan made love. He was exuberant and also apprehensive. A month passed. He seemed happy. Then one night he said, "I'm going to Sutton Place." We were stunned.

"What happened?" I asked.

"Nothing," Alan said.

"Did she want to marry you?" Steve asked.

"No."

Then about a week later when we were driving Mr. Singer's car on the West Side Highway he told us.

"Promise you won't say?"

"Yes."

"My parents said they wouldn't pay for my tuition next term if I continued to go out with her. When I wasn't working at the market my father hired another man, made less money, and so he couldn't afford to give me anything. I'll have to stop picketing and go back to work."

"Did you agree?" I asked.

"Yes," Alan said. "It was her or college and I chose college. Besides I'm fucking Sutton Place now."

"Do you love her?"

"No, but she's a good lay."

Steve and I didn't keep Alan's confession a secret. Soon Peter also knew.

"How can we face her on the picket line?" Peter asked.

"I'm afraid to see her," I said.

We decided to confront Alan's parents. We didn't regard him as a criminal, but we saw less and less of him.

"I don't think he's evil," Peter said, "but he's dishonest." We were on the verge of sending a delegation to the market. I was no longer working for Mr. Singer. He had told me to watch shoplifters and I refused. But our delegation never reached the market. Instead Peter confronted Alan one afternoon at a Columbia-Barnard mixer.

"Why does your father rob poor black people?" he asked. "I thought he was a radical."

"Schmucks!" Alan shouted. "What else can he do? He's blacklisted because he was a Communist, and he can't get another job. The market pays for my Columbia tuition. If I don't become a doctor I'll have to work in the market, too. They don't want me to suffer as they suffered. You have no financial worries. Your fathers aren't pure. Nothing in

54

this society is untainted. Don't be self-righteous."

That night when Alan was at Sutton Place, Peter and I had a beer in the West End.

"We ought to move our Woolworth's picket line downtown and picket Mr. Singer's market."

"He's not as bad as Woolworth's," I said.

"But the fact that he reads the *Worker*, goes to my father's lectures and calls himself a radical infuriates me. The Singers aren't as poor as Alan claims. They just don't like blacks."

During Christmas vacation we met Mrs. Singer.

"What are you boys studying?" she asked.

"History," I said. "We're going to teach."

"You'll only be fired for your political beliefs," she said, "like Chris and Doug. You ought to become a doctor like Alan. It's safer." But we felt that it was our mission to rewrite the history of America and its culture. We were going to take picks and shovels, dig away at the earth, and uncover the past which had been buried by Roy Cohn and Joe McCarthy. We planned to write a textbook celebrating the heroes and heroines of our childhood—Eugene V. Debs, Thaddeus Stevens, Tom Paine, Theodore Dreiser, Frederick Douglass, Mother Bloor, and Elizabeth Gurley Flynn. And we even decided that our pen names would be E. Jefferson Gordon and J. Seth Raskin.

In 1960 we took a twentieth-century American history course from Professor Hank Mirstein, a popular teacher and a tough marker. In 1940 he cooperated with the investigating committee and retained his job while Chris refused to testify and lost his. Mirstein won immortality in the college for one sexist remark— "A woman placed on a pedestal is a woman taken out of bed"— and for his conservative lectures on the thirties.

"I was at City College in the Red decade," Mirstein confessed, raising his bushy eyebrows and peering into our faces. "I know the Communist experience from the inside and I reject it. I have passed through the fire. For a brief, flickering moment in history Communism held out a vision of hope for men and women, this poor clot of humanity, huddled on the earth. But the Hitler-Stalin pact of 1939 showed us that our dreams were false. I got off the train. It was a painful parting, and none of you, I feel, can appreciate the depth of anguish and suffering, because some of our comrades stayed on the train. What was most difficult to see—though I did see it—was the necessity of confession, purgation, washing our souls free of the dust which that red journey deposited. Only the weakest, the most selfish, could not reject the party, admit their errors, and seek absolution among the great, good mass of the American people." He picked up a piece of chalk, went to the blackboard, and drew a straight line. "At first I believed that Communism was here (he pointed to the far left end of the line) but I learned that that concept is false." He paused and drew a circle. "This diagram comes closer to the truth. Communism and fascism fall to the same point at the bottom of the circle, and liberalism rises to the top. Liberalism, not Communism, is the true enemy of fascism. Fascism and Communism are not opposites but are identical. Extremes meet at the bottom. It's dialectical."

I was angry at Mirstein. I sat in class brooding, put down my pencil, and refused to take notes.

"Maybe Mrs. Singer is right," I said. "How will we graduate if our professors are like him?"

"He once refused to meet my uncle," Peter said. "The only way to get an A in this course is to say what he wants to hear."

Chris Gordon introduced us to the Cuban diplomats at the UN. They appreciated his works on American history and enjoyed meeting with him.

"Do you like New York?" Peter asked one of the young Cubans.

"We'd rather be in Havana because this is the belly of the beast, but the revolution dispatched us to Manhattan and we have come."

"Did you fight in the revolution?"

"We were in the mountains with Che and Fidel." The Cuban diplomats were younger than we were. I was nineteen, and I hadn't fired a gun or liberated a city; I wasn't a socialist ambassador. I was underdeveloped in affluent America. We talked to C. Wright Mills about his visit to Cuba, read his book *Listen, Yankee,* and hung a Cuban flag in our dorm room. We were Cubaphiles because Fidel had stayed at the Hotel Teresa in Harlem rather than a luxurious East Side hotel, and because Che boasted that he would sleep in a hammock in Central Park and live like a guerrilla in the jungles of New York. We liked the bearded Cubans because they wore army fatigues, because they were unpretentious, enthusiastic, because Nikita Khrushchev and old Red Russia hugged Fidel and new Red Cuba.

Peter's paper for Mirstein was about the Spanish American War in 1898; there was no mention of our Cuban friends, or Che or Fidel, and I thought that he was consciously leaving out his feelings so that he would get a good grade. Mirstein gave him an A-minus and criticized him for using too many left-wing sources.

I wrote a paper about Julius and Ethel Rosenberg. Every day I took my pencils and notebooks and went to the stacks of Butler Library to read thousands and thousands of pages of newsprint captured on microfilm. I lived in the pages of *The New York Times, The Daily Worker, Le Monde* from 1950 to 1953, and long after I left the library the headlines and photos were imprinted on my mind. I also obtained the official transcript of the trial from the Committee to Free Morton Sobell. Sobell had been found guilty of conspiring, along with the Rosenbergs, to steal the A-bomb secret. He was serving a thirty-year prison term on Alcatraz, the rock. I went to the committee's office in the Flatiron Building on Twenty-third Street. An old man took me up in the caged elevator, left me on the sixteenth floor, slammed the door shut, and returned to the ground floor. The corridors in the maze were narrow and crooked, and most of the electric light bulbs were burned out. Room 1603. No name. I knocked on the opaque window and entered suspiciously. The office was cramped. There were two desks, several file cabinets, a radiator which hissed and rattled. Two women were filing envelopes.

"Can I help you?" the younger woman asked.

"I want to buy a transcript of the Rosenberg trial. Is this the committee?"

"Yes. Just a minute. We packed them away. They're collector's items." She went into the adjoining room and in a few minutes returned with three dusty green volumes.

"What do you want them for?"

"I'm writing a paper on the Rosenbergs."

"My name is Helen Sobell. You are . . .?"

"Jonah Raskin."

"If you can help to pardon my husband, please . . ."

I left abruptly, afraid that I had made a mistake by giving my real name to Mrs. Helen Sobell. Why couldn't I have thought faster and said "Smith" or "Jones"? If the room was bugged by the FBI, I would be investigated. If the list of people who wanted to free Morton Sobell was seized by the police, I would be called before the House Un-American Activities Committee.

How pathetic it was. In 1960 I thought that Morton Sobell would never be freed. Why did his wife and mother persist in that drab office day after day. Probably they had no other choice. They kept on just to keep on, out of habit or like the rain which falls because it falls. They had no money, no secretary, no embossed stationery, and no one knew about Morton Sobell. Did dust gather on him in Alcatraz as it gathered on the transcript of his trial? I was angry at Helen Sobell and her mother-in-law. Why did they still have the illusion they could free a husband and son? They had no allies, no Fidel, no Che, no Red Army. What could two old women do? Nothing. And yet every day they came to the Flatiron Building, went to the sixteenth floor, unlocked the door, turned on the light, and went to work to free Morton Sobell. It was incomprehensible. They, not I, carried on the heritage of Julius and Ethel Rosenberg, for they refused to surrender, to acknowledge defeat, refused to disappear into the depths of Brooklyn and allow Morton Sobell to sit quietly gathering dust in Alcatraz. Against all odds, against every reason, they were obstinate for Morton Sobell.

A month later, as I sat in class, Professor Mirstein returned my paper. I saw the C and read his devastating comment:

> *You haven't proven your case. It seems to me that the Rosenbergs were indeed guilty. I do agree with you, however, that the death penalty was unnecessarily harsh, a slight blot on the record of American justice. Perhaps they should have received life imprisonment, but that's another story. I can't help but feel that you became emotionally involved in this paper, and that it suffers accordingly. Maybe next time you'll stick to more neutral material. Finally let me say that I feel that if you had listened to my lectures you would have avoided this error. Please pay attention, and take notes. I am not an unfair man, but your hostility and lack of respect are more than anyone can stand to bear.*

Peter read my paper and Mirstein's comment and said, "You should have done more research."

"You sound like Mirstein reviewing one of your uncle's books," I said. "I got a C because I expressed my feelings and my politics."

"Politics isn't everything."

"If you talk like that you'll sell out."

"You don't have a brain."

"Fuck off."

"Kiss my ass." A month later, I left the history department and began to study literature, and our friendship cooled. As freshmen we thought we were a perfect match, but by the middle of our sophomore year we recognized that we were very different people.

III. STATUTES OF LIBERTY

One afternoon I took the Broadway local uptown to City College to hear a talk by a member of the American Communist Party. But the school administration had canceled the speech.

"A public institution of higher learning," a dean said, "cannot offer its facilities to a Communist. We are a neutral institution and take no stand either for or against Communism."

"You allow Democrats, Republicans, generals, corporation executives to speak," a woman shouted. She was dark and looked Greek or Italian. She wore a red bandana over her head, big hoop earrings, a billowing skirt, leather sandals, and a matching handbag.

"Why don't you invite Adlai Stevenson to talk?" he suggested. "Why do you insist on Benjamin Davis?"

"Mr. Stevenson isn't a Communist," the woman said. "He's free to speak whenever and wherever he wants to."

When the argument ended I introduced myself to the woman and explained that I belonged to Action, a political organization on the Columbia campus, that we'd be willing to sponsor a speech by Benjamin Davis. "We'd like to hear what the Communist Party has to say," I told her, "and I think we can convince the administration to allow it on the grounds of freedom of speech."

I was the vice-chairman and organization man of Action. Peter Gordon was the chairman and the main spokesman, Steve Raab thought of himself as the theoretician, the *eminence grise* working behind the scenes; Alan Singer was the diplomat and the compromiser; and Kurt Thomas, an art major, shy and fair-haired, was the propagandist, the spy uncovering the university's business interests. Kurt showed us that the "House of Intellect," as Jacques Barzun, provost and professor extraordinary, called Columbia, was a "House of Profit." We called ourselves Action because we wanted students to shed their apathy, fifties cool, and Columbia College boredom and burst onto picket lines and demonstrations, listen to soap box orators, sign petitions, join study groups. Faculty members and students found us suspect and called us a "front group." We claimed we had no ideology, were an independent radical political group, and were neither pro- nor anti-Russian. But the more we declared our independence, the more we asserted that we were not a monolithic organization, the more the students suspected that we were a doctrinaire party. Fraternity leaders, administrators, Trotskyites, and Anarchists all said that we were a Communist-front organization.

We were attacked in precisely the same way our parents had been attacked in the fifties. Moreover, our strategy had been exactly like theirs. They hadn't told us how to organize, but when we did political work we imitated what they had done, for theirs was the only politics we knew from first-hand experience. We discarded their label, "progressive," and called ourselves by a new name, "Radicals," but we didn't publicly say we were Marxists, Communists, Socialists, or revolutionaries.

"Why is it, if you're not a Communist-front group," my friend Tim asked, "that the first person you invite to speak is a Communist?"

"Because Communists are denied the right to speak," I said.

"They don't give Anarchists the platform either," Tim said. His father was a radical from the 1930's, a Jew, a professor of American literature at Harvard, and his mother was from a wealthy old-line, New England family. Tim lived in the smallest room on campus; once it had been a closet where the maids kept their brooms and mops but he claimed it and now it was packed with his bed, desk, motorcycle, piles of Anarchist books and magazines, a banjo and guitar, and pictures of Emma Goldman and a bearded man.

"Is that Marx?" I asked.

"No, that's Bakunin," Tim said, "Marx's Anarchist enemy. I don't trust Action. I know what the Communists did to the

Anarchists in Barcelona in 1936. They were worse than Franco. If you were running Columbia, you wouldn't let us speak."

Professor Hans Boker of the Religion Department asked us two questions before he agreed to be the faculty advisor for Action. "Are you Anarchists?" he asked.

"No," Peter said.

"Are you planning to blow up buildings?" I laughed and Peter said, "No." I was surprised and puzzled, for I hadn't conceived of the idea that a political group would use dynamite. My nervous laugh made Professor Boker suspicious of us. He paused a few seconds before shaking my hand.

Josepha, the woman I had met at City College, helped us plan the Davis speech. We became friends. On Sundays she invited me to dinner at her parents' apartment in Washington Heights. Mrs. Spiegel was an alcoholic and usually stayed in bed with the door closed. I was nervous because the Spiegels were German Jews and my parents had warned me against German Jews. The first thing Mr. Spiegel said was "Let me see your shoes."

"What?"

"Take them off." I did. He looked at them carefully. "They're OK, but next Sunday when you come I'll repair the soles." He showed me his cobbler's tools and pointed to a photograph of Sacco, the Italian Anarchist shoemaker. "I'm prepared for the next depression," he said. "I made a study of occupations and discovered that of all workers shoemakers fared best in the economic crisis of the 1930's. People gotta walk, right? And when they walk they gotta wear shoes. I'm going to get to their heads through their feet. Organize the feet first, that's the key. From nine to five Monday through Friday he was an accountant, but he spent his spare time in shoemakers' shops, learned the trade, and on Sunday afternoons he repaired shoes in the living room—"just to practice for the coming depression."

"What's the second depression?" I asked. "My economics teacher says there won't be one."

"Is he a Trotskyite?" Mr. Spiegel asked. "Watch out for them Trotskyites. I had a mess of trouble with them when I was with Harry Bridges and the dockworkers in Seattle." Mr. Spiegel told me fascinating tales of "organizin' de workers" and "underminin' capitalism" in the 1930's.

"Sundays aren't what they used to be," he said. "We'd pile

into an old beat-up Ford, drive into Central Park and ram into the Cadillacs and Rolls-Royces of the plutocrats. That's the way we had fun in those days. Fun I tell you. We weren't stick-in-the-muds like the young guys around today. They're all revisionists."

One Sunday Mr. Spiegel handed me a bourbon and asked, "Do you know how Josepha got her name?"

"No."

"We were expecting a boy; 1943, it was after the Battle of Stalingrad, the turning point of the war, the Germans were retreating in the snow back to Berlin and the Russian people were making heroic sacrifices. What else could we call our son but Joseph? We were disappointed when she was born, but what the hell. Josepha's close enough. She's our little Stalin. Say, why not take a look at this." He handed me Stalin's essay on the National Question. "Next Sunday I'll ask you a few questions to see how much you understand."

Mr. Spiegel was working in the campaign office of Stanton de Haaland, a candidate for congress. "I'm spying," he said. "I haven't used my real name and I put on a moustache and dark glasses before I go downtown. When the secretaries leave the office I go through the files. Haaland has ties with the Air Force. There's a secret base in Arizona and he knows where it is. I want that information." Josepha tried to persuade me not to go.

"It's one of my father's wild goose chases," she said. "He likes to wear disguises."

"What harm can it do?" I said. We did mailings, stuffed letters, sealed envelopes. When the secretaries went out for lunch I stood guard while Mr. Spiegel picked the locks and went through the files. But he never found anything.

"It's wonderful to see kids in love," he said to me one afternoon when we were addressing envelopes. "You're mature young people, but take the necessary precautions."

Like me, Josepha studied French and Russian. We did dramatic readings of *Le Rouge et le Noir* and *The Idiot*. I was Julien Sorel and Prince Mishkin, and she was Matilde de la Mole and Nastasie Fillipovnia. We stayed up late, lying on her bed covered with a bright yellow and brown Mexican blanket, and talked about Dostoevsky, Stendhal, romantic love, and suicide.

Josepha and I went to parties, drank vodka, recited Mayakovsky, danced, but we never made love. Her bedroom was like a hothouse; luxurious and solitary tropical flowers entwined but didn't embrace. We got drunk and made out, but when I tried to soul kiss, touch her breasts, or take off her clothes she'd stop me, get up and suggest we talk about Benjamin Davis. We spent weeks planning for his speech, negotiating with the administration. At first Columbia didn't want Davis on campus; then the university officials decided that Columbia would look better favoring free speech, even for a Communist. We had to arrange the schedule with Davis too, but Peter, who had known him from childhood, was the only one who was willing and unafraid to meet this awesome Red.

One afternoon I picked up the phone. "Action central," I said. "This is Benjamin Davis of the Communist Party," the voice on the other end answered. I was intimidated and afraid. I had never before heard anyone say on the phone that he was a Communist or a member of the Communist Party.

"It's for you, Peter." I let him do all the talking and arranging, but Kurt resented his role. He felt that Peter was an egotist and elitist, who enjoyed being the chairman of Action not because it was politically or morally right but because being the number one student radical brought power, prestige, status.

"It puts you in the limelight," Kurt said. "You behave exactly like the fraternity leaders. They're right wing and you're left wing, but you're all individualists. You take the credit for yourself and don't give us any.

"The dean's office doesn't want to renew my scholarship next term," Peter said. "I'll have prestige, but I won't be in school. Why don't you become chairman of Action and see just how friendly people are."

Steve Raab resigned from Action a few days before Davis's speech.

"It's counterproductive," he said, "because we won't also invite a fascist to speak. It's better not to invite anyone to speak. Students will think we're revolutionaries, and we've got to appear liberal, at least for another two or three years. We need a long-term strategy."

Peter and Josepha argued about the arrangements for the speech. She wanted to set up a table and sell *The Communist Manifesto* and *The Daily Worker* in the lobby of the auditorium, but Peter opposed the idea. Furthermore, he was threatened by her political ability, and he tried to isolate her.

"She's an outside agitator, a Red from City College," he said. "We have to keep the slate clean." I tried to preserve the organization, prevent people from arguing, get to "Davis Day" without a crisis.

"All these conflicts can wait," I said, but instead they intensified and before the day arrived Action was nearly destroyed. Early one morning Mr. Spiegel arrived in my dorm room and dragged me off to South Jamaica to see his mother.

"This is the middle of a crisis," I said.

"You can't let politics interfere with humanity; she's a wonderful old woman." Josepha's grandmother lived in an old railroad flat. "The neighborhood's changed," Mr. Spiegel said, "but I want you to see how German workers lived in 1919. The apartment is the same now as it was then. Sure there's a television set, but the furniture, the curtains, the stove—all the same." Mr. Spiegel showed me the bedroom. "My father was a Wobbly. He was a sheet-metal worker, used a hammer all his life. In bed asleep at night, his arm would move automatically as if he were hammering in the factory. My mother couldn't stop that arm." We bought Grandma Spiegel a sixpack of beer, chatted with her in the kitchen, and then drove back to Columbia.

The political scene was becoming richer, more complicated. There were Anarchist, Wobbly and Communist traditions, and I felt my political dimensions were growing. Mr. Spiegel was a wonderful teacher. He came to Davis's speech.

"He's the best of the old lot," he said. Professor Dodge, a civil libertarian and philosopher, a tall crotchety man, introduced Davis. But he was stunned when Ben Davis, Chris Gordon's old friend, said "comrade" and embraced Peter on the stage. Even Peter was uncomfortable. A thousand students gathered to hear Davis talk in McMillan Theatre. They laughed at his jokes. ("We're financed by Moscow gold," he said, then drew out his empty pockets.) He was a black man, but he looked, dressed and talked like an intellectual. He didn't sound like a Communist agitator; he was a reasonable, kind man, and he persuaded the audience that anti-Communism was silly.

"Do I look dangerous?" he asked. "Do I look like a spy? I'm an American citizen, yet the State of New York has taken away my driver's license because I'm a member of the American

Communist Party. Don't you think that I should be allowed to drive legally?" The audience answered with a resounding "Yes." The Communist Party and the sons of the old left had won a victory at Columbia. We celebrated; Davis had defended Communism but he made Communists appear gentle, warm, harmless Americans. He hadn't embarrassed us.

The campus changed, people took sides, debated Action, and especially the idea that students should concern themselves with national and international issues, not just the homecoming dance and the spring fraternity weekend.

"How strange, how absurd, what does Columbia have to do with Benjamin Davis, or HUAC, or nuclear testing?" the president of the fraternity council said to Peter in a college debate. "We're here to get a degree, drink beer, root for the Lions. That's all. Don't bother me."

The day after the Davis speech, Josepha and I went to a Spanish restaurant. We drank a carafe of sangria, shared a seafood paella, flirted, teased, lured one another. We devoured lobster, clams and shrimp, sang sad, sentimental Spanish Civil War songs. Josepha looked more and more like an Andalusian woman, the heroine of the Abraham Lincoln Brigade in Barcelona in 1936.

It was a chilly April night, but we walked in Washington Square Park, stood under the arch and hunted for constellations. I felt the city couldn't hold my energy, so we took the subway to South Ferry, put five cents in the slot, and went for a ride on the Staten Island Ferry. "We're headed for Europe," Josepha said. "It's wonderful to be out on the water." We watched the captain at the wheel, bought hot dogs and soda at the snack bar. The ship was crowded with young couples, and older men and women going home from offices in Manhattan. Passengers were asleep on the seats. Lovers kissed. The city was behind us. The ferry gave me a sense of adventure and travel. I looked above and saw two constellations—Orion, the hunter, and Cassiopeia in her chair. The water was still, but the wind was sharp. The Statue of Liberty grew larger and larger as the boat moved further and further from the shore. It was a majestic and silent woman of death, corroded by the sea and turned a mossy green. We stood at the prow near the guardrail. Two kids watched their balloons float over the water. I put my arms around Josepha and kissed her. She looked green, too, but I

65

closed my eyes and kissed her again. She was cold.

"I'm going to walk back and watch the receding skyline," she said. "Want to come?"

"No, you're always looking back. Why not look ahead to the other side?"

"Maybe I don't want to go where you want me to go," she said, wrapping her black scarf around her neck and adjusting her Russian fur hat. She walked back growing smaller and smaller till she disappeared around the curve of the ship. I paced up and back, wondered what Julien Sorel would have done, what Prince Mishkin would have said. *Do I dare? What will she think? Maybe she'll walk back. I'm an idiot, a fool. I'll have to think of something to say, find a wedge to open the conversation, something political, something funny, so she won't think I'm being obnoxious.* She was standing at the edge of the ferry. The skyline was beautiful.

"Isn't it stunning?" she said.

"We're almost in Staten Island." I put my arms around her.

"Not now."

"If not now, when?"

"Later." I walked to the bow and watched the ferry zigzag toward the pier. The cars sped off, the passengers sprinted home. I shuffled my feet and walked off the ferry alone.

That was the end. We stopped seeing one another, except at demonstrations when we nodded hello.

"Did you ever sleep together?" Peter asked me one evening in the dorm.

"No, never," I said.

"Steve would say you were crazy. What was it all about?"

"Josepha was the spirit of the revolution. She was an addiction, a craving. Having an intense asexual relationship was an adventure. In the books we read and the movies we watched we were always fascinated by agonizing, alienated relationships. Lovers who didn't or couldn't love were more appealing than the happily married couples."

I stopped going to class but wandered around the Village, took the F-train to Brooklyn to visit Billy, my counselor from summer camp, went to the Thalia Theatre in the afternoon to see Fellini and De Sica films, and to the East Side Cinema to see Antonioni and Bergman films. It was wonderful to feel alienated. I felt cynical about politics. Going to the movies by myself induced a profound mood of loneliness. Antonioni's world was perfect: everything was full of reverberations—a scrap of paper, a light bulb, a drop of water. I wanted to feel loss and sorrow. Peter and Kurt yelled at me for not doing political work.

"You've got one-track minds," I said. "Don't you appreciate culture?" Occasionally, when I wanted company I tagged along with Billy and his girlfriend. At Figaro's we drank coffee, and at Coney Island we strolled along the boardwalk. Billy was casual and violent about women. He hadn't changed much since I knew him the summer of 1954. He met strange women, talked with them effortlessly, went to bed with them frequently and immediately. And it all seemed to me, as I sat in the living room and listened to him fucking in his bedroom—clean and efficient. When I was twelve, I worshipped Billy's sexuality. Now, I was both threatened by and attracted to it. He was a professional, and "chicks dug cool cats." He was suave, enigmatic, and he was always, as he said, "in the sack searching for the perfect lay, the classic fuck." I wanted to be, but was afraid of becoming, Billy, the professional "ass man."

I tried unsuccessfully to reach Josepha, and my cousin Paula told me that she joined CORE, was living with a black man in Bedford Stuyvesant, Brooklyn, and talked as if she had lived on 125th Street and Lenox Avenue her whole life.

"She's running away from something," Paula said.

"It won't last." I said, thinking of Alan Singer's brief affair with a black woman. Wait till Mrs. Spiegel finds out. I found myself hating her, wanting her to be unhappy like me, and I also imagined that Josepha's relationship was sick, perverse.

Mr. Spiegel took me and my cousin Paula out to dinner one Friday night. We had blintzes and sour cream, beef and barley soup.

"I suppose you've heard about Josepha," he said. "I haven't told my wife, but it's hard around the house with her away. I know you're sad. Normally I'd have said that Josepha hated herself and wanted to reject me. For a while I thought she was sexually confused. What do you think?" he asked.

"I'm sure you're right Mr. Spiegel," I said, thinking that Josepha did hate herself. But I didn't want to make Mr. Spiegel any more depressed than he was.

"You're right, he must be a fine man. If my daughter likes him he must be wonderful. I'm willing to bet you he's another Paul Robeson. Wanna come uptown with me?"

"No thanks, Mr. Spiegel, I'm gonna stay at my cousin's house."

When spring term ended Mr. Spiegel invited me to visit his friends in the Smoky Mountains. Billy invited me to go to Europe with him and "learn the ropes." I went with Billy because Europe seemed the ideal place to refine my cult of alienation. Mr. Spiegel was always in a good mood and it would have been impossible to be depressed in his presence. London, Paris, Rome offered new scenes for the bored, lonely, sensitive student. In Nice I met a French woman from Paris. She smelled of ripe Brie cheese. One night after we went dancing in Cannes she said that she had lost the key to her hotel, that it was too late to wake the concierge, and could she stay with me at my hotel. I invited her home.

I was suddenly afraid. My French vanished and I couldn't talk. In the hotel room we turned our backs to each other, undressed partially, stealing glances at each other's bodies to see which items of clothing we hadn't removed. *Are we going to sleep or make love? Should I put the Trojan on now or later? Do I ask her if she wants to make love, or do we just do it? Will it be any good? What would Billy do?* My head was dizzy. I didn't know if I could control myself. I wanted to be good. She kissed me and pulled me on top of her. *She surely could feel my erection now. She'd know I was excited. The body doesn't lie.* I was naked. I was exposed. There was no armor, no padding, no uniform. She took off her bra and underpants. I reciprocated and took off my underpants. *Has she made love before? Is she a virgin? Can she tell I'm inexperienced. Maybe I'll come right away. That would be the worst thing. I've got to satisfy her sexually; she's got to come. Otherwise I'm a failure. French men must be good. I'd rather not come than her not come.* I mounted her, kissed her, tasted the Brie cheese, buried my head in the pillow, and concentrated on her vagina. She didn't move, but she moaned, and so I moaned too. Then she shouted, dug her nails into my back, and I pushed harder and harder and came. *Did she come?* She didn't say and I was afraid to ask. But she smiled and wrapped her legs around mine. Something inside me had snapped. I fell asleep.

In September Billy and I returned to New York. I took the

Long Island Railroad to Huntington, and felt a deep hostility rising in me toward America. The wretched railroad, the ugly junkyards, the decrepit, snarling passengers. I felt a sickness inside, a desire to return to Paris and travel in Europe. *How could this be the most powerful nation in the world? It was dirty, vulgar, cheap, ugly.* The passengers were hostile and unlike the friendly passengers in European trains who shared their bread, cheese, wine, and fruit.

My parents met me at the station. I hardly recognized them; they looked like funny, grotesque midgets with gigantic smiles. Peter was waiting at home. We shook hands. In the evening we went to a bar.

"Mr. Spiegel wants to see you right away," he said. "He claims he's uncovered a right-wing spy network." Then he handed me a letter from Josepha. It put our relationship and my summer in perspective. It was the first letter of its kind I had ever received. It helped me to understand my feelings. It was a beginning.

Dear Jonah,

In July I went South and was arrested in Mississippi at a sit-in. I spent four weeks in jail. I thought about you a lot. Jail was awful: we had cold bologna and weak tea, the toilets didn't work. But there were black women who taught me history, and songs. We talked about our families, and sex. I'd like to see you. I hope you don't listen to Steve Raab. He thinks I went South because I'm sexually neurotic. That's not true. Maybe I was unhappy and confused when we spent time together. I have problems, but I'm not politically active because of sexual repression. You stopped political work after our relationship ended. How do you explain that? I know there is a connection between sex and politics, but you aren't political because you're sexually frustrated. That's as absurd as saying we're political because our parents were political. But I know dozens of kids at City whose parents were Reds in the 1930's, but they only care about degrees and jobs. I'm still living with Basil in Brooklyn. He's studying psychiatry. Why don't you visit? We haven't any friends, although my father has been wonderful. I'll cook dinner, and you can tell us all about Europe.

Love, Josepha

CHAPTER
FIVE
MOTHER AND DAUGHTER

Sheila wore a white dress, stockings and high heels; her long brown hair was arranged in a bun. I wore a green summer suit, a white shirt, a blue tie, and new shoes. We sat in Judge Harold Livingston's chambers on the twenty-first floor of the Foley Square Courthouse. It was August 28, 1964; the first anniversary of the March on Washington and Martin Luther King's "I have a dream" speech. We waited for the honorable Judge to declare a recess in a trial and perform the ceremony. We were going to be married. All sound was muffled. It was quiet. We were perched high above the street. When the wind blew, the building swayed. My mother dozed in a comfortable armchair. My father and Sheila's mother peered out the window at the landmarks on the horizon.

FLASHBACK ONE: COURTSHIPS

Sheila and I met in September 1963. She was a Barnard freshman, I was a master's student in American literature at Columbia. Sheila was Stella's best friend, Stella was Peter Gordon's girl-friend, and Peter was my best friend. Our peers rather than our parents had encouraged our union. When we met I was living with two couples: Tony Meyer, a former editor of *The Columbia Daily Spectator,* a graduate student in journalism and a reporter for the *Times;* Susan, a Radcliffe student and anthropologist; Paul, a graduate student in Latin American history; and Carol, a French woman and a ballet dancer. We didn't call ourselves a collective or a commune, but we shared the work, had house meetings, cooked and ate communally. Everyone was coupled off, no one was married and everyone was officially against marriage.

The major showpiece in our apartment was a nine-foot-high mural, extending the length of one wall. It was painted in seven days by Kurt, then in his first year at Yale's School of Architecture. At the center of the mural was a young black woman wearing a pink dress, leading the 1963 March on Washington. She carried a sign which said "Civil Rights Now." On the far right was Pope John XXIII holding his hands to pray and standing on a box inscribed with the words "pacem in terris." On the far left was Fidel Castro, smoking a cigar, carrying a gun, wearing an olive green army uniform. There was smiling JFK, with neatly combed hair, a snappy, pin-striped suit. Facing him was fat, balding Khrushchev, wearing a conventional 1950's-style suit, and holding the shoe he had banged on the table at the UN. At the top of the painting there were two competing slogans—"World Revolution" and "Peaceful Co-Existence."

We ate most of our meals, talked, and played cards in a large kitchen. The wallpaper was decorated with strawberries and brioche, and every morning we ate our fried eggs, bacon, English muffins, instant coffee, and dreamed about the perfect breakfast of the future—warm brioche from the bakery with rich butter, and ripe, red strawberries covered with thick, heavy cream and crunchy sugar.

Sheila and her mother Emma lived together on the seventh floor of a new twenty-five-story apartment house. There was a balcony offering a beautiful view of the skyscrapers below the Park. Sheila's paintings hung on the wall in her bedroom; a balalaika and a six-string guitar rested against the wall. Sheila was big-boned, and her brown hair reached down below her waist. On school days she wore white sneakers, dungarees, and neatly ironed shirts with flower prints. In September we had picnic lunches on the Barnard lawn, studied in the library, walked in Central Park. The air was sharp and clear, the leaves were brown, red, yellow, orange. Kids played touch football. At home in the evenings she memorized her Italian verbs, read Wittgenstein and Kant, and I read Henry James's novels. We listened to the Beatles, went to see Jackson Pollock's paintings, and watched old films on the late-night movie.

Sheila was independent and self-confident. She had a quick mind, she was compassionate, and she wanted to devote her life to radical political activity, as her father had done until the day he died. It seemed as if she could do everything well; she could dance, sing, act, write, paint. But she was also hard on herself, very demanding and very rigorous. It was difficult for her to live up to the standards she set for herself.

The more time we spent together the less time we spent in the civil rights and peace movements. But in October, before we were a solid couple, we demonstrated to protest a speech by Madame Nhu, President Diem's sister-in-law, in McMillan Theatre. Tim, who was still living in the smallest room on campus and was still an Anarchist, listened to her speech. "She insists South Vietnam is democratic," he said, "even though Saigon policemen clubbed an American reporter." On Broadway Josepha carried a sign which read ",Victory to the Viet Cong."

"Won't that alienate liberal and uncommitted students?" I asked her.

"The Viet Cong represent the Vietnamese people," she said. Tim handed Sheila and me a sign he had painted. It read: "No Nhus is Good News."

"It's about time you joined the Anarchist faction," he said. For an hour we picketed. Tim had brought a dozen raw eggs with him. He went to a balcony overlooking the theater exit; and when Madame Nhu stepped out he dropped the eggs. They splattered on the sidewalk and the yolks soiled her shoes.

Secret Service men in dark glasses eased her into the back seat of a Cadillac limousine.

"Get him," someone shouted. The Secret Service men cleared the crowd of students away from the car. The chauffeur began to drive off slowly. Two students pounded on the roof, then retreated. I knew I had to act. I handed Sheila my picket sign, climbed the stairs and ran along the steps toward Amsterdam Avenue. I caught up with the Cadillac, looked into the open window at Madame Nhu—the Dragon Lady—dressed in an elegant black kimono. Her daughter sat beside her. I looked back, two men were running toward me; the chauffeur accelerated. I looked at the Dragon Lady; she rolled up the window. A plate of glass separated us. I cleared my throat, spat and watched as Madame Nhu instinctively turned her head. The saliva oozed down the window. A hand reached up. I twisted my body and raced off campus.

An hour later in our apartment, Sheila lectured me.

"Promise me you won't do anything like that again. You and Tim are both crazy."

"I promise," I said, half teasing, half serious. I had frightened myself. I had acted spontaneously. No one had given me an order, but I remembered descriptions of students attacking Nixon's car in Latin America. Intuitively I knew that I could act as they had acted. That fall and winter we went to very few demonstrations. It was a mad time and we looked for safety.

The fall of 1962 had been crazy, too. Then we expected the world to end. Nuclear destruction—the worst fear of the 1950's—was imminent. In the warm Caribbean Russian ships and American ships were going to collide; missiles would be launched, and New York and Moscow would be destroyed. At Columbia, Professor Mirstein predicted World War III. The West End Bar was deserted, and in the dorm students in intimate circles were uttering their last, profound statements. I spoke to Josepha on the phone. Alan went home to Scarsdale; Kurt, Peter and I listened to Kennedy's speech on the radio and sent a telegram to the White House urging peace between the U.S.A. and Russia.

A year later Sheila and I watched the national tragedy on TV: President Kennedy murdered in Dallas. We embraced each other and shut out violent America.

"It's a time for love and intimacy, not for demonstrations or protests," Tim said.

Emma mistrusted me when she first met me. "She says you're a dishonorable seducer," Sheila reported. "My mother told me not to sleep with you. She says I'm too young."

"If she casts me as a seducer," I said, "I'll take the part." At first we made love in the afternoon. Then every morning Sheila arrived at my apartment at eight AM, before her first class, took off her clothes and got into bed. She wasn't passive, wasn't a victim.

"I need a diaphragm," Sheila said after we had been sleeping together for a month. "You have to come with me."

"No," I said, "it's your job."

"If you don't come, we won't make love."

"I'll come." In the waiting room I was petrified. I buried my face in *Life* magazine and nervously glanced at the women patients. The doctor entered, looked at me, then went back into his office.

"Is it OK?" I asked when she came out.

"Yes, I've got it," she said. "We'll have to hide it at your apartment.

Going to the doctor with Sheila was a sign of my willingness to

74

take emotional risks, to be committed. Sheila and I had fun making love; and there was passion too. We shared intellectual interests, argued about books and movies and felt relaxed and at ease in each other's company.

"What do you see in him?" Emma asked Sheila. "He looks like a heap of old clothes to me." But slowly her resistance declined. She changed her authoritarian, repressive tactics and became a liberal. She tried to co-opt us. "Wait till your eighteenth birthday," she said, and took us to expensive restaurants and the theater, bought us gifts. "Wait, wait," she insisted, not knowing it was too late, and offering me the collected works of Henry James as a present.

Emma had long gray hair, wore glasses, smoked cigarettes and coughed all day. The Gordon twins were from the academic intellectual old left. Emma's old left was in the unions and in the government. I had read about the radical women of the 1920's and 1930's—Mother Bloor, Mother Jones, Elizabeth Gurley Flynn—but they were historical figures from a distant era and had little to do with the old left world of the 1950's. I identified the old left with men not women.

Emma was fifty years old.

"I'm the third daughter of a third son, born on the third day of the third month in 1913, married in 1933, and I have three kidneys," she said. Her parents were Russian emigrants, settled in Brooklyn at the turn of the century. She was thirteen when her father died; her mother remarried and asked Emma and Vanessa to leave home.

"You'll only get in the way," she said. So the two sisters moved to an apartment in Manhattan. Emma finished high school and went to Hunter College and met Irwin, a Columbia College graduate with a good-paying job, at least for the bleak year of 1933. Irwin's parents were Russian revolutionaries, fugitives from the czar's police because the 1905 Revolution had failed. They sailed to New York, settled in Brownsville, declared war on bourgeois values in the New World, spoke against private property, never set foot in a synagogue, rejected organized religion, scoffed at middle-class marriage, but lived together for forty years. When his radical friends got jobs in Roosevelt's New Deal administration, Irwin and Emma moved to Washington. He worked under Harry Hopkins; Emma organized restaurant workers. Charlie, their son, was born before Pearl Harbor, Sheila was born in 1946, the year of Churchill's Iron Curtain speech at Fulton, Missouri. Then Roosevelt died, the war ended, Truman entered the White House, and the investigators subpoenaed Emma and her husband to testify about Communism. They both took the Fifth Amendment, refused to answer questions, were fired, blacklisted, and retreated to cold New York in the winter of 1953.

Irwin couldn't find work. He and Vanessa's husband, a Swedish-born economist, investigated by Roy Cohn and forced to resign from his post at the United Nations, became small-time landlords renting to middle-class whites in Washington Square. Emma and Irwin moved to Brooklyn Heights, bought a big house; Grandma Sadie, still hating the church, marriage, private property, joined them.

In 1954, with Charlie and Sheila in school, Emma joined the PTA and worked with the NAACP, with black parents and ministers for integrated education. Charlie was big, clumsy, and gentle, a mathematical genius, uninterested in politics: he puttered in the basement with radio equipment and chemicals. Sheila intimidated him, teased him. She was Irwin's favorite and she was allowed to stay up late at night to listen to political discussions. Sheila read Tolstoi, and Ilf, and Petrof. She argued with her conservative teachers, was supported by her parents who were summoned to the principal's office to account for a young girl spouting atheism and socialism. Charlie graduated from high school, went to Columbia, his father's alma mater, and moved to Manhattan.

Irwin's fatal heart attack occurred in 1963. He fell to the sidewalk on Forty-second Street, hit his forehead and died immediately. But for a long time no one on that busy street stopped to investigate or help. When the police phoned and told her, Emma collapsed. She saw no reason to live. Sheila was in despair; then she went to a psychiatrist, the father of her high school boyfriend and the author of *David and Lisa,* a book about the love affair between two young people in a psychiatric hospital. Slowly, she became more hopeful.

Most of the time Emma was enthusiastic and optimistic. She showed us her collection of political buttons from three decades —the 1920's, 1930's, 1940's—and conjured up the heroic struggles of the past, "the beautiful yearnings," "the endured sufferings,"

76

"the strivings," "the urgings to be free." Occasionally she was melancholy and depressed. She mixed a gin and tonic, closed her eyes, and listened to a recording of Schubert lieder. For a long time I mistrusted her emotions. She was melodramatic, sentimental, romantic. On Rogues Path there was little place to express emotions openly. Sam was often angry, but he was rarely sentimental, and his optimism was much more guarded than Emma's.

Emma had friends but no lovers. She was a very eligible widow. The houses Irwin had built or renovated provided her with a steady income, and Sheila and I spent her money on food, alcohol, vacations, clothing. Emma was intelligent, attractive, affluent. Alone and single she was an anomaly in the dining rooms of her married friends. She was a threat but also a great prize. A small steady stream of old left widowers came to woo her. Sheila and I rejected all of them. They were merged into one archetypal suitor: bald, fast talking, elegantly dressed, an ex-Red, now a brilliant fund raiser and corporation executive. They drank bourbon and reminisced about old friends.

Joe Benton, radical student at CCNY in the 1930's, reporter for *The Daily Worker,* resigned from the party in 1954, Ph.D. in 1960, political science professor at Michigan State.

"His kid Willie committed suicide last year," Emma said. "They say he was very unhappy. Old Joe takes it as a reflection on himself."

Nina Davis, CIO organizer, fast talker, "classy dame," the sexiest lobbyist on Capitol Hill; two kids from her first marriage —one in a mental hospital and the other a student radical at Berkeley.

Fred, State Department man, a friend of General Stilwell's, attacked by McCarthy. In 1951 packed his belongings, left his wife and kids, went to Peking.

Evelyn, Kentucky working-class woman, factory organizer in the South, married, deserted by her husband, hounded by the FBI, lived alone with a seven-year-old son. Alcoholic, constant fear of agents, continual phone calls, mysterious visitors, the constant appeal to "cooperate, talk." Compulsive crying, desperation, committed suicide, Davenport, Iowa, 1956.

Emma talked about the past, but she always introduced the immediate issues of 1963 and 1964. Her suitors were no longer in radical organizations. They had radical sympathies, but they had lost interest, were afraid or wanted comfortable lives. They gave donations, went to benefits in Town Hall, and watched their children become involved in the civil rights and peace movements of 1962, 1963, 1964, or else become junkies, go crazy, join the army. The old friends came, talked revolution because Emma wanted to, talked marriage because they wanted to, then left embarrassed or ashamed but rarely angry, and they no doubt immediately considered other eligible widows, because six months or at best a year later, they called and announced that they had remarried. She wished them the best of luck; Sheila and I nodded our heads. What would we do with Emma?

Because Emma didn't remarry, her old married friends patronized her. So, she in turn patronized her friends; the Marxist publisher and his wife who was anxious for acceptance in established intellectual circles where she could show off her furs; the couples who underwent Freudian analysis together, went to Europe every summer, sailed to Bermuda in the winters, and had never been separated from each other for more than a long afternoon. They had contempt for Emma because she was a widow who was still politically active, young, enthusiastic, and she had contempt for them because they lived rigid, boring upper middle class lives and no longer participated in political activity.

Emma's closest friends were single, old left women and young people—Kurt, Adam, Stella and Peter. We spent long hours arguing about the Sino-Soviet split and black nationalism.

Integration was still the main demand of the black movement, but it was countered by the cry of Black Power. We watched as a whole movement shifted tempo and direction. And we felt the intensity of the shift in Emma's whole being. For ten years she had devoted her energy to integration. Now, the most radical blacks wanted separatism. Emma was shaken. Tentatively, feeling her way, she argued with us that neither separation nor integration, but equality, was her aim.

We began to view the United States as a worldwide empire. We turned our attention away from Europe and toward the Third World. Emma subscribed to *Tricontinental;* we anxiously awaited its arrival from Cuba so that we could read the accounts of guerrilla movements. We would play Scrabble or chess and talk. Emma suggested that blacks within the U.S. constituted an internal colony.

"That's not Marxist," Steve Raab said, moving his pawn. "Where's the class struggle?" He was a first-year law student and insisted that "Law schools were training grounds for revolutionaries. Look at Robespierre, Jefferson, Lenin, Castro—all lawyers." He rejected Emma's argument. "If blacks try to do it themselves they'll be wiped out like the Nazis' extermination of the Jews," he said. "It's suicide. They need white allies."

"You can't tell them how to run their revolution," Sheila said. "We have to organize white people so they won't be racists."

We played game after game and argued late into the night about whether blacks were Africans, Americans, or Afro-Americans. Whether equality between whites and blacks could be achieved under capitalism or would occur only after a socialist revolution.

"What do you think of marriage?" Emma asked me one evening when she was darning socks.

"It's a bourgeois institution," I said half believing what I said and half being a wise guy. Everyone in Sam's and Millie's generation was married. A few couples had had Red weddings—in the 1930's they were married by the local head of the Communist Party, but when the revolution didn't come they were married by "bourgeois officials."

"You're afraid to take responsibility," Emma said, choosing a needle. "Read Engels's *The Origin of the Family, Private Property and the State*. He attacks bourgeois marriage and the bourgeois family, but believes that monogamy will exist under socialism, that equality between one man and one woman is possible. People who aren't married are sad and neurotic. There's nothing better than marriage."

"If we're in love," I said, "why do we have to get married?"

"I'll tell you," Emma said. She was examining the hole in the sock. "When I was a teenager I lived on a commune called April Farm. It was owned by a wealthy, young anarchist by the name of Charles Garland, known to his friends and wives as "Barley." People were free to live on his peach farm, provided that they picked the fruit when it was ripe. Dozens of young people came and stayed all summer, but especially in late August, to harvest the crop. There was free love, oh, yes, and everyone slept around. No one had a separate room, or a private mattress. Oh boy, I know one-night stands; they're dreary, boring affairs. At April Farm everyone was unhappy. The commune collapsed because of the chaotic sexual relationships. It was lousy for women but the men were miserable too. People have deep strong feelings for one another. Don't be afraid of marriage." She had finished sewing; I put on the mended socks.

One weekend in May, Sheila and I went to Huntington. The air was warm, the water was cold, but we swam anyway, barbecued steaks on a grill at the beach and went to a drive-in movie. The Rogues Path house had always been dominated by men. Sam, Daniel, Adam, and me. At last there was a woman in the house my mother could talk to. On Saturday evening Sam and I watched a Dodger baseball game on TV. He had wanted to talk to me for a day and a half. Finally during the seventh-inning stretch he asked, "You and Sheila get along well?"

"We've been living together."

"Millie and I are happy for you both." It was his official blessing. Then he asked: "Have you thought about marriage? We're not bohemians, but Communists. We don't believe in free love. Millie and I have been happily married for twenty-five years. I think it's a good institution and if you want to organize ordinary people you'll have to live like them. True Communists aren't eccentrics. They live solid, respectable lives."

Suddenly there was an incredible burden, and at the same time an incredible release. Sam's political rationale was cumbersome and unnecessary. One married if one was in love, and also if social backgrounds weren't at odds. I wanted to get married but the thought of marriage was an irrevocable act, a final solution. None of my college friends were married. My father made me feel it was legitimate to get married. All the next day I thought about marriage and that night in bed I asked Sheila and she said "Yes." It was easy; there was no argument, and no debate. A simple question and a simple answer. Marriage.

FLASHBACK TWO: THE CAREER

In 1962 when I returned from Europe I panicked. I was a college senior without a future. What would become of me? It seemed as if there was no alternative but to go to graduate school. I couldn't continue to be the alienated world traveler with a copy of

Steppenwolf in my back pocket. I couldn't inhabit the Thalia Theatre and the West End Bar. And I didn't want to become a political organizer. Radicals didn't make a living passing out leaflets. Our peers looked down at the student radicals who graduated from college and became Communist Party or Socialist Workers Party organizers. They were amateurs.

As radicals on campus we had enemies among students, faculty, and administration but we were fairly safe. We had been at campus demonstrations, at Washington marches, but we were all accepted to first-rate graduate schools. None of us had to pay or to sacrifice for our student radicalism. The Cold War of the 1950's had retreated to the polar regions, and for us living in the temperate zone of 1962 it looked like there was room for radicals inside the belly of the college.

Because I liked to read novels I decided to go to graduate school in English literature. I identified with Marcel Proust living in his cork-lined room, remembering the past, the *petit madeleine,* with Dostoevsky's underground man, living in a blue funk, and with Raskolnikov wanting to confess his crimes and be punished. My senior year I lived alone in an L-shaped room facing Broadway. My bed was surrounded by books. On one side were *An American Tragedy, The Titan, Sister Carrie.* On the other side were *Women in Love, Sons and Lovers, The Wings of the Dove, The Golden Bowl, The Portrait of a Lady.* I read Lawrence, Dreiser, James. I read so much that my mind became a growing electric plant. It seemed like red and blue lightning bolts charged and enlarged my mind. The roots of the electric plant pushed up toward the surface, split open the hard, dark earth, sent up stems and flowered in orange, yellow, green, and violet ideas.

Peter and I had long discussions about the academic alternatives available to us. We didn't want to become like Chris Gordon, socially isolated and personally callous. When we looked at the Columbia professors there was a wide variety of types. One of them was Daniel Bell. In 1962 I applied for an opening in Bell's seminar on literature and revolution, and he interviewed me in his office. One of his questions was:

"Do you know any Communists?"

"Is this the House Un-American Activities Committee?" I replied.

Bell laughed. "I'm not interested in investigating your political beliefs," he said. "I want to know if you're open minded or closed minded. If you're a Communist or associate with Communists you'll be closed minded, you won't learn. It's not a question of politics or repression. It's a question of education."

Professors like Daniel Bell made Columbia a treacherous college. They taught the exciting courses, like Literature and Revolution, but they used the classroom to teach liberal anti-Communism. Bell's rival in the Sociology Department was C. Wright Mills. We read his books, took his courses, and admired his values. Mills was a radical and he was inside the academic world. He showed us that there was another alternative between the extremes of Chris Gordon's isolated radicalism and Bell's fame as a liberal conservative. Moreover, we admired Mills's life-style. He wasn't pompous, or disdainful, or egotistical. He was funny, and dynamic. He had friends, traveled, attacked the power elite, celebrated labor intellectuals, praised the creative energy of the Cuban Revolution. He was a Texan, wore cowboy boots, and rode his motorcycle on campus. His office files, packed with notes and clippings was a storehouse of knowledge. "What will he write next?" we wondered. We even enjoyed his silly Marxist puns.

"There are many Marxes," he said one day in class. "Marx the agitator. Marx the economist. Marx the historian. Marx the philosopher of history and Marx the humanist. There is no one Marx. Each one of you will have to earn his own Marx." We rejected Gordon's way and chose Mills's way, in part because Chris Gordon was cynical about Mills. "He's not a genuine Marxist. He's a revisionist," he said. Chris Gordon couldn't express generosity. We became Mills's followers, and when he died in 1962 it seemed especially urgent to learn from him.

Peter fought for a niche in the history department. It wasn't easy. His professors were suspicious of him because he was a Gordon. The name alone made him guilty; they visited the "sins" of the father and the uncle on the son and nephew. They thought that he was really a Marxist ideologue carrying his father's colors, and only masquerading as a student without an ideology. "One day," Mirstein predicted (a friend in the department reported his remarks), "the day he's given tenure, he'll think it's safe to come out. Then we'll hear the propaganda, the tirades, the rhetoric. Now he sounds cute, but just you wait. I say we stop him now."

82

Other professors argued that he wasn't a good scholar, that he was as careless a researcher as his Uncle Chris. "That's just an excuse," our History Department friend said. "Peter is brilliant. You're afraid you'll be investigated. You don't want to dirty your hands." Peter became the focal point for political intrigue and debate in the department. He couldn't be forgotten or neglected. He wouldn't go away. The scholarship to Cambridge had to be given to a student and he was the obvious choice. The absence of his name from the scholarship list would have made the department's motives suspect. Students would have demanded an investigation.

The key man in the situation was Richard Hofstadter, ex-radical, the most prestigious professor in the Columbia History Department and the establishment historian we most admired. We learned our sociology from Mills's *The Power Elite* and our American history from Hofstadter's *The American Political Tradition.*

Hoftstadter's first teaching job was at City College in 1940. In the wake of the committee investigations of radicals he was hired to fill Doug Gordon's vacant position. Twenty years later Hofstadter was the number-one American historian and Doug Gordon was teaching at Great Neck High School. Hofstadter was also Peter Gordon's tutor and it was in his power to determine Peter's future; if he certified him Peter would find the doors of academia open; but if he refused to write a recommendation Peter would have a rough time. If Hofstadter backed the son of a Red, the son of a man he had superseded twenty years ago, Peter would receive the scholarship.

Peter had one close friend on the history faculty—Professor Patrick Connelly, an energetic, popular and eccentric man who taught Civil War and Reconstruction history. He was well known because he appeared regularly on television; he was liked because he treated students as his friends. He was a bachelor and lived at home with his mother. Professor Connelly suggested to Hofstadter that the college send Peter to Cambridge, England. After Cambridge he would definitely not be a vulgar Marxist, the most odious species of intellectual in the eyes of the Columbia elite. At worst he'd be a sophisticated Marxist, a maverick like C. Wright Mills. But the administration balked at the idea of Peter's going to Cambridge. After all he was the chairman of Action, he had literally embraced Benjamin Davis, had picketed at Woolworth's. He would be a poor representative of Columbia College in England. A battle ensued between the liberal and conservative factions. Initially Hofstadter objected, but when presented with the portrait of a Gordon with a British accent and a continental flavor, he changed his mind and his vote.

Hofstadter himself wasn't an investigator, nor did he support the investigations, but like it or not he owed his first job to the investigators. In 1940 he had supplanted the father; in 1963 his first instinct was to block the path of the son. But for some reason—perhaps because he felt guilty about Doug and Chris and wanted to make amends, to be remembered for his generosity, perhaps because he was entrenched and powerful and could afford to be lenient, perhaps because he felt that Cambridge would bleach the redness out of Peter—Hofstadter decided that Peter ought to receive the scholarship to Cambridge.

But for the first time ever in the history of the college two scholarships to Cambridge were awarded.

"If we send a radical to Cambridge," Mirstein argued, "we have to send a conservative as well." So Peter and a conservative student sailed for Southampton together.

While Peter studied under Hofstadter I was spellbound in Lionel Trilling's course on modern literature. Even Susan Sontag came to his lectures on Kafka. Dignified, gray-haired Trilling was erudite, cultured, acted like an English scholar and a gentleman. He juggled history and literature, ideas and culture. After the textual critics, the agonizing hours scrutinizing poems in seventeenth-century literature classes, his lectures were sophisticated. Books were related to society. Trilling quoted Marx and Engels, talked about social classes, the French Revolution, Veblen, modern art. And the books Trilling presented to us were wonderful. *The Magic Mountain, The Trial, Swann's Way, Ulysses, Women in Love.* There was excitement in his classes; we believed we were the future intellectual elite. Trilling offered us a rare opportunity to enter the cathedral and create with him the cultural rituals of the New World. Trilling exuded power. When he stood before us in Hamilton Hall and lectured about bourgeois culture, the bohemian artist, the opposing self, the liberal imagination, we sensed that we were first-class citizens of the twentieth century, sitting elbow to elbow in Montparnasse cafes

84

with James Joyce, Marcel Proust, Thomas Mann, and T. S. Eliot. His power was compelling. Trilling held out the holy grail of the elite culture, and we knelt at his feet.

His manners were often offensively aristocratic. Trilling was no democrat. He insisted that everyone defer to him, that deference was necessary for proper social intercourse. He talked like a stuffy Cambridge don, and he often seemed to be a character out of a Trollope or a Thackeray novel rather than a Columbia professor. In his office he always made us stand, as if this were the Prussian army and he were the officer in charge of new raw recruits. We talked, and he balked when I suggested that Conrad's *Heart of Darkness* and Melville's *Benito Cereno* were about race, colonialism, and violence. My views were too overtly political, too bloody, too committed for his taste.

At the end of the semester I rushed to the registrar's office to see my grade posted on the bulletin board. I received an A. Trilling had singled me out, I told myself. He has recognized my ability, even though I'm a radical. I must be good. I could be great.

Peter and I passed through the portals of Columbia College and emerged on the other side with recommendations from Hofstadter and Trilling and suspicions from our friends.

"How can we trust you?" Raab asked. "Maybe you'll sell out, maybe you'll become the new Mirstein. After all wasn't he a radical in the 1930's?" I think he was challenging himself with the question, too.

In 1963-64 I wrote a master's thesis on Henry James. For years my favorite author was Theodore Dreiser. I was intrigued by the relationship between sex and power in his novels. His titans, financiers, geniuses were portraits of America's kings. In *An American Tragedy* he exposed the American dream. "You can't succeed," he said. "The poor don't become rich. The outsider doesn't become the insider. The awkward adolescent doesn't marry the beautiful aristocrat. The road ends in prison not the White House."

Dreiser's fictional world presented, I thought, what C. Wright Mills offered in *The Power Elite* and *White Collar*. To study Dreiser would be to extend Mills's thought and analysis of American culture.

But I discovered that Trilling detested Dreiser. He thought he was vulgar and crude. Maybe I was wrong. Maybe I admired Dreiser because I was a vulgar Marxist. Since Trilling was brilliant, since he worshipped Henry James, I decided to read James. If I praised Dreiser, Trilling would have contempt for me. He'd think I was shallow minded.

"But that isn't the case," I told myself. I thought that I was a complex thinker. By reading and studying James, I convinced myself I'd enrich my imagination. I wanted to advance toward Trilling's realm of pure thought. I became an esoteric thinker. I put away *An American Tragedy, Sister Carrie, The Titan* and surrendered myself to *Portrait of a Lady, The Ambassadors, The American, The Golden Bowl, The Bostonians, The Princess Casamassima*. Soon James's doomed, sensitive, aristocratic young women were as alive in my imagination as Josepha Spiegel had once been. James's books taught me the beauty of defeat, the aesthetics of loneliness. His characters chose psychological incarceration; they surrendered gracefully. Moreover, there were no heroes, everyone was equally corrupt; everyone was someone else's prisoner, everyone was someone else's jailor. Exquisite irony. Dreiser's America faded away. James's Europe possessed me. I devoted so much time and energy to reading and studying James that I began to feel like his innocent Americans in decadent, beautiful Venice. I knew that the city was undermined by the sea, that the beautiful betrayed woman was dying alone.

What would I do? Studying literature at Columbia made me cynical and pessimistic. I became a Jamesian, and my devotion to James was the sign of my collaboration with the liberal anti-Communists who had stepped on the Gordons in their rise to power, and fame. I bowed down to Lionel Trilling's god: Mr. Henry James.

I wanted to become an intellectual, a professor; I wanted to be accepted by Trilling, to be a part of his elite world. I felt myself being sucked up into the belly of Columbia, and I was terrified.

When Emma half-jokingly suggested that I was selling out, I responded with a joke.

"Yes," I said. "I'll be like Whittaker Chambers, I'll turn into a rat." I knew I could make accommodations for my own security and comfort, and that frightened me. I was afraid, but not of repression as I had been in the 1950's. I knew I wasn't going to jail or to the electric chair. But I seemed to be advancing toward the university chair, and the ease, comfort and elitism of the academic world—symbolized by the endowed prestigious chair of literature, Trilling's seat of honor—forced me to compromise, to collaborate. I was silent. I convinced myself that Dreiser was crude, that James was sophisticated and that Trilling, though not a radical, was more brilliant than any left-wing critic.

FLASHBACK THREE: TOBACCO PROFESSOR

My first teaching job was at Winston-Salem State College in North Carolina. Winston-Salem was a large, busy city, conspicuous for its statues of Robert E. Lee, Jefferson Davis, and its memorials to the Confederacy. It was a tobacco town. The city smelled of tobacco, tars, nicotine, the sickly sweet smell of aromatic pipe tobacco. The tobacco factories dominated the city, established the class hierarchy, governed the relations between blacks and whites, determined the nature of work, and clouded Southern minds. People talked, walked, sweated tobacco, died with cigarettes in their mouths and smoke curling in the air. Without it there would be no Winston, no Salem, no town, no people, no life. Tobacco tied everyone together. It brought me to Winston-Salem State College. My paycheck was signed by the Comptroller for the State of North Carolina and wasn't he, too, a pawn of the tobacco companies?

I lived in a small musty room in the men's dormitory. The first week of June the campus was empty. Students hadn't yet returned for the summer session. The dining hall wasn't open so I ate in the one restaurant within walking distance of the campus. But I had no appetite. I was nauseous. I lost weight. I was afraid to eat the food. The large black woman who worked behind the counter and mumbled incoherently was a terrifying figure to me, as I imagine I was to her. Why was I eating in an all-black greasy spoon in the poorest black section of Winston-Salem? I must be a strange breed of white man. I chewed my grilled cheese sandwich slowly, carefully, and swallowed hard.

At night I couldn't sleep. I wanted to board the next bus to New York, go back North to Sheila and my friends. I wanted to escape from the smell of tobacco, from the heat which sat on the cabins, tobacco fields, sharecroppers. I was a lonely white man floating in the black South. I had exiled myself, banished myself voluntarily to this poor, crumbling invisible world no one cared about. I slept alone. One night I had a terrifying dream. On Eighth Street in Greenwich Village there was ice and snow, icicles hung from the awnings and frost made crazy beautiful patterns on car windows. Sheila and I walked together through the snowdrifts to the Astor Place subway. She dropped a token into the slot and passed through the turnstiles. I gave change to the attendant in the booth, but instead of a metal token, I received a piece of ice the size of a token. The Sea Beach train arrived. Sheila got on the subway car. I raced toward her but when I reached the turnstile I looked into my palm and saw that the ice had melted. The train and Sheila departed. I woke up, smelled stale tobacco, and heard the sound of black voices. The next day I collected a pocket full of change, and called Sam from the dorm pay phone.

"I want to leave," I said. "I can't stand it. I'm afraid and lonely."

"You've got nothing to fear," he said. "Be strong, stick it out. You have a job to do, it's an obligation."

"But I miss you, Sheila, my friends."

The next afternoon I sat outside the men's dorm on the lawn in the hot sun, sweated, and cried. The superintendent of schools drove by in an official state car. He stopped and sat behind the wheel with the motor running.

"I hear you want to leave," he said. How did he know? Had someone overheard the conversation with my father? Had I talked in my sleep? Or could he tell merely by looking at me?

"My people need education, and you have the skills. Give yourself a chance. I'll take you to the Greyhound terminal now, but why not stay, and see how you like it?" He drove off. I looked at the red brick buildings, the parched grass, the tobacco fields in the distance and decided to stay.

I became friendly with Bob Brown, a black historian, the only black in his class at Harvard who had chosen to teach in all-black schools in the South, rather than be the token black at a white school in the North. He was the saddest man I had ever met; he was separated from his wife and kids, he was hounded by the FBI because he was defending W. E. B. DuBois, who had just joined the Communist Party, and he got into trouble because he went out with a white woman in town. Bob and I drank together and got into fights in town. He sang the blues, and we nursed our wounds in the back room of a black bar.

I taught English literature, American literature, and freshman composition. All my students were black. The chairman of the department, Miss C. C. Robinson, was in her thirties, lived with her mother near the campus, and applied skin lightener to her hands and face. She was dainty and graceful and her diction was perfect. Miss Robinson wanted me to teach sentence structure, participles, and gerunds, and not black literature, but I changed the curriculum, and we read Richard Wright and James Baldwin, discussed Thoreau, Martin Luther King, civil disobedience, and the civil rights struggle. The students understood and admired King but thought that Thoreau, my hero, the nineteenth-century New England radical, was crazy. His refusal to pay his taxes and his symbolic night in jail were incomprehensible. And why, they asked, did I choose to talk about Richard Wright's violence and Baldwin's homosexuality? Weren't there nicer topics?

In August, Sheila came to Winston-Salem. She got off the bus and went to Raskins's jewelry store to buy a wedding ring. Sol Raskin was a third cousin and he asked, "What's a Jew doing teaching the coloreds? They can't learn." On the campus we told the college president, the faculty members and the students that we were married, and no one doubted us.

At the end of the term I evaluated my stay in Winston-Salem. I had arrived in fear of blacks but left in fear of the whites in town who called me a "nigger lover" and wrote letters to the town paper attacking the New York Jew who "ought to go back North and let Southern whites and blacks solve their own problems, peacefully, as we have always done, and will continue to do." Sheila and I were accepted in the black community; we went to black homes, parties, barbecues. Sheila directed a successful production of Edward Albee's play "The Death of Bessie Smith" in the Baptist Church, and brought excitement to the quiet campus.

At the end of August we returned to New York. Winston-Salem reinforced our decision to get married. It would be impossible to live together in a Southern town and not be married. If we had not lied and said we were married, I would have been fired, and we would have caused a scandal.

Judge Livingston rushed into the room. My mother woke up. Sam and Emma walked away from the window, and Sheila and I stood up. The judge gulped down a glass of water and performed the marriage ceremony. I put the ring on her finger and we kissed. We had waited and waited and now it was over.

Emma had wanted Reverend Milton Galamison, a black leader in Brooklyn, to perform the ceremony in his church because he was an old friend of the family, because she had worked closely with him in school integration struggles and because he had known Sheila since she was a little girl. But I refused to have a religious ceremony. I was indignant. I would not be married in a church by a minister, so Harold Livingston, a corrupt judge, married us in a cold, official ceremony.

Emma had arranged a party for Sheila and me to celebrate our marriage and our departure for England. To me it seemed unnecessary, a waste of money, a bourgeois extravagance. "It's only money," Emma said, "and it gives me great pleasure." We left Foley Square Courthouse and went to the wedding reception at the Tavern-on-the-Green in Central Park. There were hundreds of guests—my relatives and friends, Sheila's friends and relatives, but mostly Emma's friends. There was a band, a group of Emma's old friends from the 1930's who once played at Soviet-American friendship rallies, CIO dances, and benefits for the survivors of the Abraham Lincoln Brigade. They played out of tune, and they butchered the Beatles' songs, but they were drunk and happy. At the end they played "The Internationale." It was a wonderful festival for the old radicals and the new radicals.

My Grandma Dora—my only living grandparent—took me aside and whispered her approval and handed me a $100 bill. Chris and Doug Gordon argued about the Sino-Soviet dispute. Billy danced with Josepha. Adam got stoned, picked up a saxophone and played with the band. The Singers boasted about Alan's medical school career.

Mark Pearlman from the Seattle dockworkers union compared notes with Red Johnson from the Chicago meatpackers union. Larry Stollman and Richard Kamer, two old radical lawyers and the masters of ceremony, analyzed the Supreme Court. Nina Davis, Emma's old friend, came from Los Angeles with her new husband and danced all night in her bare feet.

We all danced, first the twist, then folk dances and finally the hora. All the old Jews and the young Jews joined hands, formed a circle, whooped and hollered, and spun round and round.

My mother and father were quiet. They sat by themselves, ate, got drunk, and shook the hands of Emma's friends who came to their table to say hello.

When it was over we were exhausted. On our wedding night we slept at Emma's. Instead of making love Sheila and I counted the money we had received. The next day Emma took us to Kennedy International Airport. She drove up Eighth Avenue. At Frederick Douglass Circle we saw six white policemen beating a black man. Their white hands went up and down, the clubs pounded his flesh. He was motionless and silent, and when we boarded the BOAC flight to London that image remained in my mind.

CHAPTER
SIX
JONAH BECOMES JOMO

Fayerweather Hall, the university center for the study of political science, was built in the 1930's from granite rock blasted and excavated from the island of Manhattan. In 1964 I had attended Professor Lapin's talks on Henry James in the lecture theater on the ground floor. In April 1968 Fayerweather Hall, renamed Fayerweather Commune, became my home during the Columbia Insurrection. But it was, at the beginning, a terrifying home. Only at the end was it a house of joy. Fayerweather was a crucible. "Stand and deliver," the walls said. "Who are you?" the windows asked. "You ran to England. Now you can't run any more. Choose."

It was not the locks, not the iron bars on the windows, and not the barricades that made Fayerweather Commune a prison. The prison was in my mind. The revolutionary commissars of time and space sat only in the citadel of my own imagination. I was free to leave or to stay, and I knew that sooner or later I would have to decide. Did I belong inside the commune or outside the commune? Was I a communard or a solitary and lonely I?

From a window on the seventh floor of Fayerweather I could see Peter Gordon's office in Philosophy Hall. Like me, he had his Ph.D.; like me he was an assistant professor. But he wasn't in Fayerweather, and neither was his wife Stella. She had joined the Democratic Party, was canvassing for Eugene McCarthy, and Peter was teaching Afro-American history. He was a good teacher, a radical, but the black students had walked out in the middle of his lecture about Nat Turner, had demanded a black studies program, black professors for black courses. Sheila had walked out, too, and so had Peter's own cousin, Uncle Chris's daughter, a brilliant graduate student active in radical politics. Peter continued to lecture. He didn't stop. I admired him. He wasn't confused. He assumed that what he was doing was right. I wasn't sure about anything. I was unsure about marriage, teaching, the revolution, myself. But sooner or later I'd have to be sure about something.

Most of the new tenants in Fayerweather were sure they didn't like the old landlord. So they expropriated the hall, and transformed it into a commune, like the Paris Commune of 1871, they said; a free world, like the jungle zones liberated by the Viet Cong, they argued. I listened skeptically. Maybe so. Maybe this was the revolution come to life. Maybe the red flag on the green roof, proclaiming solidarity and independence, taunting administrators, policemen, right-wing students, and anguished liberals was a sign of the living rebellion.

The communards had dared to disrupt the city within the city, the little feifdom governed by the trustees from *The New York Times,* CBS television, the New York District Attorney's Office, and the Chase Manhattan Bank. In 1962 Peter and I had picketed the university and demanded the formation of a cooperative book store, but Action, unlike SDS, never acted to halt the university's flow of chaotic business. Kurt Thomas had exposed the House of Intellect when we were undergraduates. Now, once again, he revealed that behind the House of Liberalism Columbia was a House of War, a House of Counter-Revolution, that Columbia professors worked for the Institute for Defense Analysis.

The black students unmasked the House of Power, for Columbia had seized public property in Harlem, had cut down trees, overturned the soil. The Lords of Morningside Heights prepared blueprints for a white gymnasium. The architect's plans indicated a service entrance where black boys could enter at special hours and mix their sweat with white boys' sweat and swim in the white boys' pool.

Class bells rang on the hour, but no students obeyed their call. The sacred rituals of the college were halted. For nearly a decade students entering the library were confronted with a heroic oil painting of Dwight David Eisenhower—President of Columbia University before he was elected President of the United States of America. No one defaced it, and no one turned Ike's eyes to face the wall. It was simply neglected. The Eisenhower years were finally forgotten.

There were a few daring acts. Buildings were seized. Sheila, who had never felt that property was sacred, had taken a brush dipped in red paint and had written on

94

the wall of Hamilton Hall, "No Gym."

"It's just like France or Italy," one astute sociology professor remarked, writing the slogan and her name in a book. The leaders of the insurrection had even used naughty words like "bullshit" and "Up against the wall, motherfucker" in the presence of faculty members. This was the very mob Professor Mirstein described in his lectures on the eighteenth century. The world was turned upside down; professors who had been standing on their heads their whole academic lives were forced to stand on their feet, and they were dazed and confused and insisted that we return to the era of headstanding.

"You've made a nice gesture here," Professor Alistar Bond said, "but violence will get you nowhere. If you persist in staying inside these buildings, making this absurd demand for amnesty, you'll ruin all the good you've done. Amnesty is nonsense. If you've done wrong you must be punished. I beg you, please, come back to class, come back to your teachers, come back to Columbia." But we persisted. We remained inside our sanctuary, our utopia, lived in the noise, and the filth, ate peanut butter and jelly sandwiches on white bread, camped on the marble floors, and waited day after day for the police bust, for the sound of sirens, the nightsticks and the mace.

There were meetings all day long and intense debates about the war, racism, liberal intellectuals, democracy and communism. We became strategists and tacticians overnight. We were always engagé. We read *The New York Times* account of Columbia and discovered that it wasn't an objective paper, that it backed the university and attacked us. We watched the black students in Hamilton Hall to see what they would do next, because we felt that they were the vanguard of our rebellion. We listened to rumors about "famous" Tom Hayden who was across the campus in Mathematics Hall with the Motherfuckers. We became conscious of SDS, a powerful, dynamic organization, and a new generation of movement spokesmen like Mark Rudd, Ted Gold, John Jacobs. It seemed as if we had traveled through several historical stages in one week. We thought that we were like the Russian revolutionaries of 1917, and we thought that we, along with students in France and China, were going to make a world youth revolution. We were convinced that we were confronting American power itself; we told ourselves that we wouldn't be co-opted, that repression would make us only more rebellious, that we were creating a new alliance between blacks and whites, that we would establish counterinstitutions—our own university, co-ops, unions, radio stations, newspapers and communes.

I was the honorary professor of Fayerweather; I was teaching at the State University of New York and commuted back and forth on the Long Island Expressway from the revolution on the Columbia campus to the prerevolutionary classroom at Stony Brook. In the morning I rolled out of my sleeping bag, went to the bathroom, pissed, washed, sat down with paper and pen, prepared my lectures, read the literary magazines, then drove to Stony Brook, speeding all the way. In the afternoon I lectured on Dickens and Shakespeare, corrected examination papers, had conferences with students, chatted in the faculty lounge with my colleagues, then drove to the city, went to SDS meetings, wrote leaflets, attended rallies, marched in the streets.

Who would have guessed," Hal said, "that the professor carrying his well-worn, underlined copy of *King Lear* also throws rocks at police cars on Amsterdam Avenue?"

"Shakespeare would know, but not the professors of Shakespearean drama at Columbia or Stony Brook," Sheila said smiling. She had never been as happy, as full of joy before.

I wanted to be a scholar, a professor, and also a student revolutionary. I had divided, confused loyalties. In my mind there was a running debate between a student radical and a professor. "Either/or," each one said. "You can't be in the middle." At Stony Brook I told no one I was living in Fayerweather. I wore a tie, was clean shaven, and calmly smoked my pipe. I was afraid that if they knew I was at Columbia, a participant in the revolution, undermining my alma mater, I would be isolated and ostracized. I would never receive tenure. I also didn't want my former Columbia teachers to see me in the commune. I didn't want to offend them or upset them because in their eyes I was a loyal, and promising protégé; they recommended me for grants and promotions, encouraged my research, paid for lunches and drinks.

Many of them, like Richard Hofstadter, had joined civil rights marches and antiwar protests, but now that the University was under seige they affiliated with the police, with order and authority. So I sneaked around campus and prayed that I would not encounter Lionel Trilling. If he recognized me entering Fayer-weather or carrying a Viet Cong flag, he'd snub me and never again recommend me for a job. Inside Fayerweather I was also uncomfortable; everyone else was a student, and this was a revolution against, among other things, professors. What right did I, a professor, have to join with students? I was a disloyal academic, fraternizing with the enemy, my friends. They didn't quite trust me, my Ph.D., or the title "professor" I was unwilling to discard. Who was I deceiving—students, professors, myself?

The chairman of the Stony Brook English Department had surely heard a rumor through the professorial grapevine. One day he summoned me to his office, closed the door, and confiden-tially said, "Your reappointment comes up next week, but there'll be no problem, none at all, unless, of course, you intend to make a stink. I dislike stinks. Hurry on now, it's past two; you'll be late for your lecture, and you don't want to keep those eager minds waiting."

In Fayerweather I took a new name for a new life. My scholar-ly articles for *Essays in Criticism* and *Notes and Queries* were published under the name Jonah Raskin. Students called me Doctor Raskin, or Professor Raskin. I published all my articles for the underground press under the pen name Jomo, and in Fayer-weather the communards called me Jomo. I wasn't trying to hide my identity but self-consciously to assume another identity. In Fayerweather Professor Raskin gradually withdrew and Jomo gradually emerged.

I had only a few friends in Fayerweather. I was an English professor impersonating an Englishman wandering through an American revolution. In September of 1967 Sheila and I had returned to New York after three years of voluntary exile in England. In large part, I had chosen to leave the United States in August 1964 because of the war, the violence. I was married and a student and so not eligible for the draft, but tens of thousands of young Americans who were eligible for the draft were forced into exile. In the mid-1960's I was so estranged from the U.S.A. that I fled abroad, rejected a mad, self-destructive society, and became, like Trilling, an Anglophile. Americans lived and died by the gun. Living in New York I knew I couldn't close the door to my room and work on my Ph.D. The violence would be outside my door. So I traveled 3,000 miles to Manchester to get a Ph.D.;

the sound of machine gun fire wouldn't unnerve me as I sat in the Manchester Central Reference Library.

When we returned to the U.S.A. in 1967 it seemed as if we went directly to the demonstration at the Pentagon. In 1967 the country was different; there were hippies, there had been a summer of love, there was a counterculture, rock, the Lower East Side, marijuana, SDS, Black Panthers, Yippies. The Old Left World and the Civil Rights movement of the early 1960's had retreated. At first I was wary of the new left; Fayerweather was my first bittersweet taste of it. In Fayerweather. I thought of myself as a rock chipped away from the mountain of the old left. I resented the new radicals for their arrogance, for their failure to acknowledge our part, the role of Action in 1961-64 in creating the possibility for the Columbia Insurrection of 1968. One afternoon I overheard three SDS leaders talking about their relations with the Panthers. I eavesdropped on their conversation until they noticed my presence.

"There's a cop listening, cool it," one of them said, and I walked off. I wanted to be a part of that fascinating discussion, but I couldn't prove I was a radical. I had no valid credentials to offer. Sheila was much more at home, because in England she had wanted very much to return to the U.S.A. and become active in the movement. She resented the fact that I had taken her away from radical politics. Fayerweather was where she had wanted me to be for years.

The first-floor lounge in Fayerweather, the center of the building, was always filled with people, but when I walked around I felt as if I was meandering through a crowd of strangers in the lobby of a theater during intermission. Students stood about gossiping, drinking, eating. In the far corner of the room a freshman from Omaha was usually asleep. Occasionally he'd wake up and ask, "Are the police coming?" "Not yet," a friend would answer, and he'd pull the blanket over his head and go back to sleep. Others were stoned, or were drunk, or read books, or wrote poetry. Everyone had his or her own way of surviving.

In the late afternoon I'd return to New York from Stony Brook, borrow a friend's identification card (you needed a Columbia ID to get on campus and I had none of my own), then crawl through a guarded passageway and return to Fayerweather. In the lobby I looked for Tony Meyer, my old roommate from

Central Park West. He had just resigned from *The Washington Post* and joined *Liberation News Service*. In September, before he started to work as a reporter and before I started teaching at Stony Brook, we had bought herringbone tweed suits at Halstead's men's shop, new suits for new professionals, new images. But after two months, after the Pentagon demonstration and Stop the Draft Week, we both hung the suits in a closet. In September, when he returned to New York after a year in Brazil, he confessed to Sheila and me that he was a homosexual, that he had been a homosexual since high school and throughout college. In Rio de Janeiro, thousands of miles away from his friends and parents, he had lived openly for the first time. In Fayerweather he was still a closet homosexual, but the door was beginning to open, and he was starting to emerge from hiding. We sat down together and he remembered painfully the antifag jokes that we had made for years. Tony was a red and a fag, an underground fag in an underground culture, repressed by both the old and the new left.

Emma had always said that fags in the movement were liabilities because they could be blackmailed by the FBI. "They'll inform on radical friends," she said, "rather than be exposed as homosexuals."

My father was afraid that Adam and Kurt Thomas were having a homosexual relationship; they spent long weekends together, and Kurt took hundreds of photographs of Adam. Sam wanted to foreclose any incipient homosexuality. He snooped on Adam and Kurt.

Tony condemned both Emma and my father for their intolerance. He criticized everyone who repeated a fag joke and demanded that we also criticize people who told jokes about homosexuals, as we criticized people who told anti-Semitic or anti-black jokes.

Sheila had three close friends in Fayerweather. They ate supper, studied, went to meetings and the movies together. They gossiped, held hands, embraced; I resented their camaraderie because I was outside. I was suspicious and jealous. Little by little Sheila stopped cooking supper, doing housework, asking me my opinion, and more and more she spent all her time at political meetings, at the Hungarian Pastry Shop with strangers, drinking hot chocolate and talking, or at the Law School Library.

Her friend Lorraine came from a wealthy wasp family, had studied at Radcliffe, and was a graduate student in art history at Columbia. To her, Jews and radicals were exotic and sexual, more sexual than blue-eyed, blond-haired Massachusetts aristocrats in her home town. She swooned over pictures of Algerian guerrillas, Chinese Red Army soldiers, and SDS leaders at Columbia, as rock or movie fans swooned over their idols.

"Isn't Che sexy?" she said. "I'd have gone to the mountains of Bolivia with him." Lorraine's family was Episcopalian and Republican. She fell in love with the son of an old left union man and became a radical. They got married, then, after a year, separated.

Lorraine was the first person who convinced me that disliking Russia didn't mean not wanting a revolution. "Russia is a repressive society," she said, "but that doesn't stop me from wanting a revolution here. Because it failed there doesn't mean it's bound to fail here or that we should give up at the start." I wanted to point to a real, not a mythological, country where humane socialism existed. It seemed logical to me that if people thought that all previous revolutions had failed to change the quality of life they'd be opposed to a revolution in the United States.

"I like the Chinese Revolution," Lorraine said.

"But maybe one day," I said, "you'll become cynical and think they failed too. You'll call Mao another Stalinist." Hal, another friend, overheard our discussion.

"That's why Fayerweather Commune is valuable," he said. "We're creating a small version of the future society here. People can see and live the alternative society now." Hal and Lorraine both forced me to stop using the hammer and sickle to rate Redness.

Hal was one of the few Columbia law students who participated in the rebellion. He was an excellent orator and an aspiring Clarence Darrow. For Hal, Fayerweather was a House of Joy; he sparkled, was relaxed, confident, and always prepared to seize and liberate another building, fight the jocks, execute an act of daring and bravery.

Hal's father was an old union man, a Communist organizer, a tough, hard worker. Sheila and I met him a few weeks before the Columbia Insurrection. Hal had invited us to his parents' home in Brooklyn for the first night of the Passover Seder. His father wore a yarmulka and tallis, read the Hebrew, and performed the rituals, and then we feasted. Hal's father was in his sixties, short, bald, with a bad heart, retired from work in the General Electric plant, but he still hated "the bastards," as he called the Rockefellers and the Fords, and the "copperheads," as he called the false witnesses like Whittaker Chambers. Hal loved his father and accepted the Passover rituals, but he rejected his father's politics. He disliked the discipline of the old left; he didn't like the idea of a party, or a party line, or a central committee.

"My father always tells me to postpone gratification of pleasure," he said, "but the revolution is about sex and dope now, here, in Fayerweather."

Sheila's other close friend was Richard, also a law student, from California, the son of a multimillionaire, who used his money to start a free school for black kids. He and Sheila worked together in a civil rights organization for law students. They investigated charges of discrimination in housing and higher education and brought suit against the institutions under the laws enacted in the civil rights legislation of 1966. Hal didn't trust Richard.

"I guess it's my father's working class influence," he said. "Anybody that rich makes me uncomfortable. Even when he gives it away he makes me more uncomfortable."

At first I thought that Sheila, Lorraine, and Hal were simply good friends. Then I thought that Sheila was having an affair with Hal.

"That's absurd," Lorraine said. "They're just good friends. If I were you I'd watch out for Richard. He's sneaky. He tried to make me."

"Do you like Hal?" I asked.

"He's sexy. I could if I were to let myself go."

"It looks to me as if Sheila is using Hal as a shield for her affair with Richard."

"There's something secret going on, but I'm not sure what. It reminds me of the end of my marriage. It's all too familiar," Lorraine said.

"Don't say that."

"Maybe I'm wrong." She shook her head.

I was suspicious of the revolution in Fayerweather Commune, in liberated territory, because my marriage was ending. I didn't know whether Lorraine, Hal, and Richard were my brothers and sisters or were conspiring to deceive me. From the outside their relationships were enigmatic. Like Grayson Kirk, the president of Columbia University, I once had authority. I was the head of the household. Now, the earth was rumbling under my feet.

"Can't we talk," I asked Sheila. "I can't go on like this."

"I've gone on *like this,*" she said, "for years. Whenever I wanted to talk, you told me you were busy. When I told you I was jealous of your friendship with Josepha you laughed at me."

One quiet afternoon we left Fayerweather and walked to Grant's Tomb. We went inside and looked at the large wooden caskets of Julia and Ulysses S. Grant lying side by side under the dome. There were a few tourists talking in whispers, and the uniformed guards kept an eye on the black kids throwing rocks at the marble lions.

"Do you want to leave me?" I asked.

"I don't know."

"What do you know?"

"Sometimes I want to take my guitar, say goodbye to everyone, get into a bus, and go away."

"Where would you go?"

"Anyplace."

"Do you love Hal?"

"I love him only as a friend."

"What about Richard?"

"We talked about it."

"Did you do it?"

"No, but we wanted to."

There was a sledgehammer pounding in my chest. Blood was rushing to my temples. I pounded my fist against a glass case containing memorabilia of Ulysses S. Grant: his pen, his cufflinks, a cigar box, a photograph of him resting his hands on Julia's shoulders. A guard rushed toward me.

"You'll have to control yourself young man," he said. "This is a national monument."

"OK," I said. I unclenched my fist.

"What's happening now?" I asked Sheila.

"Nothing. What never was is over now."

"The next time I see him I'm going to bust his head open."

"If you hit him it'll make it seem as if something significant really happened."

"But if nothing happened," I said, not believing her explanation, "what's bothering you?"

"Everything. My life, us. There's a lot of resentment inside. I followed you around, went to England because you wanted to, lived there because you wanted to, but I don't intend to trail after you and your career anymore. I was only seventeen when we started living together; I feel like I've missed a lot. I don't want to live and die and even after death rest beside you, like Julia Grant resting beside her husband in the awful tomb. A marriage can be as nightmarish as that couple lying in those polished mahogony coffins."

"But we can't let it. That's up to us."

"But you have let it. You never told me you loved me, always made me say it, shut me out of your room, your life. You'd have thought you were married to Joseph Conrad. You've hurt me. I remember Peter and Stella's wedding. You sat with Josepha. I heard you say 'We're not married, we haven't compromised.' She believed you, her eyes lit up, and you wanted not to be married so you could go to bed with her. I felt awful, but I said nothing. You always acted as if you weren't married; now when I don't want to be defined as a married woman you insist that we look, behave, talk like a married couple."

"Is that why you don't wear your wedding ring?"

"Wearing a wedding ring doesn't make us married. For years I wore a ring, but you never did. You don't even have one. Is that equal? You're stronger than I am. You're always threatening me with your physical power."

Hal wanted Sheila and me to stay together. One Sunday morning we left Fayerweather, took a break from the insurrection and went to his apartment for brunch.

"Richard is a Milquetoast," Hal said. "He's got nothing on you. Sheila just wants someone she can push around." Hal was living in an apartment on West Seventy-ninth Street. When we arrived at eleven AM the breakfast table was set. There were bagels, bialys, cream cheese, black and green olives, lox, whitefish and caviar.

"Champagne, folks?" he asked, taking chilled glasses from the refrigerator and opening a bottle. "Here's to you two." We sat at the table and he cooked an onion and cheese omelette. We ate and drank for two hours, finishing off with Irish coffee, with thick whipped cream, and Danish pastries.

"How about some dope? It's dynamite." He rolled two joints, put one in my mouth, the second in Sheila's and lit them. It was good grass. Hal was still hungry, so he took two gallons of ice cream from the freezer. He took china bowls and teaspoons from the closet.

"No, not them," I said. "they're too small, they're for midgets." Hal brought large salad bowls and wooden serving spoons to the table and we scooped out mounds of ice cream. We were digging at the earth, carving out valleys of chocolate and coffee. I looked at my arm and it was the arm of a giant. My body had grown. I was the giant in the story of Jack and the Beanstalk. I started to laugh, and I laughed so hard that I cried, looked at Sheila and she and Hal laughed, and I stopped crying and started to laugh too, as the ice cream ran down the sides of my mouth. The ice cream was melted, in a swirl of colors and patterns. I knew I was normal-sized Jonah, but I was also at the same time giant Jomo, a giant as large as Leviathan.

In the afternoon we walked in Central Park, rented a boat and rowed on the lake. After the chaos of Fayerweather, it was calm and quiet. But Sheila and I went back to our Riverside Drive apartment, made love, a brutal, hard loving, showered, got dressed for a continuation of Hal's party. I put on a white suit, a blue lawn shirt, a yellow silk tie, my beads, and sat on the bed and watched Sheila shave her legs, dab perfume on her neck and wrists, apply lipstick and mascara. She put on her see-through bra, an old, but finely preserved sheer dress of organza, and high-heeled shoes.

"Why do you dress like that?"

"I like to."

"You like everyone to see you half naked?"

"When you thought you owned me you wanted me to expose myself all the time. It's my body, I'll do what I want with it."

We walked back to Hal's apartment. He had prepared steamers, mussels, and shrimps, bought with money borrowed from his girlfriend. There was champagne, dozens of people, eating, dancing, drinking. A friend of Lorraine's was stoned and drunk; she started to take off her clothes and stood in the middle of the living room in her bra and underpants. Then she went into the bedroom, came out holding a

Mexican whip, walked up to me and said, "Whip me."

"No."

"I like it. I want to be whipped."

I was stoned; I was still both normal-sized Jonah and giant Jomo, and I was afraid that if I picked it up, the whip would grow in my hands, that it would become an enormous whip which would lash our bodies. We would be powerless to stop it.

"Jomo, you're crazy," Hal said, "she wants to be whipped." He took the whip, grabbed her around the neck, snapped the whip in the air, pushed her against the wall. He wanted to whip her but knew it was wrong, so he lashed her ankles and then beat the wall yelling "bitch, bitch."

I walked into the bedroom and sat down in an armchair. I heard the whip crack in the next room and Hal laughed. Sheila came into the bedroom. She was barefoot.

"Why didn't you whip her?" she asked.

"It's not my idea of fun," I said. She stood in the doorway, looked down at me as I sat in the chair, raised the whip above her head, and cracked it. It missed my left ear by inches, but I felt the air part. Then she turned her back and walked out.

"She's crazy," I said to myself, and then I thought "Maybe the only way she feels unintimidated by my physical strength is to hold a whip in her hand. Maybe that's the only way to equalize and counterbalance the threat of violence from me. I want to get out of here, want to get away from the giant which has taken possession of me." Late that night we returned to the campus. There were cops throughout the neighborhood. Political tension was high. We went to sleep on the floor of the lounge.

The next day I was normal-sized Jonah. Before I drove to Stony Brook to teach, Hal and I talked in Fayerweather.

"I feel like I'm going crazy," I said.

"Tell her who's boss."

"I've been bossing her for years."

"Then be loving."

"If I'm loving she's suspicious. I always thought the revolution was a simple but hard fight. We combated the enemy out there and after a long struggle won. But in this revolution—if it is a revolution—there are personal problems, neuroses, jealousy, hate. I always thought that people who feel as I do now, people who are cynical, who have a sense of irony, were counterrevolutionary. Maybe I'm not a revolutionary."

"Bullshit. You're feeling sorry for yourself."

"I have to write a review of Doris Lessing's *The Golden Notebook* for Liberation News Service. Her radicals crack up, like I'm doing, but I don't want to believe her. I don't want to like the book. I don't like the submerged me. I want revolutionaries who are pure, strong, unselfish, happy, with settled, uncomplicated lives. The peasant with his wife, his bowl of rice, and his rifle, fighting for liberation seems to have a better life than me. He just eats, fucks, fights. What kind of psychological problems does he have? Why can't we be like revolutionaries in Vietnam or the Congo?"

"Then we'd be bombed or napalmed and wouldn't live long enough to have psychological problems."

One morning I woke up in Fayerweather and remembered a nightmare. With all the sleepless nights, the poor food, the physical overextension, and the nervous frazzle, I was sick. My body was weak, I had a slight fever and a cough. I wrote down the dream and my feelings.

> *Sitting.*
> *Wanting to throw a punch.*
> *Hating.*
> *In the night below, doors opening, closing.*
> *Waiting.*
> *Imaginary keys turning in real locks.*
> *Uptown, downtown;*
> *Looks, glances, touches, shouts, joy.*
> *Betrayal, cross-examination, lies.*
> *Buildings liberated.*
> *Love and friendship mocked.*
> *In dreams the liberated building is a whale.*
> *Swallowing the sea, I swallow everything.*
> *Saliva drips down my throat, down the corridors,*
> *I awake vomiting, spitting bile,*
> *Alone, now and always. Fists clenched.*

I was preoccupied with my own psychological dilemma, but I had always believed that psychology was counterrevolutionary, that psychiatrists had neglected social conditions and claimed that problems stemmed from personal neuroses and anxieties. No revolutionary had psychological problems. Lenin wasn't anxious about his wife and marriage in 1917; Mao fought Chiang Kai-shek and the natural world, not his wife, on the Long March. Or if he did, it wasn't in the history books. Didn't that mean that revolutionaries should not be concerned with personal problems, at least not in the midst of the revolution? Couldn't they wait? Why did this crisis in our marriage have to happen at the same time that the political crisis was taking place?

I didn't want to believe Doris Lessing's descriptions of the psychological crackup of revolutionaries, their madness in 1956 when the hegemony of the Communist world was also cracking up. I didn't want bizarre affairs, strange passions, nightmares. But I looked inside and saw that I didn't fit the image I wanted. Something was wrong. Either I was sick, a bourgeois decadent who didn't belong in this liberated building, or this mini-revolution wasn't really a revolution, but a mad outburst, destroying good and bad, treating the healthy and the unhealthy equally. Who were the true and who were the false revolutionaries? What was revolutionary behavior? Did revolutionaries feel love and jealousy, or were those feelings reserved for the rich, the decadent, the dying? If Communism meant sharing, why did I feel possessive? I had to discover and reevaluate my emotions, to plot the politics of emotions.

If this was the revolution, then perhaps revolutions weren't wonderful. Perhaps Henry James was right, after all, perhaps the sensitive men and women who had lived within the old regime, enjoying the intellectual and social freedoms which only affluence could offer, did experience the revolution as a prison, as tragedy. Maybe the Columbia Insurrection was my guillotine. Life in liberated Fayerweather meant jealousy, and jealousy looked like a banker with bulging pockets, a top hat, and a pin-striped suit.

The bust was coming, and I had to decide what to do. I examined my own feelings and was surprised to see how deeply the fear of being arrested and losing my job, of having professor taken from Raskin and being left with Jomo, had sunk into my soul. Why should I sacrifice a career as a Marxist professor for this revolution in a dirty building, a peanut butter and jelly revolution? But I decided that it was the only thing to do. Suspicious as I was of the radicals, Columbia was worse.

I knew that I couldn't live with myself if I wasn't in Fayer-weather when the police came to bust us. The revolution would go ahead and leave me behind. I knew that if Sheila was busted and I wasn't we'd be further separated, that we'd never resolve our problems. She could always say that we had real political differences, that she was in the revolution and I was outside the revolution, and that these differences were sufficient to end our marriage.

I realized that my personal life and my political life were entwined. One part didn't stop and wait for the other part to catch up. Our personal crisis couldn't be resolved in a vacuum. We had had disagreements for a year, but, whenever Sheila had wanted to discuss them, I had said I had to go to a meeting or to the library. Now, in Fayerweather Commune I wanted to discuss our relationship because I felt powerless and weak. I was no longer in control. But the Columbia Insurrection, the police, the revolutionaries would not wait for us to resolve our differences. We had to participate fully in the rebellion and also at the same time try to understand our marriage. Not to be in Fayerweather for the bust would be to retreat back to the 1950's. It would mean placing my own body in deep freeze. I too would become an ice man.

I wasn't an SDS member, but I'd sit in and be arrested on my own, on behalf of my own central committee, with my own demands and program. Let SDS members sit in and be arrested too, I had my own cause and their protest would not interfere with mine. I decided not to leave Fayerweather the night of the bust, because I wanted to cut my ties with Columbia professors. If I had to choose between the professors and the students, I'd choose the students. If I had to choose between a job and no work, I'd choose no work. I didn't want to remain loyal to the Columbia English Department.

When I was an undergraduate and received an A from Trilling and a pat on the head, my friend Steve Raab suggested that I could become the "pet Marxist literary critic of the bourgeoisie." I took his suggestion half as a compliment, because he thought Marxists should infiltrate the bourgeoisie, and half as a cruel joke, because a pet is docile, is kept on a leash, and knows its master. A pet Marxist literary critic would be protected by the bourgeoisie from the maverick, vulgar Marxists. He could have his warm corner, but he would have to swallow the snide comments from his liberal colleagues, would never be given real power, and would be cut off from Marxists on the outside. In 1962 I wasn't sure whether or not to be a pet Marxist. But in 1968 I knew that I didn't want to be the pet of the English Department.

When I was working on my master's thesis on Henry James, the editor of the college literary magazine asked me to write a review of Maxwell Geismar's *Henry James and the Jacobites,* a critique of the cult of James. I liked the book; it helped me understand my own peculiar attachment to James and to strengthen my criticisms of the Columbia professors who admired James. But at Columbia Geismar's book was subversive. Trilling didn't like it. Lewis Leary, the chairman of the department, vilified it in our seminar. I saw two choices—to write a favorable review or an unfavorable review. If I praised Trilling's enemy, then I, too, would become Trilling's enemy. That I couldn't do. If I attacked Geismar and defended the Jamesians, I could sit quietly and wait for the rewards to drop from Trilling's hands into my lap. But I couldn't lie. So I took a third choice—I did nothing. I was paralyzed. I wrote no review at all. In 1968 I wanted to end my paralysis.

In Fayerweather lounge the night of the bust the communards danced to the Beatles. There was no longer a prison in my mind. I had chosen. The carpet had been rolled up, tables and chairs pushed aside, and oil paintings of famous trustees taken down from the walls. Hundreds of people danced, shouted, hugged and kissed each other. The tenants were no longer strangers in the lobby of a theater but brothers and sisters weaving in a ritual dance. We sang the words of the Beatles' songs, danced round and round in a circle. Tony went into the center of the circle, waved his arms, and swirled round, took out his draft card, set fire to it, and people danced round and round, clapping their hands, stamping their feet, leaped into the air. Then Hal went to the center of the circle, struck a wooden match and burned his draft card too. There was a center of fire, of light in the midst of the darkened hall; I watched, started toward the center of the circle, drew back, then plunged forward, pushed through the maze of dancers into the vortex, and lit my draft card. Tony and Hal and I joined hands, and swirled round and round, and embraced, and Sheila kissed Tony and Hal, and looked at me half smiling, and half suspiciously, as if asking me "what right do you have to burn your draft card, professor, what right do you have to dance with your brothers?"

The recording ended, the dancing stopped; we were exhausted. Then we saw a slide show. A folk singer and a journalist who had recently returned from Cuba put up a screen and set up their projector. We sat down in a semicircle, and looked at images of Cuban sugarcane cutters with their machetes in the fields, new housing projects, and schools in the countryside, Fidel Castro addressing a crowd in Havana and Che smoking a cigar. It was the end of April in New York and still cold, but the images of the bright Cuban sunshine, the warm Caribbean waters, the luxurious trees and plants and the glorious revolution brought the tropics to this temperate zone in Fayerweather. Before the slide show ended someone announced that the police had arrested the communards in Mathematics Hall and were forming ranks outside Fayerweather. The screen was taken down, the images of Cuban sunshine put back in the box of slides, and grim Fayerweather was before us.

We had a choice to make: to stay in the lounge, sit on the floor, and link arms in passive resistance, sing "We Shall Overcome," and let the police drag us outside to the paddy wagons (the SDS leaders were going to sit on the floor); or if we wanted to be charged only with trespassing and walk out to the police wagon on our own two feet, we could sit in a classroom. Hal, Sheila, and Lorraine huddled together in the lobby. Hal and Sheila decided to stay in the lounge; they wanted to make a complete commitment. Lorraine and I decided to go to a classroom. I was still the professor, still more at home in a classroom than sitting on the lounge floor with the leading communards. We kissed, as if we were saying goodbye to the past, our lives, our histories, and making an irrevocable act. Lorraine and I sat down together, held hands and waited for the police. The blackboard hadn't yet been erased, and there were still a professor's last scribblings.

I had no idea what time it was, but I hoped that it would soon be over, so that I could be bailed out, released from jail, and go to work. I felt strange that I was not with Sheila, but with our friend Lorraine, that between us there were unspoken ties, a jagged history, hostility and friendship both. I was confident, calm.

110

Since we had decided to be busted, our marriage crisis seemed less immediate.

The police broke down the barricades with axes, stormed into the building, separated the men from the women, asked us our names and addresses, and took us out the main entrance past the garbage, the rubble, the broken furniture, and into a New York City bus. We were driven to jail at 100 Centre Street. The cells were already packed and we were moved from one cell to another, from one floor to another. I didn't know what floor we were on, what time of day or night it was, what was happening to us, whether or not we would appear before a judge. There were eighteen of us packed into a tiny cell, and not all of us could sit down at the same time. Someone had a radio, and we listened to the news. Since Columbia events dominated the broadcasts we felt that we were the makers of history, that we had joined with the Red Guards, the Chinese cultural revolutionaries, French students, and their incipient revolution in Paris.

Still, I wanted to be released, and to teach my courses. It would be OK to be an hour or two late, but if I missed the entire day they'd be suspicious. Would they believe that it was a coincidence that I was absent on the day that the Columbia students were arrested and sent to jail? What kind of alibi could I concoct? How could I hide a police record? How could I hide Jomo from Stony Brook?

We weren't fed, hadn't eaten for hours, and were all hungry. Everyone was irritable, and sleepy, and wanted rest and freedom. Unlike Fayerweather, the Tombs was a real jail. Here were bars and thick walls, real keys, real locks, fat jailers. We couldn't come and go freely, couldn't dance or make love or listen to the Beatles.

Two factions developed in our cell, each with its own ideology, leaders, and political strategy. The first and largest group argued that if we behaved we'd get fed. Prisoners who recognized authority and didn't ask questions were well treated, they said. The second faction argued that if we protested we'd be fed soon, on the grounds that the state never gave anything unless the people protested, demonstrated, organized. One kid took off his shoe and banged it on the iron bars. A student in the other faction tried to grab the shoe, but the shoe eluded both of them and flipped into the main corridor, beyond our reach, but within plain view of the turnkey who picked it up and carried it off.

I wondered if we'd ever get out. Maybe we'd be in for another night. Maybe we were lost in the Tombs, like characters in a Kafka story. I tried to remember *The Trial*, tried to recall my lecture on Kafka. My cellmates were getting on my nerves. It was cramped, and the never-ending radio broadcasts were irritating. I wondered about Sheila, wondered if I was missing something important, wondered if she was missing me, or thought better of me because I had been arrested.

There were no windows, no opening to the the outside, no wind, no fresh air. A rumor spread: judges were especially severe with prisoners who weren't Columbia students, for they were outside agitators. I began to worry that I'd be singled out and given special punishment, that of all the prisoners I'd be held the longest. Perhaps I could tell the judge that I had gone to Fayerweather, not out of political commitment, but to see my wife, and that I had gotten caught in the round-up by accident. I had tried to leave, but the cop arrested me.

I closed my eyes and thought about running through green meadows. I was running alone with no one else, with no one running beside me, no one trying to catch up with me, and I wasn't trying to pass anyone. There was no starting point, and no finish line. No one to time me, in fact no time at all, just endless space, moving effortlessly beneath my dreamy feet. My arms were spread wide apart. I was running without exertion or strain. My legs were stretched out, and I bounced off the soft earth, off the spongy grass in the yellow and green meadows, bounded off the red and brown leaves in the glistening woods. Running to nowhere, breathing cool, fresh air, running for liberation, from prison, bounding like a deer which has never seen, and never will see a hunter with a gun.

Finally we were given tea and bologna sandwiches. Then John Mage, a friendly lawyer, entered our cell. Here at last was a connection with the street, fresh air, sidewalks, from the world where I could run free, stay free. If they'd let me off this time I'd never break the law again. A short time in a cell and I was ready to be obedient. The lawyer told me that it was five o'clock in the afternoon. I had missed all my lectures at Stony Brook and my absence had surely been noticed. The chairman of the department was probably adding two and two and getting Jomo, the revolutionary, in prison. A whole day had gone, a day was missing, ripped out of the calendar and thrown away.

At last I was taken out of the prison cell and led into the courtroom. I stood before the judge in black robes. I was charged with trespassing and disorderly conduct. But when the lawyer told him that I was an alumnus of Columbia I was released on my own recognizance.

"Can I go now?" I asked.

"Yes, yes, get out."

"Walk out that door," I told my feet. I put one foot before the other, as if walking through deep snow. There were dozens of people around me, but I couldn't see anyone's face. All I could see were the swinging doors before me, the doors leading to running. Maybe the judge had made a mistake. Maybe he would realize that I was a criminal and he would call me back. Then I'd have to make a dash for the exit. But there was no shout from the bench. I walked through the deep snow, reached the doors, pushed ahead and emerged in a crowded hallway.

There were hundreds of people shouting, pushing, pulling, hugging, kissing, crying, laughing. There were parents lecturing their kids, couples staring vacantly into each others' eyes, cops guarding criminals. I pushed through the crowd looking for Lorraine, Tony, Hal, but the first person I saw was Peter Gordon.

"What are you doing here?"

"I taught your classes at Stony Brook."

"Thanks."

"Your students knew you had been at Columbia. You'll never be Professor Raskin again. Jomo has finally reached Stony Brook."

"It was bound to happen, and I'm glad. Life will be less schizophrenic."

"Jomo." I looked up. It was Emma. She was smoking a cigarette. "Sheila's out of jail too. We've been looking for you for hours, but there was no record of you anyplace. So we just waited and expected you'd find us. Here's Hal."

"What happened to you?" I asked.

"The cops beat me. A doctor put fifteen stitches in my head. Then I wasn't arrested."

Sheila rushed forward and gave me a hug and a kiss. She looked tired; her legs were bloody, for the police had dragged her down a flight of stairs, and along a gravel path, her face toward the ground. She had become a spokeswoman of the Columbia rebellion, respected for her ideas and her solid commitment. She had given all her energy to the Columbia movement and now, after a day in jail with her sisters from Barnard and General Studies, she felt a sense of joy and achievement. We had taken the bust OK. We could be proud of ourselves. We smiled at each other and went downstairs. The elevator operator looked at us as if we were hardened criminals. We walked out the front door, out of the prison house, onto Centre Street, and piled into Emma's car for a slow ride uptown in rush hour traffic.

CHAPTER
SEVEN
"DECEMBER 9TH: A DAY IN THE LIFE"

Winter. A cold night. Unreal Manhattan. Christmas trees. Red and green lights. Rush hour traffic. Affluent shoppers. Secretaries hurrying home. The world's loot on display.

A fete in New York and a funeral in Chicago. Richard Nixon was at the Waldorf Astoria receiving an award from the Football Coaches Association, and Fred Hampton lay in an open coffin ready for burial.

It was December 9, 1969. Nixon announced the first draft lottery; the names of prospective corpses were picked from a hat and shipped to Vietnam. On December 4th Fred Hampton and Mark Clark, two Black Panthers, were killed by the Chicago police. On December 6th the Rolling Stones played at Altamont; Meredith Hunter drew a gun and rushed toward Mick Jagger and a Hell's Angel killed him with a knife. All week people talked about blood, orgies, death, madness. The decade was coming to an end, but the mood seemed more appropriate to the end of the century. The 1960's were dying and the 1970's were busy being born.

My own life was in upheaval. On December first Sheila and I separated. After living together for six years we decided to live apart, live with other people. Inside I felt hate and bitterness. I felt like a stick of human dynamite, primed to explode and aimed in all directions. I was confused. My anger had gotten the better of me. I couldn't see Sheila clearly, appreciate her revolutionary activity or understand the importance of women's liberation for her.

Sheila had been in Chicago in a Weather collective for most of November. She had become a Weatherwoman. After Thanksgiving she flew to New York.

"You've been lying all fall," I said. We were sitting in our bedroom. The bed was unmade, the curtains were drawn. Cuban revolutionary posters surrounded us. The first thing I saw when I got up in the morning were guerrillas from Africa, Asia, Latin

America holding spears, bows and arrows, rifles, anti-aircraft guns, ancient and modern weapons of resistance.

"A letter came for you," I said. "I opened it. It's from Gregory. He tells it all—your romance in Cuba, Pittsburgh, Chicago. Why did you lie?"

"Who said I lied?"

"Now you're lying again. I believe this letter. He says he loves you, wants to live with you."

"OK. I lied, hit me. I'm evil. Take your revenge."

"Why did you have an affair in Cuba?"

"Because you weren't there. I was lonely. I was attacked for my bourgeois marriage. Everyone was sleeping around. I didn't want to sleep with everyone, so I became friends with Gregory."

"Why didn't you ever say?"

"I was afraid."

"I don't feel good about Cuba."

"That's stupid."

"It's a land of secrecy and deception."

"My relationship with Gregory in Havana is one thing. Cuba is another. It's a revolutionary society."

"I'm not going to become anti-Cuban, but your affair sours the revolution for me. I want a Cuban paradise. You went to meet the Cubans and the Vietnamese in Havana, but you also went to get away from me."

The next morning I didn't come home. I had been spending a lot of time with Marsha, Hal's sister. She was twenty years old and had long brown hair, wore lots of make-up. She made her own clothes: long dresses, bright orange or purple, shirts with mirrors, fringe vests. She had dropped out of New York University and was working in a law office. We had gotten to know one another when her boyfriend was in prison, serving a two-month sentence for rioting and inciting to riot. On July 26th, the anniversary of the Cuban revolution, Marsha and I celebrated with Hal and his wife. Sheila and Hal were no longer friends. While she dropped out of law school, went to Cuba and joined Weatherman, and while our relationship deteriorated, Hal dropped out of political activity, got married, and concentrated on law school.

"He'll be a liberal lawyer," Sheila said. "We don't need more lawyers, we need revolutionaries."

116

I never talked to Marsha about my marriage crisis, but she knew all about it from Hal. On December 1st we walked home from a meeting.

"Wanna come up for a cup of coffee?" she asked.

"Yes." In the kitchen we talked and ate cake. I kissed her.

"I want to make love," I said. She laughed.

"I don't think we should. I know what you're going through."

"Tonight." I lifted her up, carried her down the hallway into her bedroom, and dropped her on the mattress.

"Jomo, this is crazy."

"I want to." She laughed. I took off her necklace, pulled off her sweater, and kissed her.

"What are you doing?" She put her sweater on. I took it off and unfastened her bra. "There's no stopping you is there?"

"No."

"I give up, but let me put in my diaphragm."

"We made love hour after hour. I was tense, shaking, couldn't come, and went home early in the morning. Sheila was asleep. I got into bed and woke her.

"Where were you last night?"

"Out. When are you leaving?"

"This afternoon."

Sheila packed a suitcase, threw away her jewelry, miniskirts, long evening gowns, her shoes, sold her law books, and moved to a Weatherman collective.

December 9th, Nixon, the nation's number-one football fan, was in New York. In October and November when demonstrators marched outside the White House, the South Vietnamese Embassy, and the Justice Department, *he* watched football on television. I hadn't played football since high school. I disliked its violence; it was warfare on Saturday afternoon, but it was also a game of agility, grace, intelligence. The Football Coaches' award to Nixon made the game a farce. Giving Nixon a football award was condoning the B-52 air strikes, the strategic hamlets, the napalm, the torture.

And Fred Hampton was dead. Black Chicago passed through his home to see his body. Twenty-one years old. No one on Park Avenue seemed to know or care. The long line of mourners went to offer testimony of their love for Fred. Fred Hampton's people. The black people of Chicago, waiting in line to see the face, to watch the lips which would move no more. I listened to a recording of his voice. "I *am* a revolutionary. I *am* a revolutionary," Fred said. A biography of Lenin lay conspicuously on the floor. His mattress was bloody. His door was punctured with bullets.

I didn't want to believe it, but anyone could have predicted it. Huey P. Newton was in prison in California; Eldridge Cleaver had chosen exile rather than return to prison; a dozen New York Panthers were in jail, held on $100,000 bail and charged with conspiring to blow up railway stations, the botanical gardens, police stations; Bobby Seale had been bound and gagged in Judge Julius Hoffman's courtroom in Chicago and was charged in Connecticut with murder and kidnap. Prison, exile, bondage, and now death. Even Roy Wilkins and Arthur Goldberg were outraged and called for an investigation.

There were two demonstrations in the street on December 9th. One protested the war in Vietnam, another protested the murder of Fred Hampton. The people gathered in the same space, but the peace demonstrators weren't grieved by the death of Fred Hampton. One student asked, "What does Fred Hampton have to do with Nixon and Vietnam?"

"It's the life energy against the masters of death," a Yippie, with his face painted red, orange, green, said.

"No violence, please," the student said. "Peace, peace." He held up his fingers in a "V".

"Fuckin' peace creep," the Yippie said.

For an hour we marched round and round in a circle on Park Avenue, outside the Waldorf. Police with spurs on their boots drove their horses into the crowd. The mounts reared back. Mouths opened wide. I look at the iron bit between the horse's teeth. We retreated.

"Ten years ago," I said to Marsha, "I was picketing against segregation at Woolworth's on Thirty-fourth Street."

"Now you're on Fiftieth Street," she said, "that's progress, you're moving uptown." But I was too angry to laugh at her remark.

What next? I said to myself. I've picketed, sat in, signed petitions, sent telegrams, attended teach-ins, burnt my draft card, fasted. They all seem insufficient. Sending a telegram to Mayor Daley, inviting Roy Wilkins to speak at a rally, phoning my congressman—they were all inadequate responses to the murder of Fred Hampton, and to the bombs over Vietnam. Telegrams and sit-ins didn't work. Revolutionary violence was necessary.

I reached into my dungaree pockets and felt the smooth, ancient glacial rocks, gathered in Riverside Park outside my apartment before I took the subway downtown. Soon. Soon. The time was coming. I had argued with the Weathermen all fall against street violence, but now I felt that they were right. There was a war going on. We had to take the side of the blacks. We had to force the pigs to overextend themselves, to expose them, and to go on the offensive. There were a dozen Weathermen in the streets. I recognized them all, nodded hello to Elizabeth, a friend of Sheila's, a Weatherwoman, an organizer for the Days of Rage. She was carrying an umbrella, and she waved it in the air to acknowledge my presence.

I had come to the demonstration with a guerrilla theater group. On the sidewalk on Park Avenue we performed our play. We had costumes, props, a Nixon mask, a Rockefeller mask, a policeman's uniform, a plastic machine gun, a model airplane. But the mounted policemen drove their horses into our midst, disrupted the street theater, seized the props and masks. The picket line continued. But Fred Hampton's people—a thousand demonstrators—marched west on Forty-ninth Street and north on Fifth Avenue. The lights flickered. Southbound traffic was halted. I reached into my pocket, drew out a smooth, oval stone and heaved it. It punctured a window at the office of the Portuguese airline. A kid marching alongside started whistling the Rolling Stones's "Street Fighting Man," and I chanted the words to myself: "The time is ripe for violent revolution." I arched one stone after the other; the whole plate glass window collapsed. A kid with an aerosal can of red paint sprayed a slogan on the wall of the building "Off the Pig."

At the corner of Fifth Avenue and Fiftieth Street I picked up a round club lying in the street near the curb. It was smooth and fit nicely in my hand. Rockefeller Center was on the west side of the street. The statue of Atlas holding up the globe, and the giant Christmas tree beyond the ice skating rink (it was dwarfed by the skyscrapers) were illuminated by spotlights. Silent, medieval St. Patrick's Cathedral was lit up, too, for Christmas. I stood in the middle of Fifth Avenue. Hundreds of people were swirling around, flowing like a river. I looked uptown and downtown, watched the demonstrators carrying silkscreen banners with a silhouette of Fred Hampton and the slogan "Avenge Fred." Someone was hovering close by. I turned around. It was Elizabeth.

"I saw what you did," she said. "The Days of Rage in Chicago was like this. We ought to hit Rockefeller Center." Then she walked away and disappeared in the crowd.

"I guess she isn't afraid," I said to myself. "She faces fifty years in jail if she is convicted. And she was the one who first told me about Fred. Funny."

Six months earlier I didn't know of Fred Hampton's existence, hadn't heard his name. Elizabeth worked closely with Terry Robbins and Mark Rudd to organize the Weatherman Days of Rage in Chicago, October 8-11, 1969, the demonstrations called to protest the Conspiracy trial, to celebrate Che and the Viet Cong, to make, as Elizabeth said, "revolutionary violence by white youth a reality in America." In the summer of 1969 when Sheila was in Cuba, Elizabeth invited me to work in the SDS National Office (a year earlier, in July 1968, I had joined SDS), to write pamphlets and leaflets (we called them "shot-guns" because of their shape and size and because working on a "shot-gun" sounded better than working on a leaflet). My first project was to write a "shot-gun" on political prisoners. Jomo was going to be the propagandist for the revolution.

There was a crisis my first day at the SDS National Office. Elizabeth and I parked her Chevy on West Madison Street and saw five black kids surround two SDS members on the sidewalk outside the entrance and take their wallets. By the time we reached the door the kids had run off. We pounded on the iron door (it was always locked). The officer of the day peered through the keyhole and let us in. At the morning meeting the robbery on the street was the main topic of discussion. Workmen were putting iron bars on the windows to keep out robbers who had broken into the building and stolen typewriters; their hammering and drilling was distracting.

"If a kid tries to rob me," Marty said, "I don't care if he's black or white I'm gonna belt him." He chewed on his glasses as he talked.

"You do that and their older brothers in the B. Stone Rangers will vamp on us," Terry said. He had a pen and a pad and took notes on the meeting.

"They're potential black guerrillas," Elizabeth said.

"Taking a wallet from me isn't revolutionary," Marty said. "The Mafia are thieves, too."

"And we can learn from them," Terry said and jotted that idea down.

"Can't we talk to the Panthers?" Marty asked.

"The chairman's in jail," Terry said, "besides we're not getting along with the Panthers. They've been intimidating our printer to do their leaflets before he does ours."

"The Panther men have been hassling the women in the office," Liz said.

In the afternoon she and I went to a Mexican restaurant, ate tortillas, tacos, refried beans, talked to the chef in Spanish, and planned the "shot-gun" on political prisoners. The whole discussion was colored by the incident on the street and the morning discussion. Liz argued that all blacks in prison were political prisoners.

"If the black kids who steal from us are caught and sent to jail, are they political prisoners?" I asked.

"They steal because they have to survive, and survival is political. Take Fred's case."

"Who's Fred?"

"He's the chairman of the Illinois Black Panther Party. He's a great orator, and he's in jail now for stealing $70 worth of ice-cream bars from a Good Humor man."

The "shot-gun" was never written, because we had disagreements about who was and who wasn't a political prisoner. At the end of my first week in Chicago the police raided the Black Panther office, shot and wounded three Panthers. There were more immediate problems than writing "shot-guns." There were doctors to see, lawyers to speak to, a press conference, and a strategy to plan.

Now, Fred Hampton was dead. I heard the sirens. New York. In Chicago the mourners were passing before the open casket. "I *am* a revolutionary." I swung the smooth, round club in the air, ran to the sidewalk, and looked into the display windows at Saks Fifth Avenue Department store. There were elaborate Christmas

121

decorations—miniature Santa Clauses, reindeer, and artificial snow. The mannequins were dressed in expensive evening gowns, silk nightgowns, bikinis for winter vacations in the Caribbean.

I was alone. Marsha was marching with Emma. The guerrilla theater group got lost in the crowd, the red and black banners of Fred Hampton filled the air. I heard the sound of breaking glass and sirens. The roar was deafening.

In October and November we had had long discussions about Bobby Seale. When he was bound and gagged in Hoffman's courtroom the other defendants sat, watched, didn't protest. I remembered what Liz had said then. "How could Hayden, Hoffman, Davis, sit back and watch them shackle a black man and do nothing? That's American history. Blacks are enslaved, white liberals sit on their hands." I remembered the drawing of Seale chained and gagged. And the white defendants were free to come and go, get stoned, eat leisurely breakfasts, buy newspapers on street corners. But what streets did Bobby Seale walk in Cook County Jail? What freight trains did he ride in the night? Could he see the North Star through the prison bars?

"They knew they could kill Fred," Elizabeth said, "because we didn't act after Seale was shackled. "They escalated from rope and cotton to guns and bullets."

The noise was louder. The lights were brighter. The mannequins looked seductive, like real women. Charge accounts. Expensive clothing. High society. I had to do something. "The pigs are coming," someone shouted. Fred was dead. If we didn't protest now we'd all be dead. Bobby Seale shackled in a chair and Fred in his coffin.

I raised the club, the glass cracked, the mannequin in an evening gown toppled over. Someone inside the store screamed. I looked at my own reflection in the glass and then watched it shatter into thousands of pieces one after the other. I smashed six large plate glass windows. The window displays were destroyed; the mannequins were dismembered. The sound of the glass breaking was clear, sharp, resonant. The sidewalk was covered with jagged pieces of glass. I ran east toward Madison Avenue.

Three hippies with bellbottoms, tie-dyed shirts, and fringe jackets ran toward me. Were they friends or enemies? I thought of the football field. I was a fullback carrying the ball. The goal line was a few yards away. I lowered my head, lifted my knees

122

high and bulled my way forward. The middle linebacker went flying over my shoulders, hovered in the air for a second, and then landed screaming on a sheet of cold, clear glass. Two guards tackled me. Two ends hit me with sticks. I was surrounded. Clubs on the football field. There was no light. The sky above was dark. The hippie football players were beating me on the skull; I raised my hands to protect myself, but their blows drove me down to the sidewalk. My knees buckled, and I collapsed, breathless, chest heaving. The air was cold, but my head was warm, wet, and sticky. I exhaled deeply, looked up from the sidewalk, and caught a glimpse of Elizabeth still holding her umbrella and running uptown, chased by the police. The hippie beating me on the head had a badge. He had a gun. My wrist hurt. It was cold and heavy. Was it cut? Was I bleeding? I looked down and saw that I was handcuffed. Who's hand was locked in the other handcuff? The cops blocked my vision. Then the legs parted and I saw that incredibly I was handcuffed to Pat Ryan, who had been my roommate for the last two months. We were bound together. We were under arrest. A police captain in blue stood over us and gave orders. "Take them to the Eighteenth," he said. Pat—still holding his pipe and his tobacco pouch, and wearing a red shirt—and I were pushed into a police car.

Pat was a schoolteacher; his wife Liza was an actress. In the early 1960's Pat acted in horror movies (he played Frankenstein, or the space monster, or the mummy) and he also performed in romantic comedies (he danced, sang, courted, and won the heroine). Then he became disgusted with Hollywood, went back to college, and got a job teaching in the High School of the Performing Arts. Liza was German, had learned about America first from black GI's stationed in Berlin after the Second World War, and then from Patrick when he was traveling in Europe. She was beautiful and she too had been an actress—tall, thin, red hair, sharp nose—had played Jenny Diver in Brecht's *The Three Penny Opera*. Pat had played Macheath. They had acted in the German State Theatre, resigned after a dispute with the director, started their own street theater group, and performed in the streets of Berlin. In 1968 they came to New York and formed a street theater group at Columbia. When Sheila moved out of our house, they moved in.

Pat and I were put in the custody of Patrolman Rocco

Finocchiaro.

"If you guys want war, I'll give you war," he said. He pushed us into the back seat of a patrol car, locked the door ("just so you don't try to be heroes," he said) and drove us to the 18th precinct. With his nightstick he prodded us into the squad room, unlocked the handcuffs, and handcuffed each of us separately with our hands behind our backs.

"Try something," he said. "I'll kill you cocksuckers as easy as I killed the V.C." He hit me on the nose, cracked a bone, beat me in the back of the head, then whacked Pat in the face. He shoved me into a chair and started asking questions.

"Are you a Weatherman?" I looked down at my shoes. "Won't talk." Finocchiaro brought his stick down on my head. A dark, bearded demonstrator was thrown to the floor; a policeman jumped up and down on his ribcage and kicked him in the face.

"Have mercy, mercy," he cried.

Finocchiaro pulled us upstairs and locked us in two different cells. We were separated by a wall. I was afraid of being taken to another jail, and of being alone. Being handcuffed together had been painful. When Finocchiaro pulled or pushed Pat, he in turn was forced to pull me or push me along. We collided with each other. But being handcuffed together also meant that we couldn't be separated. The cuffs brought a connection. I lay down in the cell. It was hard on the floor. Maybe jail would be OK for a while.

For six months Sheila and I had lived neither together nor apart. In June she was in Chicago. I was in New York. In July and August she was in Cuba and I was in Chicago. In September, October, and November she was in prison in Pittsburgh, and in the SDS National Office in Chicago and occasionally came to New York. All summer and fall I had asked her to choose.

"Join Weatherman and leave me, or stay with me and quit Weatherman," I said. "It can't be both."

"I want both."

"They won't let you."

"Our marriage is our affair."

"Not when the official Weatherman policy is 'smash monogamy' and Liz is trying to wreck our marriage."

After the Columbia insurrection of 1968 Sheila and I had lived together for a few months, but the tensions between political activity, my job, her school, Stony Brook, New York, and other relationships were aggravated. In the spring of 1969 Elizabeth came to live with us in New York. She brought two avocado plants, a suitcase, and a guitar. At first I thought I might get to like her. She and Sheila played guitars together, sang English love songs (their favorite was "Young lovers are many, but sweethearts few/If my love leaves me, what shall I do"). They went on college speaking tours, wrote a book on the movement, organized radical lawyers.

Liz, like Sheila, had always been fascinated by the law; her father had defended labor leaders in the 1940's and a woman charged with being an atom spy for the Russians in the 1950's. Liz's father wanted her to go to law school. Every March she applied, was accepted, and every September she decided not to enroll. She admired her father's ability but rejected his political strategy.

"The old left argued their cases on technical not political grounds," she said, "and they were always in the courtroom appealing, never in the street demonstrating." Liz's father was a brilliant lawyer, calm, dignified. He wore suspenders, had white hair, and a bad heart, aggravated by Liz's arrest in Chicago during the Democratic Convention and her commitment to Weatherman.

"My father defended Communists," she said, "but he was never in the party. He was always an independent, unaffiliated radical. I always thought of myself as an independent radical, too."

"Weren't you in SDS?"

"I was in SDS projects, but I never joined SDS. I wasn't a card-carrying member. Weatherman is the first, the only organization I've ever belonged to."

"I bet we had similar experiences," I said.

"I remember one supper at Bryn Mawr," Liz said. "There was a picket line in the afternoon, and I was the only undergraduate there. No one would join me. Later, at dinner, I stood up, lifted my plate and smashed it against the wall. No one stopped eating or said a word. They didn't even look up from their plates."

After college Liz went to Russia, lived with a Russian family, ate black bread, cabbage soup, warm milk, and honey. Liz liked Russian rivers, lakes, forests, the Russian people, but not the Soviet government.

125

"The Russians need another revolution," she said. "If we lived in Moscow we'd be doing the same things there as we're doing here."

"Who's going to make the Second Russian Revolution?"

"The Russian hippies I met in Leningrad," she said. "They're like us, live communally, don't believe in marriage, or private property. They're artists."

Living with Sheila and me in the spring of 1969 Liz was morose. Her boyfriend was in Cuba, building houses for the Cuban government, and she had an affair with a young radical filmmaker. She was also in a women's consciousness-raising group with the man's wife. One night she came home from the meeting and said "Larry's wife said she'd kill any woman who was sleeping with her husband."

"What did you say?"

"Nothing, but I'm going to drop out of the group and end the affair."

The prison floor was hard. I looked up at the bars; two cops were typing. Finocchiaro was talking on the phone.

"I want you to take a look at Raskin," he said. "I think he's a Weatherman." What's a Weatherman? If a Weatherman is against marriage then I'm not a Weatherman.

Sheila always seemed to be caught between me and Liz. I represented marriage, a bourgeois life-style, and the academic world ("You're like those European Marxist intellectuals," Liz said, "you'll never do anything").

"You prevent Sheila from becoming a revolutionary woman," she said. I didn't want to be found guilty of being a male chauvinist or a counterrevolutionary, so I listened to Liz's criticism and tried to evaluate it. But I resented her. She was living in our apartment, off my salary.

Every Sunday we had big breakfasts in our living room. There was Irish linen, Spodewear china, omelets, coffee and cream, lox, bagels and cream cheese. One Sunday in June we got into our favorite topic of conversation—marriage.

"Marriage puts women in prison," Liz said.

"Bullshit. Chou En-lai and his wife were both on the Long March, both were revolutionaries. They didn't inhibit one another."

"This whole breakfast is bourgeois."

Hal was eating with us. He picked up a pumpernickle bagel. "How could a bagel be bourgeois?" he asked. "You're eating too, so you've got the bourgeoisie inside you. You just hate yourself."

After the Days of Rage I went to Chicago to see Sheila. She had pleaded with me to demonstrate, but I refused. It was crazy to announce you were going to trash and then trash. And how could anyone live in a Weatherman collective. No one had his or her own bed; it was filthy. Everyone was terrified of everyone else. I always had a feeling of claustrophobia in a Weatherman collective, always felt isolated, felt hate, felt as if we were doomed and suicidal. In Washington before an antiwar demonstration in the fall of 1969 I stayed in a Weatherman collective. Before going into the street everyone put on helmets, boots, bandanas, gathered in a small group and sang (to the tune of the Beatles "Yellow Submarine") "We all live in a Weatherman machine, a Weatherman machine." They were an integral unit; they seemed to be interchangeable parts. They liked the idea of being a machine, and they were almost oblivious of the outside world. Who would want to live underwater in a cramped submarine?

To be a Weatherman was to risk everything. It was compelling existentially because I was asked to choose to make ultimate decisions. I had been criticized for being a cautious intellectual. "You're too passive," a Weatherman said to me one day in Chicago. "We *can* create history. We *can* transform our lives." On December 9th, I had started a new life.

Finocchiaro was still on the phone. "Yes, Weatherman . . ." he said. I was a Weatherman if willing oneself into the future was an attribute of Weatherman. But my bitterest fights had been with Weatherman, and Weatherman was the catalyst which ended my marriage. In Chicago after the Days of Rage I asked Sheila to leave Weatherman and come back to New York. I wanted to try to save our relationship.

I met her in a downtown law office. The first thing she did was to cut my hair. "The police are looking for us," she said. "You've got to look inconspicuous. They're picking up hippies on the street and booking them as Weathermen." We went to Marshall Fields Department Store in the Loop. Sheila bought a miniskirt, a sweater, and high-heeled shoes, and I bought a white shirt and a jacket.

"Want to go to the movies?" I was standing in front of a mirror in the men's clothing department.

"No, I've got a meeting now."

"Can't you ever go to the movies in the revolution?"

"Our people are in Cook County Jail. We've got to bail them out." The salesman was listening to our conversation.

"Let's get out of here."

"I'll take the jacket," I said, looking in the mirror. We walked out into the street.

"Will I see you tonight?"

"Yes."

"Don't come back with Liz. If you do I'll kill her."

I went to a friend's apartment on North Sheffield, had meatballs and spaghetti for supper and watched an old Flash Gordon movie on TV. By two AM Sheila hadn't come home so I went to bed. The apartment had been a dry goods store, and the bedroom was in what had been the stock room. In the morning when I woke, Liz and Sheila were in bed with me. Liz was naked, but Sheila was wearing a sweater and underpants.

"I hear you threatened to kill me muthafucka," Liz said.

"Yeah."

"What are you going to do about it?"

"I'll deal with you later," I said. I went out alone for breakfast.

In the afternoon Sheila and I sat in the bedroom and talked. You could hear the train as it rattled by. It was drafty and cold.

"You shouldn't have told Liz."

"You're crazy to threaten death."

"She's sick for wanting to end our relationship. Are you coming back to New York?"

"No."

"I love you."

"You don't love me, you just want a fix." I slapped her in the face, cut her lip; it bled and she started to cry.

"I'm sorry."

"You're not sorry. I'm not sorry. I'm glad you did that."

128

Nothing was resolved. The next day I went back to New York.

In jail there'd be no women. No Sheila, and no Liz. All autumn they wanted me to be a Weatherman. Now, maybe they'd be happy. "Scum bag," Finocchiaro shouted. "Wake up, you can't daydream in jail. I'm gonna give you nightmares." He put his face between the bars and spat at me. I moved my head, and the saliva oozed down the wall. Another cop, younger, blond, angular, popped into the room. His head was bandaged.

"Is this the cocksucker?" he asked.

"This is him, you can have him," Finocchiaro said.

"You see this?" He pointed to a bandage on his face. "The doctor gave me twenty-two stitches. Guess how I got cut? You. You're my boy, Raskin. I'm gonna get even, shithead."

"You can't hit O'Daley and get away with it," Finocchiaro said. I recognized O'Daley's face. He had beaten me on the street. I hadn't struck him, but I was being made the fall guy. A cop had been injured, and somebody, anybody, had to take the rap. So that's why I was being labeled a Weatherman. A frame-up. It's legitimate to mess up a Weatherman. They're not people. Someone was guilty. It might as well be me.

Finocchiaro unlocked the door to my cell. O'Daley walked in, pushed me back, and bounced my head against the wall. The wounds were reopened, and the blood began to ooze again in my hair. "You're a Weatherman, aren't you?" he said. Whatever I said didn't matter to O'Daley. He had decided that I was a Weatherman. It would give him inner satisfaction. O'Daley shoved me down into a chair and started asking questions.

"Name?"

"Jonah Raskin."

"Address?"

"250 Riverside Drive."

"Name?"

"You asked me that already." He belted me in the mouth.

"No lip from you. I'll ask you your name as often as I fuckin' want."

"Work?"

"Schoolteacher."

"A low-life scum bag like you teaches. What do you teach, Riot I?" And he laughed.

O'Daley took his hands off the keys of the typewriter and looked around. A silver-haired man in a dark green suit, polished shoes, looking like a Princeton graduate circa 1956, now a Madison Avenue executive, walked into the squad room. He looked at me.

"Is he one of them, Captain Werben?" O'Daley asked.

"He's a Weatherman all right," Werben said. "Just look at him. He's got a scar on his nose. Look at his clothes." I looked down at my boots, my faded dungarees, my blue turtleneck sweater.

"He's got Chicago written all over his face," Werben said. "And look at this." He lifted my left hand and pulled off the ring, which Sheila had given to me.

"It's one of them Viet Cong rings. He's a fuckin' traitor." Finocchiaro pulled out his gun and smashed the ring with the butt end.

"Scum bag here thought he was married to the Viet Cong."

"What do we do with him?" O'Daley asked.

"They're all yours. Watch the head and take off his glasses, so he won't get hurt." O'Daley pulled off my old English spectacles from Manchester, dropped them to the floor and crushed the lenses under his foot. Captain Werben took a Polaroid camera and a roll of film out of a locker. He loaded the camera.

"Get back against the wall," he said. I didn't move.

"You heard the Captain," Finocchiaro said and he pushed me back. Werben focused, clicked the button, the shutter snapped. O'Daley unlocked Pat's cell.

"Come out here. What are you doing with a kike. You're a good Irishman like me, ain't ya?"

"Look at his file," Werben said. "Forty years old, a teacher, a Korean war vet, two previous arrests at antiwar demonstrations. Here's a photo. Looks like a pin up."

"I wonder where he went wrong?" O'Daley asked. "He thinks he's the Viet Cong. Fuckin' peace creep."

A policeman took us downstairs and shoved us in the back of an ambulance. We were still handcuffed.

"How are you doing?" I asked Pat.

"I'm OK," he said. "Be cool, play it by ear. It's a tight one. I wish I still had my pipe." We were driven to Roosevelt Hospital. In the emergency room a nurse asked "What did he do wrong?"

"He's a Weatherman," the cop said, "but don't let him bleed

130

too much." The nurse cut my hair and cleaned the scalp. Then I remembered that Alan Singer was a resident at Roosevelt.

"Can you page Doctor Alan Singer?" I asked.

"I'll try," the nurse said. In a few minutes my old college roommate—I hadn't seen him for two years—was putting stitches in my head.

"Can you call a lawyer and some of our friends?" I asked "We're in the Eighteenth precinct."

"What happened?" Singer asked.

"We were at an antiwar demonstration," Pat Ryan said. "They beat us on the streets." We were X-rayed, then handcuffed again and taken back to the police ambulance. Emma and Marsha were standing behind a fence.

"Are you all right?" Marsha shouted.

"Yes," I said, "there's nothing wrong."

When we returned to the 18th precinct, Paul Chevigny, a lawyer from the American Civil Liberties Union, was waiting, but a cop told him he wasn't allowed in the precinct. And because he was there, they took us off to another precinct and wouldn't tell Chevigny our destination. Finocchiaro tightened my handcuffs. My fingers were numb. We were rushed back into a squad car. I peered out the window to see where we were going. We passed Saks on Fifth Avenue and Fiftieth Street.

"Nice work, boys," O'Daley said. The windows were boarded up and the glass swept off the streets. Finocchiaro parked outside the 17th precinct. It was midnight, shift time; one group of policemen was going off duty, changing from their uniforms to their street clothes, and another group was beginning the midnight to eight AM shift, changing from their street clothes to their blue uniforms. O'Daley and Finocchiaro shoved us past the desk sergeant, into a back room. The 17th precinct had fluorescent lights, modern furniture; it was clean, and nothing like the old, dark, grimy 18th.

"We're gonna teach you a lesson," Finocchiaro said. "You won't ever demonstrate again. You can scream your fuckin' heads off, it won't do you a bit of good. And after it's over, you can squawk to your *lansman* Javits. Nothing is gonna stop me."

O'Daley pushed Pat and me into the far corner of the squad room. Finocchiaro struck me in the small of the back with his blackjack. He alternated the rhythm of his blows, and I was caught off balance. I tried to assume a defensive position, but I couldn't follow his crazy beat. I could feel my back become contorted and twisted out of shape. I flinched, and there was a spasm in the muscle.

I thought about Nguyen Van Troi. I remembered a drawing of him I had seen on a Vietnamese postage stamp. He was tied to a stake, dressed in white. He was dying, his mouth was open, and he was shouting "Long Live Vietnam. Long Live Peoples' War." Sheila met his widow Phan Ti Quen in Havana. She was delicate, small, graceful.

"There is fire everywhere in Vietnam," Phan said, "forests on fire, lakes and rivers on fire. Vietnam is a sea of fire." Nguyen Van Troi, an electrician in Saigon, had tried to assassinate Secretary of Defense McNamara in 1964. He failed, was arrested, jailed, tortured, refused to betray his friends, tried to escape, jumped from a second story window, broke a leg, was captured, tortured again, then sentenced to be executed. He was tied to a stake. The soldiers in the firing squad lifted their guns and took aim. Nguyen Van Troi shouted. The soldiers fired. He shouted. They fired off a second round and Nguyen Van Troi was dead.

Finocchiaro pulled me into the center of the room, took a long stick, and pounded my right arm and my right leg. The blows made my whole body shudder. I closed my eyes and saw my flesh laid out on a butcher block; it was blue and bloody, torn and raw, and the butcher was tenderizing it, pounding it. O'Daley grasped a pair of pliers and hit both of my elbows. They stung. It seemed as if my bones were being shattered into thousands of little pieces, like slivers of glass. I remembered the hospital. The machine. I saw my own X-rays, the white bones illuminated against a black background.

Finocchiaro and O'Daley took turns beating me. I was facing the wall, couldn't turn around, and so every new blow, every variation, every new weapon was a sudden surprise. My body was getting puffy, because the cells were breaking down, and blood flooded under the skin, like a river flooding its gates. Finocchiaro took his nightstick and rammed it between my thighs, aiming for my testicles.

"You won't have a married life anymore," he shouted. But I anticipated him, moved an inch and he missed. O'Daley pushed my face into the wall.

132

"Don't move fucker," he said. Pat Ryan glanced at me. They were beating him the whole time, too. He looked calm and resolute. He was poised. Even in the precinct we could act. This was our quintessential guerrilla theater performance. We were actors in a movie about the police and a group of revolutionaries. Pat and I were the stars. And yet I knew that we shouldn't try to escape as Nguyen Van Troi tried to escape. I thought of Larry Weiss, a Weatherman who was arrested by the Chicago police in September, escaped while handcuffed, went underground, became a fugitive hunted by the FBI. I didn't want to follow him underground. I didn't want to become a fugitive. Moreover, I didn't think that it was possible to escape. Prisoners escaped in Hollywood movies. My jailbreak would be an attempt at celluloid heroism. Pat and I were actors and pals, but we weren't Robert Redford and Paul Newman playing Butch Cassidy and the Sundance Kid.

I looked at the clock. It was one AM. O'Daley and Finocchiaro paused for a moment. My body cooled off. It was icy. I shivered. Then they started beating me again, the furnace inside my body ignited, my temperature rose and my skin felt as if it was on fire. I perspired. My pores opened, and the poisons flowed out. I was washed in my own hot, saltwater bath. My clothes were drenched. It seemed as if the cell walls inside my body were collapsing, my body was decomposing, cell by cell.

I was calm. I didn't hate Finocchiaro and O'Daley. And I felt that Pat Ryan was my brother, that Nguyen Van Troi, Fred Hampton, and Bobby Seale were my brothers.

A reporter from *The Daily News* entered the precinct.

"Hey, mister," Pat shouted. They stopped beating us, and O'Daley cupped his right hand around Pat's face so that he couldn't shout. When the reporter left, the desk sergeant told Finocchiaro and O'Daley to take us downstairs.

"It's more private," he said.

"Hey, Sergeant," Pat said, "aren't you going to break this party up?"

"Fuck you," O'Daley said, and kicked him in the groin. A black cop walked up to me and said "They ought to kill you. You're getting off easy." I wanted the black cop to sympathize. Didn't he know that Fred was dead, that Fred was his brother. He looked down at my trousers. They were sopping wet.

"Pissed in your pants, eh white boy," he said. "Couldn't hold it in."

We were pushed down one flight of stairs and we careened off the cement walls. Pat looked at me and said "Chairman Bobby." I remembered the drawing of Bobby Seale bound and gagged in Judge Hoffman's courtroom, twisting and turning to loosen the ropes, shouting into the cotton gauze, trying to speak, refusing to be silenced. Steel doors slammed shut. The corridors echoed with our footsteps and their voices.

"Move, scum bag. Still want to demonstrate?" Four cops escorted us into a small locker room with a wash basin and a table, leaned Pat in one corner facing the wall and me in the opposite corner, also facing the wall. I wasn't sure I could endure anymore. I seemed to be passing out, but I couldn't decide if I was actually losing consciousness or was performing for the police and pretending to lose consciousness. I was afraid to pass out. "Don't fall," Pat had said in the corridor. "If you do they'll kick you in the stomach, the face, the balls." So I climbed up the ladder of consciousness into a clearing. But things were beginning to fall away. The borders of my mind and my body were fugitives. I could no longer tell if I had hands. I could feel my shoulders, biceps, forearms, but then feeling ended.

"Wanna see a neat trick?" O'Daley said. There seemed to be a veil between him and me. The air was white, smoky. Everything was taking place in slow motion. He took a match, struck it, grabbed my arms, yanked them to the side so I could see them, and held a match under the palm of my left hand. I saw the match, and the blue-white flame, but I couldn't feel the heat. The match went out. He exposed my hand, and I saw an ugly red mark in the center of my palm.

I looked at Pat. He was leaning against the wall, sliding to the floor. A man in a white shirt, tie, and jacket punched him in the stomach. Then a cop tossed a bucket of cold water in Pat's face. He gasped and opened his eyes. Finocchiaro filled the bucket with cold water and doused my body. It was freezing, but immediately the cold water became hot on the surface of my skin.

It was over. O'Daley and Finocchiaro were exhausted. Finocchiaro walked slowly upstairs, pausing to catch his breath. They took us downtown to the 4th precinct. A hippie was in the squad car with us, had been arrested, and had witnessed the beating we had received in the 17th precinct. He talked with Finocchiaro about communes, underground newspapers, Joe McCarthy. The hippie knew that we had been badly beaten, and he understood instinctively that he could ease our pain by making conversation with the cops and getting them to forget about us. He told one story after another about a commune he had lived in on Martha's Vineyard.

"You sound like a Communist," Finocchiaro said.

"I'm no Communist," the hippie said. "I don't want no government by nobody. I don't want no cops in *my* country."

In the 4th precinct we were locked in separate cells. Before O'Daley closed the cell door he said "Your name is Fuck Face. Whenever I ask you your name I want you to say 'Fuck Face.'" Over and over again I said to myself I've got to remember my name. My name is Jonah. My name is Jonah. My name is Jonah.

"What's your name?" O'Daley said.

"My name is Jonah." He struck me in the chest with a blackjack. There was a sharp, stinging pain in my chest bones. "My name is Jonah. My name is Jonah." I wanted to be locked in my cell. The bars would protect me. In this foyer I was his prey. Sooner or later one of us would have to surrender to the other. Either he'll stop asking or I'll say "Fuck Face." He just wants a final humiliation. Maybe I should pretend to be humiliated and say "Fuck Face." But that's not pretending. If you say it, you *are* humiliated. It's all a game anyway. And even if I say "Fuck Face" he may want me to call myself "Scum Face" next. I'll wait before I give in. A desk sergeant walked into the foyer and yelled "Lock 'em up. It's past two. Precinct regulations." O'Daley gave me one last blow, threw me into the cell and locked the door.

"Good night, douche bag," he said.

In the morning Finocchiaro and O'Daley drove us to 100 Centre Street. My back was stiff and bent. My legs were swollen. We were brought before the judge—the same judge who had married Sheila and me in 1964. He set bail at $30,000. Emma and my father put up $3,000 cash and Pat and I were released. The courtroom was crowded. My mother sat in the courtroom and wept. Her face was pale. "Promise me you won't demonstrate again," she said. Emma fumed. She yelled at Finocchiaro.

"Maybe my son-in-law broke windows," she said, "but that's

no excuse to torture him all night. You could have killed these boys. It's outrageous."

"Are you making a complaint, madam?" Finocchiaro asked.

"You're a fascist," my father said. "You're a gestapo agent." He spat on the floor.

My father drove Pat and me home. Liza and Marsha had made some tea and soup. I couldn't keep my eyelids open, and since my legs were swollen and my arms were sore I couldn't take my trousers or boots off. So Sam carefully eased the boots and dungarees away from my legs. I looked in the mirror, but I didn't recognize myself. My hair was matted and bloody, my nose was cut. I wasn't wearing my glasses, and the image in the mirror looked blurred. There were purple and blue splotches on my back and calves. I took two demerol to kill the pain and got into bed. In the morning I remembered a dream about Elizabeth, a dark shadow with long, coarse hair, hulking over me, and another dream about Marsha, combing her long brown hair. In the dream we sat at a wooden table, under an apple tree. The warm wind scattered the blossoms. Horses grazed in the pasture.

For a few weeks I was afraid I had been permanently injured. I had migraine headaches and slept most of the time. And the coldness of winter seemed to freeze my back. Marsha came to live with me.

We had lots of visitors. One of them was Mark Rudd. "Now you're a Weatherman," he said. "I've brought you a book to read." He handed me Debray's *Revolution in the Revolution,* and we talked about John Reed, Lenin, and the Russian Revolution. "You've finally kicked the old left bag," he said, just before he left.

"Leave him alone," Marsha said. "Can't you see he's in pain." My old Columbia friend Steve Raab visited one afternoon.

"I hope you've learned your lesson," he said. "Street violence is stupid."

"That's not what I've learned," I said, taking a copy of Che's essays from the bookshelf. "This is my lesson: 'Wherever death may surprise us, it will be welcome, provided that our battle cry has reached a receptive ear and that another hand be extended to take up our weapons, and that other men come forward to intone the funeral dirge with the staccato of machine guns and new cries of battle and victory.' "

136

"You're worse off than I thought," he said.

Pat and I held a press conference and gave an account of the beating in the 17th precinct. But a spokesman for the Communist Party who had been at the demonstration accused me of being an agent provocateur.

"Only a police agent," he said, "would break windows, certainly not a peacenik. I have no sympathy for you, in fact I find your lumpen ways morally repugnant."

Mostly, I wanted to be alone with Marsha.

"I hope we don't have anymore visitors," I said. She was cutting up an eggplant and cooking tomato sauce in the kitchen. I went into the living room, put a Jefferson Airplane record on the turntable, and sat down to read, and listen. The tomato sauce and the eggplant smelled good.

My parents, Millie and Sam, in the front yard of our Huntington house in the fall of 1972.

Dancing with my wife at our wedding; August 1964. *Photo by Michael Klare.*

My youngest brother, Adam, at home, 1972.

My brother Adam, a junior high school student in the early sixties. *Photo by Michael Klare.*

The working class neighborhood I lived in from 1964 to 1967; Manchester, England.

August 1964. The summer of the Harlem riots. I was teaching at Winston-Salem State College in North Carolina. Deborah Gwatkin, beside me, was teaching Math.

At the trial of Columbia SDS member, Gus Reichbach; the Law School, 1968. I'm wrestling with the judge for control of the gavel.

At Gus's trial, doing a dance, and kicking legal briefs to the floor. *Photo by Randy Glickman.*

The New York Times article on the police torture of me. We were protesting the war in Vietnam and the murder of Fred Hampton; but in this post-Watergate world the "Anti-Nixon" emphasis of the headline is satisfying.

THE NEW YORK TIMES, SUNDAY, DECEMBER 14, 1969

2 Arrested at Anti-Nixon Protest Say They Were Beaten by Police

By THOMAS P. RONAN

Two men arrested at a demonstration against President Nixon last Tuesday night stripped off their shirts yesterday and showed bruises and welts that they said they suffered in a beating by the police.

The two, Jonah Raskin, 27-year-old assistant professor at the State University at Stony Brook, L.I., and Robert Reilly, 40, a lecturer at the Baldwin School, 160 West 74th Street, said their legs showed similar injuries.

They told a news conference at Mr. Raskin's apartment, at 250 Riverside Drive that they suffered head injuries when they were arrested and then were kicked and beaten by policemen. They said the beating lasted for about 45 minutes in a basement room at the police station at 167 East 51st Street.

They said that the Police Department's Civilian Complaint Review Board was investigating the incident and they were interviewed and that pictures of their injuries were taken by representatives of the board on Thursday.

A spokesman for the Police Department said it would not comment on the matter.

The two men, among the 65 arrested during and after the demonstration, said they had been charged with felonious assault, rioting and incitement to riot. Mr. Reilly said he had been freed in $2,500 bail and Mr. Raskin in $500 bail when they were arraigned in Manhattan Criminal Court on Wednesday.

About 3,000 youths demonstrated against the President and his war policies while he was attending the National Football Foundation's awards dinner at the Waldorf-Astoria.

A small group of the demonstrators went on a rampage as far as Rockefeller Center and broke windows in six stores. Of the eight policemen injured, one was an inspector struck in the face by a stone and another was a patrolman hit with a lead pipe.

Mr. Reilly and Mr. Raskin said they were taken first to the 18th Precinct station, 306 West 54th Street, and from there to Roosevelt Hospital.

They said that after they were taken to the East 51st Street station and, while they were handcuffed, policemen took turns beating them with nightsticks and blackjacks, and one policeman repeatedly kicked them.

REMEMBER THE NEEDIEST!

Four days after I was beaten and tortured by the police; my living room in Manhattan, December, 1969. *Photo by Carol Stein.*

(above) My brother Dan and his wife, Ann Weissman, 1972. *Photo by Sam Raskin.*

(below) Michael Meeropol, oldest son of the Rosenbergs, with his kids Veronica Ethel and Gregory Julian; Springfield, Massachusetts, fall 1973. *Photo by Sally Stein.*

The "Wanted Poster" for Lionel Trilling I designed and printed in 1972 after I didn't get tenure at Stony Brook.

With Robby Meeropol, the Rosenbergs' youngest son, in Springfield, Massachusetts. We're working together on an article about Robby's parents. *Photo by Sally Stein.*

(opposite, above) Eldridge Cleaver and Tim Leary at the Algiers airport, 1970. *Photo by Larry Mack.*

(opposite, below) Tim Leary's birthday party in Algiers, October 1970. *Back row:* Marty Kenner, Anita Hoffman, one of Leary's friends; *front row:* Stew Alpert, Tim, Brian Flanigan. *Photo by Jonah Raskin.*

Pat, Bob, Maisie, me, Marty, and our dog Lily on the roof of our 89th Street building; Christmas 1973 in Manhattan. *Photo by Camilla Smith.*

CHAPTER
EIGHT
TOWNHOUSE EXPLOSION

I. MARCH 1970

Two Weathermen and one Weatherwoman were dead. At first I was shocked and surprised. Then, on reflection, it seemed fated and inevitable. I began to construct a justification and an explanation of their deaths.

"They were stupid and careless," I said to myself. I was angry at Weatherman for endangering *my* own safety. The FBI knocked on *my* door to ask me questions. The Chicago police came to *my* apartment with bench warrants for the arrest of three fugitives who had gone underground: Bernardine Dohrn, Kathy Boudin, Kathy Wilkerson, now presumably living with assumed names and new identities. The cops looked surprised when Bernardine Dohrn wasn't available, as if they expected her to be sitting in my living room and knitting, waiting to be arrested. The cops opened drawers, poked under the sofa, and looked behind the bedroom curtains. They had no search warrant and they found nothing.

"Maybe the police will indict me," I said to myself. I know the Weatherpeople. I was in Chicago. I went to the last public Weatherman meeting—the War Council—in Flint. Maybe that's enough evidence to charge me with murder and conspiracy to commit sabotage. Guilt by association. Guilt by former friends, ex-comrades, and the wife I was separated from. Sheila had disappeared. I had no idea where she was. But Teddy Gold, Diana Oughton, and Terry Robbins were dead, and their bodies were in the ruins of Mr. Wilkerson's townhouse on West Eleventh Street in Greenwich Village.

"It tells you how desperate things are," Marsha said.

"It's the biggest action in Weather history," Hal announced. In the days following the explosion I read all the newspapers I could find and listened to news reports on radio and television. I wondered whose body they would find next in the rubble. Would there be more bits of fingers, hair, and flesh among the plaster, wood and glass? What was the explanation? How deep would they have to dig to find the answer? A newspaper reporter told me that the police had found a piece of paper with my name on it in the ruins of West Eleventh Street. I didn't know whether to believe him or not. Maybe he was working with the FBI. I had never been inside Mr. Wilkerson's townhouse, and I wondered why the police wanted to place me at the scene of the explosion.

"I'm sure the cops made up that story," Marsha said. "They want you to crack up and cooperate."

"They work like that," Hal said. "They indict you on phony charges and tell you you can get off if you talk. To clear yourself you'll have to concoct a case, along with the police, to frame Weatherman."

"And if I don't talk," I said, "they'll lock me up for something I didn't do." The townhouse explosion occurred on March 6th. It rocked the foundations of my mind. I was haunted by the specter of Weatherman and the police. On the night of March 10th I woke up suddenly at three AM.

"What's the matter?" Marsha said.

"I had a weird dream," I said, "and I want to write it all down now before I forget."

"I'm going to sleep," she said, rolling over. I got up, took pencil and paper and wrote down the dream as best I could remember. It went like this:

I was standing on a country road with two boxers (dogs). One of the dogs was bleeding from the eye. He had been shot. A crowd had gathered. I knew that some other living creature had been killed, and I was afraid that the corpse and the gun would be discovered in the tall grass. A police car was parked a quarter of a mile down the road. I was afraid that the crowd of people would attract the cop's attention, that he'd discover the body and arrest an innocent bystander. But the crowd disappeared; the dog with the bloody eye vanished and the scene changed. I was lying on the grass along the road, inside a rectangular glass house. I was visible from all sides. I couldn't hide, couldn't burrow underground like a mole, but I felt safe behind the glass because I was so completely in the open. Visibility, rather than invisibility, would protect me.

140

The next morning I got dressed, went outside, bought a loose-leaf notebook and gave it a name. On the first page I wrote:

Jomo's Dream Explosion Book

I copied down my dream and from then on recorded all my townhouse dreams and a lot of townhouse stories.

Townhouse myths spread everywhere, proliferating endlessly. Everyone had his or her own scenario; plots and motives were hatched to explain the explosion. One weekend I visited a middle-aged schoolteacher in Washington, D.C.

"It was suicide," she said. "They drove themselves to exhaustion and despair. At the end Teddy Gold faced a brick wall. There was nothing left but death." Her husband, an employee in the Department of Commerce, disagreed. We were eating supper. He swallowed his bread and butter and said, "It was probably an accident. The dynamite was probably stored improperly, or a circuit may have been shorted." The next day I visited a Virginia commune and listened to scenarios about the sexual rituals in the townhouse.

"Diana Oughton was a lesbian," an eighteen-year-old woman said. "She was torn away from her lover by male chauvinist Weathermen pigs and sent to her death."

"Bullshit," a man said. "I bet they had dynamite orgies. I bet the Weatherwomen stuck the dynamite up their cunts."

The press called the townhouse a "bomb factory," and the Weathermen psychopaths, but I wasn't satisfied with that explanation. I tried to put myself inside the townhouse before the explosion and to look out the windows with Terry Robbins and Diana Oughton. February 1970. Greenwich Village, Washington Square Park, beautiful old brownstones, the Women's House of Detention, junkies and smack on Eighth Street, the Panther 21 pretrial hearings at Centre Street. There were rumors of an impending American invasion of North Vietnam or Cambodia. On campuses it was quiet. It looked bleak.

That night—March 20th—I had my second townhouse dream.

I dreamed I was in Ratner's Restaurant on Second Avenue eating mushroom and barley soup with Ethel Rosenberg. Bernardine Dohrn walked in and sat down. She

141

*was wearing a disguise, and she said that her underground
name was Polly. Ethel kissed Bernardine and handed her an
envelope filled with money. I cut open a bagel. There was a
typewritten message inside: "Go to Avenue C now." I got
up and left. Ethel Rosenberg and Bernardine Dohrn had
their arms around one another. They looked like mother
and daughter.*

II. TEDDY, TERRY AND DIANA

I remembered Teddy Gold, Terry Robbins, and Diana Oughton
with mixed feelings. Short, dark-haired Terry was a relent-
less engine, pistons driving without remorse or pity. I didn't
like him, and I suspect that he didn't like me because he thought
I was a liberal academic. Terry made me feel that I was wasting
my life. I met him in Chicago in the summer of 1969. He always
paced nervously back and forth in the SDS National Office,
shouting and directing. He was reading Malraux's *Man's Fate,* a
novel about Chinese terrorists in the 1920's.

"It's about us," he said. "The assassination at the beginning is
incredible. You ought to assign it in class, professor."

"It's distorted," I said. "The revolutionaries are just fanatics."
Occasionally we talked about literature and culture, but Terry
always returned to the theme of armed black men and women
making war in America.

"The civil war between blacks and whites *has* begun," he
insisted.

"But the country *is* changing peacefully," I answered. "There's
gradual improvement."

"Blacks are being murdered in the streets." That was his final
word. There was no further discussion of the question.

I knew Teddy Gold at Columbia and from the New York
Weatherman collective. Teddy seemed innocent and naive, but he
was tireless, dedicated to the revolution and determined to do
what was right. He followed collective discipline and was abso-
lutely loyal. In the fall of 1969, before the Days of Rage, he was
euphoric.

"The revolution *is* coming," he said, "and we're making it." In
July and August he had been to Cuba and was profoundly transformed by the meetings with the North and South (Viet Cong)

Vietnamese. Teddy believed that Weatherman could create a base area in Brooklyn, as Che and Fidel had established a base area, or foco, in the mountains of Cuba. Teddy Gold was an internationalist who loved Brooklyn—the old home of the Dodgers, Prospect Park, Coney Island—and the possibility of guerrillas in Brooklyn fulfilled his wildest fantasy and his deepest need. The revolution would take place at home.

I was friendly with Teddy, but we had once fought bitterly. At one Weatherman meeting Teddy insisted, "The army directs the party, the gun determines our politics." I was convinced that the army and the party had to be separate, that the guerrillas had to be controlled by the party strategists and theorists.

"You suck, Gold," I shouted, rushing toward him, but his friends held me down, and we never actually exchanged blows. After the townhouse explosion I remembered that hostile, angry meeting, and I felt guilty. I was sad that he was dead. I had never really apologized for my hostile remark.

Like many other Weathermen, Teddy Gold was an anomaly. He walked the streets of New York and Chicago dreaming about Havana and Hanoi. He had grown up in New York and was a New Yorker to his bones, an American kid who loved fifties rock 'n' roll so much that he added his own revolutionary lyrics to the old tunes. He was a walking baseball encyclopedia. He could give you Lou Gehrig's lifetime batting average, Satchel Page's strikeouts. He played stickball in the street, jogged to the park to play basketball, wore sneakers and a T-shirt.

One day we talked about Sheila. We were living apart and she was working with the lawyers on the Weatherman cases from the Days of Rage.

"Are you depressed?" he asked.

"Not so much now," I said.

"I remember the end of a relationship," he said. "I came home one day and found a friend in bed with my girlfriend. I closed the door, sat down in the living room and cried."

"That's natural," I said.

"I was crying because I was jealous and angry, but a Communist ought to share, not hoard his love. Still I felt betrayed by my comrade." I was feeling especially cynical and I muttered between my teeth, "We've all been betrayed."

In the winter of 1969-70 Teddy was doing research for a

history of SDS, the mass student organization which Weatherman had consciously dismantled because they believed that it was liberal and not revolutionary. But I couldn't take Teddy seriously anymore. I thought he was trying to con us. Most Weathermen had given up all hope for white people. Since they treated hippies, Yippies, freaks, and students with contempt, their attempt to organize them seemed dishonest and opportunistic. And yet, maybe, just maybe, it was a genuine attempt. But by then it was too late. Looking back at Teddy's effort to reconstruct SDS—after the townhouse explosion—it took on new meaning and looked like a sign of his isolation, a reaching out for friends, a cry for help, and for the radical family of the past. When no help and no friends came, he walked into the basement of Wilkerson's townhouse. And once he went underground there was no exit to the street and the surface of everyday life.

The last time I saw Teddy he was sitting cross-legged on the floor. It was at the Flint War Council. He was wearing thermal underwear, expecting nasty weather. There was a recess in a meeting. Teddy looked weary. He had come to the end of the road, and wanted to rest, but even as he dropped he pushed himself forward to reach his goal, to live like his brothers and sisters in Cuba and Vietnam.

As for Diana Oughton, I knew very little about her. She and her boyfriend, Billy Ayres, came to our apartment late one afternoon in June 1969. Diana was wearing dungarees, a short-sleeved shirt and sandals. I was wearing a suit, though I did have an asparagus stalk in my jacket lapel—my Yippie badge of recognition. Sheila wore a long dress, high-heeled shoes and makeup, and we were on our way to a National Lawyers Guild dinner at the Hilton Hotel. Billy and Diana didn't have tickets, but we agreed that it would be legitimate for them to crash the gate, so they joined us. We were ripping off the wealthy Hilton Hotel, not the radical Lawyers Guild, we told ourselves.

The main reason for attending the banquet was that Morton Sobell, codefendant with Julius and Ethel Rosenberg, had been pardoned, freed from jail, and was the honored guest. Sobell had long, gray hair, wore sneakers, and looked like a middle-aged hippie. I was amazed that he was out of jail. Nine years earlier, in 1960, I had thought that he'd be in jail for the rest of his life, but the efforts of his wife, his mother, and thousands of people all

144

around the world, year after year, for nearly two decades, had secured his freedom.

"Sobell's incredible," Hal said. He too was an honored guest, and had sat beside him on the dais, a representative of the new left. "He understands Black Power, and he even digs women's liberation. There's nothing stuffy about him."

After dinner and Sobell's hopeful speech, Billy, Diana, Sheila and I went to Trader Vic's. We talked about the Sobells, the Rosenbergs, the old left, monogamy.

"If I was sent to prison I wouldn't want you to form a 'Free Billy Ayres Defense Committee,' " Billy said to Diana. "Women who fight simply because their husbands are imprisoned don't do shit for the revolution. If I'm busted you can forget me."

"But if I were in prison," Diana said, "I'd want you to form a 'Free Diana Oughton Defense Committee,' " and Sheila shouted, "We'll be in prison as long and as often as you men, you'll see."

III. FLINT, MICHIGAN

The last time I saw Diana (Terry was in jail) was at Flint, Michigan, in December 1969. The townhouse explosion revived my memories of Flint, of the Weatherman War Council. In hindsight I saw it clearly, but at the time I didn't really understand what was happening. I didn't see any bombs, fuses or dynamite at Flint, and no one asked me if I wanted to make, plant, or throw bombs. People talked about "doing some heavy shit," and winked at me, but it wasn't until March 6th—two and a half months later—that I knew for sure what the wink and the phrase "heavy shit" referred to. Looking back I saw that—figuratively speaking —the clock on the townhouse bomb was set at Flint. The underground organization and a program of armed struggle were planned at Flint, but I didn't hear any clocks ticking, and I regarded Flint mostly, not as a political meeting, but as a bizarre revolutionary happening. There were speeches and discussions; at endless rap sessions people poured out their life stories, their deepest secrets. They probed and tested each other's revolutionary commitment. But I remember a nonstop spectacle, dance, orgy. I performed. I was Jomo the jester, the Yippie, the street fighter. At Flint I wore a large Canadian navy coat, which looked like a 1905 Russian Cossack's uniform and an orange scarf which

I twirled in imitation of Mick Jagger, and I smoked dark Cuban cigars. I threatened to go to Flint in drag to parody the Weatherman cult of homosexuality but had chickened out. As it turned out, the coat, scarf, and cigar were more than an adequate costume.

Mostly I remember dancing. Men danced with men, women danced with women. A group of Weathermen, including myself, did a ritualistic macho scarfdance in the center of the ballroom. Men kissed each other, women made love to each other. We played Sly Stone's song "Thank you for letting me be myself, again" but added our own lyrics—"*Qué Viva, Viva Che.*" At Flint we were wild. We celebrated the revolutionary who hated and banished the revolutionary who loved. I mentioned Che's remark —"revolutionaries are guided by great feelings of love"—and a Weatherwoman said, "You're sentimental and bourgeois. Don't worry about love, just learn to hate the enemy."

At Flint I assumed that the cult of Manson and the fork, the praise for the killers of Sharon Tate, was madness. But the only way to respond to it was to parody it. So, I went to a supermarket, bought a package of plastic forks, and distributed them inside the meeting hall to Weather collectives.

As people danced they leaped into the air, kicked their feet together and shouted, "EXPLODE, EXPLODE." I, too, shouted "EXPLODE." I participated and I didn't think that I was a mad terrorist, a fanatical saboteur. I assumed that EXPLOSIONS meant bombings, but I also thought that we'd be metaphorically EXPLODING the old forms of consciousness. During the Chicago Conspiracy Trial Abbie Hoffman had said, "Jomo, we're out to dynamite brain cells," and I knew that the Yippies weren't going to use TNT. Abbie meant explosion by guerrilla theater—a lot different than a Weatherman explosion. I guess that at heart I was more of a Yippie than a Weatherman bomber. My bombs would be words and images. At the time I was writing *The Mythology of Imperialism* and, taking an image from the contemporary political scene, I had described Joseph Conrad, the writer, as the "saboteur who set the time-bomb on the twentieth-century revolution in the novel." I didn't literally mean that Conrad was an armed terrorist who placed bombs in the homes of establishment writers. No, but the effect of his books—*Heart of Darkness* and *Nostromo*—caused a literary explosion as shattering as a dynamite explosion. Every radio disc jockey talked about "dynamite" records, and almost everyone in the movement at the end of 1969 talked about bombings and kidnappings. The talk indicated our real anger, but there was an air of unreality about our talk. We daydreamed about guns and bombs.

I could not envision myself constructing a bomb. I didn't have the technical ability, and I was afraid. I regarded the Weathermen, like Teddy Gold and Mark Rudd, as white middle-class students, and I didn't think that they'd really make bombs either. If there were bombings I imagined that anonymous groups of secret revolutionaries, not the ostentatious Weathermen, would do them, because after all the point was not to draw attention to yourself and get caught.

I knew that the first action by the Weathermen during the Days of Rage was to blow up the historical statue of a policeman in Haymarket Square. That explosion was an acknowledgment of their nineteenth-century revolutionary heritage. In the 1880's a bomb had been thrown in Haymarket Square; several policemen were killed, and a group of Anarchists, who proclaimed their innocence, were arrested, framed, and found guilty. The Weathermen were also rejecting the tradition of American radicalism. They said, in effect, "We are guilty. We are bombers. We haven't been framed. Cops oughta be offed." But I assumed that an anonymous student radical or freak, spurred on by the general talk of bombings, had done the action, and not an official member of Weatherman. I didn't believe that Rudd, Dohrn, or Ayres, the people who *preached* armed struggle also *practiced* armed struggle.

For example, in November 1969, an underground organization which later turned out to be Sam Melville's group, blew up the White Hall Induction Center in New York. It was an act of sabotage against the war in Vietnam, and we welcomed it. Along with hundreds of thousands of other people—including the Weathermen—I was in the streets of Washington demonstrating publicly against the war. Sabotage by an underground organization and large demonstrations by a popular mass organization both seemed necessary, but also very distinct, separate operations. I assumed that since the Weathermen were in the streets trashing they weren't also underground bombing. In fact—contrary to most left-wing experience—they were doing both.

At Flint I talked to Teddy and Diana. I listened to Bernardine Dohrn's speech about the necessity to avenge Fred Hampton's death. I participated in the discussions, but I didn't foresee the townhouse. Maybe an astute, prophetic observer could have looked into the future and seen the ruins. But I couldn't. At Flint the Weathermen were simultaneously cogent and mad, penetrating and ludicrous. On one hand there was a coherent political analysis, a disciplined organization, an ideology, and leadership. There was an understanding of imperialism, especially the war in Vietnam, and black oppression and rebellion in the United States. There was also a firm grasp of the strengths and weaknesses of youth culture and an insistence on the importance of women's liberation. On the other hand, there was a chaotic and frenetic life-style and an intense, irrational moral fervor. The Flint fanatics, the townhouse terrorists, were American Buddhists. In Saigon the priests in their saffron robes immolated themselves to protest the war. In a perverse, though real sense, the Weather guerrillas blew themselves up on West Eleventh Street to protest the war. They knew that they'd destroy themselves, but by sacrificing themselves they believed that they'd set the stage for younger revolutionaries to succeed.

"1969-1970 is the American equivalent of the Russian 1905, or the Cuban 1953," a Weatherwoman had said at Flint. "The Russians failed in 1905, but twelve years later in 1917 the revolution succeeded. Fidel attacked Batista's fortress at Moncada in 1953, was defeated and captured, but the Moncada defeat was turned into the Havana victory of 1959. The Days of Rage is our Moncada. Flint marks the beginning of the end."

At the end of 1969 the Weather collectives became more and incestuous. They were cut off from students and freaks. Weathermen isolated themselves, and in turn the movement and the society ostracized them. In the eyes of America Weatherman was a monster. Weatherman hated the old left, old SDS; in turn the peace movement hated Weatherman. By Flint time Weatherman was in an advanced state of disintegration.

I went to Flint as Jomo the pig fighter, the hero of the 17th precinct, but I was still Jonah Raskin, the son of a fifties radical. My old left background made me skeptical about the prospects for an armed underground in the United States. Leaders of the American Communist Party indicted by the Smith Act, which made it a crime to advocate, write or talk about the violent overthrow of the U.S. government, created a clandestine organization in the 1950's. But they went into hiding; they hibernated like bears. In 1953 when I was eleven I thought that the Raskin family was going underground. It was the summer the Rosenbergs were executed. We left our home on Rogues Path and rented a bungalow on a remote beach. It was hot, dry, desolate. Only a few wild plum bushes grew in the sand. The bungalow had a 1940's refrigerator, chipped China, tarnished silverware, no television, and *Life* magazines from 1941 and 1942. I felt as if we were going back in time, away from the repressive fifties to the calmer, safer forties. We had few friends and received almost no mail. I sat in my room and read about the Rosenbergs and the atom bomb, or swam alone, hour after hour, in Long Island Sound.

One day my father came home with the paper. He dropped *The New York Times* on the kitchen table. It exploded. A banner headline proclaimed that a leader of the American Communist Party had been captured, handcuffed, and locked up in jail. There was a photograph of his cabin in the Sierra mountains. He had been in hiding for years, and yet they found him. I was a paranoid, imaginative eleven-year-old, and I thought that we were also hiding from the FBI.

From my fifties background, my old left experiences, I thought that to be underground meant to hide, to be inactive. Communist Party fugitives didn't blow up townhouses or police stations. I still accepted much of the old left's argument that violence was initiated by the right, by the state, and not by the revolutionaries. The police in the 17th precinct, not me, were violent. I *had* broken a few windows, but that didn't compare with the torture they inflicted on me. Throughout history there was the same story. The Haymarket martyrs were innocent. They were framed. The Rosenbergs hadn't stolen the secret of the atom bomb. They were innocent and had been framed, too. I grew up in the fifties understanding the importance of armed revolution and the Red Army in China and Russia, but nothing in my old left experience prepared me for armed struggle by *us,* as opposed to *them,* by American guerrillas on native soil.

At Flint when a Weatherman asked me if I wanted to join the organization, I said, "I like your politics, but I hate the collectives."

"In that case," he said, "you can't be a Weatherman." And that was that. I found life in the collectives repulsive. The Weathermen said that they would live in tribes, like apes, find food wherever it was available, camp out, create a home, use up the natural resources and move on. They'd make waste of America. They'd eat, sleep, fuck, fight. They'd build a community, rediscover man's innate being, combat the natural environment and survive. The tribes would spread the revolution and destroy the old culture. It was as if their underlying assumption was that hydrogen bombs had been dropped across America, cities were destroyed, a civil war was in progress, and a group of young American radicals had to march secretly across occupied territory from New York to San Francisco, looting and burning.

I escaped from Flint. The dancing was endless, Sly Stone's song played over and over again, and day and night dancers shouted "EXPLODE," "EXPLODE," and chanted *Qué Viva, Viva Che.* Fred Hampton's face was everywhere. My last night in Flint I slept with a woman on the altar of a Catholic church. A kind, old priest invited us in for the night because we had no other place to sleep. In the middle of the night I woke up and saw two people fucking in the pews. They waved to me and I waved back. At 5:30 in the morning the priest woke us; a group of Polish and Lithuanian women was entering the church for the first mass of the day. We got dressed and went out for coffee and doughnuts.

The Weathermen were planning a New Year's Eve party in Ann Arbor, but I left long before it started. I flew to New York, and went to an all-night party in Westchester. It was snowing. I parked the car and walked across the lawn, entering the house through the kitchen. I saw three black maids in white uniforms preparing food. In the living room the guests were high and drunk. I looked at them with hostility, pointed my index finger toward the ceiling, formed my hand in the shape of a gun and shouted "piece now," punning on the "peace now" chant. A beautiful, middle-aged woman handed me a hash pipe, kissed me on the cheek, and asked me, "How's the revolution?" When midnight arrived and the sixties turned into the seventies I found myself not with my revolutionary brothers and sisters, but with middle-aged, wealthy liberal suburbanites.

150

IV. THE FUGITIVE

A few weeks after the townhouse explosion the FBI came to my apartment to question me. I wasn't home, but a friend from Boston who was visiting me was taken into custody and interrogated. When I phoned home later in the day a man answered and said "Don't come home again."

"Who is this?" I asked, but he hung up. I phoned Marsha.

"The FBI thinks you know something about the townhouse," she said. "You'd better hide out for a while." I went to Brooklyn to live with a married couple and their eight-year-old daughter Strawberry. Harrison had been an SDS member in the Midwest in the 1960's and was now teaching French literature at Brooklyn College. He was cynical about the movement and was devoting all his time to a dissertation about Louis Aragon, the French Communist poet. His wife, Cynthia, had dropped out of the University of Minnesota, had worked for SDS, and now ran a children's day-care center and was active in a women's consciousness-raising group.

Cynthia and Harrison weren't apolitical people, but they no longer went to demonstrations, read underground papers, or visited with their old movement friends. Their apartment was comfortable. It was, I thought, a good hiding place. We ate big meals, got stoned, went to the movies, but I was still nervous, tense, and I didn't sleep well. I started to dream again, and I recorded them in "Jomo's Dream Explosion Book." My third townhouse dream was on March 31st. It was my seventh night in Brooklyn as a fugitive.

In the dream I went to a Yankee baseball game with Marsha. It was played in the 1930's: there were old cars, and clothes, soap box orators, bread lines, and soup kitchens near the stadium. In the sixth inning I left my seat to buy a hot dog. When I sat down again a man with a baseball cap was waiting for me. He asked me for names. I refused to cooperate and he took me into custody. "Phone a lawyer," I shouted to Marsha, and the man ordered, "Take her along, too." In the locker room they interrogated both of us. "Did Babe Ruth hit a home run to left field or right field?" the man asked. I didn't know, but I tried to figure it out, assuming that lefties hit to right field and righties hit to left field. The man twirled his bat. "Left, right, left, right, right, left, right, left," he shouted. "Which is left which is right?" I couldn't answer. The bat was raised over my head. Then I woke up.

In the morning, after lox and bagels, Cynthia showed me an old trunk in the living room.

"Some Weatherpeople left it here a long time ago," she said. "I don't think they'll ever come back for it." We pulled it into the center of the room and opened it. There were Cuban and Vietnamese books, *Soul on Ice, Woodstock Nation,* Beatles and Grateful Dead records, coconut incense, a hand-carved hash pipe, a fringe jacket, a pair of sandals, faded dungarees, panty hose, notebooks filled with poems, ramblings, doodlings. It was like sorting through historical relics of the sixties, the mementos of the recent Weather past.

That night Marsha came to visit us and brought news. The New York district attorney had subpoenaed our friends, my parents, and Sheila's mother, Emma, to a grand jury investigating the townhouse explosion. Was this the fifties again? I wondered. Was this the start of a new decade of investigations, informers, FBI harassment, and persecution? Were we doomed to repeat the fate of the thirties radicals? Emma had been questioned in the fifties because of her husband's activities. Now she was being questioned in the seventies for her daughter's activities. When would it end?

One afternoon I was restless, so I took the train into Manhattan and wandered around the Village. On Eighth Street and Fifth Avenue, not far from the ruins of the townhouse, I saw a man sitting in a green Ford, holding a pistol. I looked into the window. On the dash board were wanted posters for Mark Rudd and Bernardine Dohrn. I ran down the street as fast as I could.

Another afternoon I went home to my Riverside Drive apartment to get my mail. I missed the FBI by a minute or two. I had walked up the stairs while they took the elevator downstairs. My mail was disappointing. There was a letter from the Justice Department in Washington which charged that I had never registered for the draft, that I was liable for prosecution and should report immediately to the nearest FBI office. It was a lie. I had registered for the draft in 1960 when I was eighteen years old, and the letter was clearly a trick to get me to surface, to turn myself in so that they could question me about the townhouse. The more the FBI hounded me, the more evidence I had of their dragnet, the less anger I felt toward Teddy, Terry and Diana, and the surviving Weather people. I was still afraid and bitter, but I felt like a brother fugitive, if not in their underground, then in my own separate underground. I knew now that I wouldn't cooperate with the FBI to save my own skin. I forgot about Flint and my disagreements with the organization, my fights with Sheila. But I continued to have weird dreams. My fourth town-house dream was on April 3rd.

> In the dream I got a phone call from a woman. She refused to give her name, but she gave her address. When I arrived it was the 17th precinct on Fifty-first Street. I stood outside, afraid to enter, but I gathered up my courage. Inside it wasn't a police station, but a luxurious hotel run by the policemen who had beaten me. They didn't recognize me. Prostitutes were sitting in the lounge, pimps were drinking at the bar. I took the elevator to the eleventh floor, walked down the hall, knocked on a door. A Weatherwoman wearing a blond wig answered the door. We got into bed and made love. Then we got dressed and went to a restaurant for coffee. Fat white men in Cadillacs were propositioning beautiful black prostitutes. Junkies were nodding out on the street corner. We ate and went back to the 17th precinct whorehouse hotel. "I want to fuck again," the Weatherwoman said. Before we could get back into the hotel room the police captain/hotel manager stopped us. I was afraid that he'd recognize me and arrest me, but he just wanted his bribe. "That'll be $100," he said. I took out my wallet and noticed that I had fake identification papers. On my driver's license my name was Edgar Samuels. I gave the man a $100 bill and he smiled. "She's a good lay?" he asked and laughed.

That was the first dream I talked about with Harrison, Cynthia and Marsha, and from there we went on to talk about Weatherman, the townhouse, Flint. Marsha wrote a poem, which was inspired by the Weatherpeople and the townhouse. I copied it into my notebook:

153

In public places
Guarded words deceive.
The face of love
Waits patiently for night.

On dark city corners
Submerged couples surface.
Outlawed hands and faces
Communicate by touch
After daylight separation.

In sweet secret sessions
Underground emotions explode.
Clandestine lovers weave
Crazy patterns on borrowed sheets.

Usually we talked late at night, but one afternoon, when we were sorting through the trunk the topic came up again and I noticed that Strawberry was listening carefully to our conversation.

"Should she hear all this?" I asked. "When I was a kid in the fifties my parents whispered when they talked about Joe McCarthy. They wanted to protect me."

"Why shouldn't she hear," Cynthia said. "She met Bernardine Dohrn in Minnesota once. Didn't you?"

"I did," Strawberry said.

"I think kids ought to know," Harrison said. "The old left fucked up their kids by not talking to them about politics." That night, on April 10th, I had my fifth townhouse dream. It seemed to arise out of the conversation we had during the day.

I was in an apartment on West 11th Street with
Bernardine Dohrn. She was wearing a shirt and dungarees
from the big trunk, and she was putting colored beads on a
string and talking about living underground as a fugitive.
"Our need for money is almost as great as our desire for
sex," she said. I felt as if I was being asked to make love
and take out my wallet. But I didn't move. I had a photo-
graph of a football player in my lap. His arms were
outstretched as he reached for a forward pass. "Cut the
photograph," Bernardine said. I took the scissors, and cut

*out everything except the fingerprints. Then I looked up
and saw that the walls were covered with the fingerprints of
fugitive football players.*

It was the middle of April, and I was getting restless. I wanted
to end my hibernation. One afternoon Cynthia and I decided to
make a pilgrimage to West Eleventh Street. "Maybe the FBI will
be watching," Harrison said. "You'd better be careful."

"We're not doing anything wrong," Cynthia said. We took the
New Lots train into Manhattan, bought two bouquets of roses
from an old Italian woman, and placed them in the empty lot
where the townhouse had stood. Cynthia wrote a message in
chalk on the sidewalk: "With love, for Teddy, Terry, and Diana."
Then we went back to Brooklyn.

But I wasn't satisfied. I couldn't sleep that night so I got up,
got dressed, took the subway to Eighth Street, walked up Fifth
Avenue to Eleventh Street, and when the cop on the corner
wasn't looking I jumped over the fence. It was dark, chilly, and
quiet. The earth was covered with bricks, broken glass, rocks,
shattered beams. I sat down on the ground and looked into the
sky; there were no stars and no moonlight. I felt as if I was in a
dark cavern. I closed my eyes, stretched out my legs and tried to
imagine the townhouse as it had been before the explosion. I
became an actor in my own scenario.

*I see myself walking up the stairs. A man with a black
mask over his face comes to the door and lets me in. He is
wearing gloves and he has a clock in his hands. A Beethoven
symphony is playing on the radio. A naked woman with a
mask on her face also holds a clock in her gloved hands. I
hear the clocks, tic-toc, tic-toc, tic-toc, getting faster and
faster and louder and louder. "We invited everyone," the
masked Weatherman says, "but no one came. Everyone has
turned away from us." "I came," I say. "You don't count,"
the Weatherwoman says. "I tried to save you," I plead. "I
don't want to be saved," she says. The room is luxurious.
There is a chandelier overhead, wormwood panels, thick
carpets. The masked man puts down the clock and picks up
a tennis racket. "You only talk about explosions," I say,
bouncing a tennis ball on the floor.*

A dog barks. I open my eyes. There is no house, no Weatherman,

155

no clocks, or tennis racket. It is uncomfortable on the cold, hard ground, but I have more questions.

"Was it an accident?" I ask. "Nothing is accidental," the Weatherwoman says, throwing the tennis ball in the air. "Was it fated?" "Nothing is fated," she says. "In these ruins flowers will bloom. We are the first." "You are the last," I say. "You are crazed." "We are at the edge of infinity." I want them to say "Jomo, you are not at fault. We killed ourselves." But even in this imaginary conversation they refuse to blame themselves. "The pigs killed us," the woman says, "and we will have our revenge." They lead me to the door and say goodbye.

I opened my eyes, stood up, brushed off my trousers, and looked through a crack in the fence. The policeman wasn't on the corner, so I jumped over the fence to the sidewalk and felt that I had returned from the underground to the surface of everyday life. I walked to the IRT, waited an hour for a train and returned to Brooklyn.

One morning, about a week later, Cynthia went to her job at the day-care center. As she walked out the front door she noticed a man standing across the street, holding a camera. When she came back in the afternoon he was gone, but the next morning she saw him again, and I watched him from our third floor window; he photographed everyone who went in and out of the old brownstone. We spoke to the building superintendent. "Two FBI agents questioned me about bombs," he said. "They wanted to know who lives here. I told them we are all peaceful citizens."

"Maybe they're watching *you*." Harrison looked at me.

"Maybe they're watching *us* because we were in SDS," Cynthia said. Maybe they know this trunk is here." We were apprehensive and speculated that we'd be subpoenaed to the townhouse grand jury. That night I had another dream.

I went back to the 17th precinct hotel, but there was nothing left. "It blew up," a cop said. "What happened to the woman in 11C?" I asked. "She left before the blast, but the pimps and the police were blown up."

The next day we stayed home together.

"We've got to get rid of the trunk," Harrison said. He pulled it into the middle of the room and kicked it. We looked at the stickers: "Cunard Line," "Queen Elizabeth."

"If the FBI raids the apartment," he said, "we don't want them to seize it." We burned the papers and gave the clothes to the Salvation Army. Harrison saved a green corduroy jacket for sentimental reasons. That night I packed a suitcase, put my Dream Explosion Book in my back pocket, moved out of the apartment and went to stay with friends in Queens. On the subway I looked at the map. It seemed as if West Eleventh Street was at the center of New York, that circles radiated outward to the suburbs, that I was moving to the periphery.

But within a week I had to return to Manhattan. I was scheduled to testify on May 19th before a special grand jury investigating the police beating of Patrick and me at the 17th precinct. I put on a suit and tie and took the subway to Canal Street. I felt that I was plunging into the vortex. The criminal court building was alien territory. In the witness waiting room I tapped my foot nervously. Then they called my name and I went inside to testify before grand jurors who looked like Wall Street brokers. They didn't look one bit sympathetic. When I concluded my narrative the district attorney asked me one question.

"Do you call police pigs?"

"Yes," I said. "A policeman who tortures is a pig."

"Let the record show that the witness uses rhetorical language," the district attorney said. "He has a tendency to exaggerate." I wanted to call him a pig, but I walked out without uttering a word and sat down again in the waiting room. A tall, fat man who looked like a professional football player stepped up to me and asked politely, "Are you Jonah Raskin?" I looked at the flower in his lapel. "Yes," I said. He handed me a piece of paper. It was a subpoena commanding me to appear before the grand jury investigating the Weatherpeople. Ever since the fifties I had been preoccupied with investigating committees, the interrogation of witnesses, perjury and contempt. Now, I was asked to inform, to cooperate. I knew that I would not, could not, become a seventies rat. There was no way I would betray my old friends the way fifties ex-Communists finked on comrades from the thirties. I went to see a lawyer.

"I don't want to testify," I said. "I refuse to give names."

"I think I can have the subpoena quashed," the lawyer said.

157

"You're a journalist aren't you? And wasn't your wife Sheila a Weatherwoman?"

"Yes."

"Well, reporters are protected from divulging their sources. You're safe, at least until the Supreme Court changes its mind. And husbands can't be forced to testify against their wives. As long as you're not divorced from Sheila you have immunity."

A week later I was surprised again. The Weather Underground issued its first communique, a "Declaration of War," which proclaimed, "Within the next fourteen days we will attack a symbol or institution of Amerikan injustice. This is the way we celebrate the example of Eldridge Cleaver and H. Rap Brown and all black revolutionaries who first inspired us by their fight behind the enemy lines for the liberation of their people." On June 10th a bomb exploded in the New York City Police Headquarters. By then I wasn't in hiding anymore. I was attending rallies and demonstrations. I had surfaced after my few brief months as a fugitive. I met Harrison and Cynthia in Midtown.

"They've done it," Cynthia exclaimed. "It makes me feel good, and it's revenge for the beating you and Pat received."

Then Cynthia, Harrison, Marsha and I went to see Antonioni's *Zabriskie Point,* a film in which the hero steals an airplane, paints it, takes off, then lands and is killed by the police. In retaliation the luxurious home of an American millionaire is blown up. In slow motion and in color the camera shows books, food, clothing, furniture, float gracefully in the air. The explosion is beautiful. It's a terrorist ballet. A woman sitting behind me got up and left when the house blew up. She coughed and it sounded like Sheila. I turned around and jumped out of my seat, but Marsha grabbed my arm and pulled me down. "Stay," she said. "You can't run after phantoms."

In the spring of 1970 Jean Genet came to the United States to speak in defense of the Black Panthers and to do everything in his power to prevent the State of Connecticut from sending Bobby Seale to the electric chair. I met Genet in the Panther Defense office in Union Square. The New York Panthers had been indicted on bombing conspiracy charges and were in jail without bail. Genet would come into the office in the morning, and we'd chat. He wore a black leather jacket and faded dungarees, and he

158

smoked thin cigars. He was mostly quiet, and he had a whimsical smile, but when he talked about Seale he became intense and earnest. I was embarrassed and shy in his presence, but I was anxious to know his political opinions. Finally I summoned up my courage. I thought out my question first in English and then asked him out loud in French:

"*Que pensez-vous des* Weatherman?"

He took a puff on his cigar, his expression became serious and he said, "*Les Weatherman ont des petites bombes. Les Etats-Unis ont les grandes bombes à Vietnam.*" Saint Genet had spoken.

CHAPTER
NINE
EXILES

I. ROME

We arrived at six AM. Our flight from New York was short but we were nervous.

"Will we make it?" Jennifer asked.

"Who knows," I said. "Maybe we'll be hijacked." We left New York in an atmosphere of terror. Palestinian guerrillas commandeered a 747, held the passengers hostage, demanded the release of political prisoners held in Israeli jails, and, when no prisoners were released, the Palestinians escorted the passengers from the jet and blew it up. At JFK airport we were thoroughly searched.

"Dohrn, Dohrn," the customs man said. "The name sounds familiar."

"You probably knew her father," I said. "He was a salesman, did a lot of traveling."

"Nice-looking chick," he murmured to me, pointing his chin at Jennifer. She was wearing a long skirt, dark glasses, and her brown hair was in a bun. "Where are you two love birds going?"

"Rome," I said.

"You're going to see the pope?"

"We're going to see the pope."

"What have you got in your rucksack?" He opened it, pushed aside the clothing, and drew out a book in a soft leather casing. "What's this?"

"*The Book of Changes,*" Jennifer said.

"I'm opposed to changes," the customs man said.

"What about books?" I asked.

"Don't be a smart alec," he said. "What's this?" He held up the I Ching sticks.

"They're magical," Jennifer said. The customs man sniffed them.

"They don't look dangerous," he said, "but you're both weirdos."

161

The 747 was almost empty. After dinner we took off our shoes and put on slippers provided by the stewardess. The overture to a Verdi comic opera was playing on the loudspeaker system.

"My former friends in the California Communist League," Jennifer said, "would disapprove if they knew I was going to see Tim Leary and Eldridge Cleaver. We read Stalin, and I worked in a bra factory to organize Chicano women."

"You've changed," I said. "How about throwing the Ching." She took out the sticks and the book. On the inside cover there was a red, yellow, blue and green rainbow and a black lightning bolt—the symbols of the Weather Underground—and the words, "This book belongs to Jennifer Dohrn." She threw the sticks and read from the book. It was "Fu/Return (the turning point)."

> After a time of decay comes the turning point. The powerful light that has been banished returns. There is movement, but it is not brought about by force. The old is discarded and the new is introduced.

"Is Eldridge Cleaver going to return?" I asked.
"There's more," Jennifer said.

> Societies of people sharing the same views are formed. All selfish separatist tendencies are excluded and no mistake is made. In winter the life energy, symbolized by thunder, the Arousing, is still underground. It must be strengthened by rest, so that it will not be dissipated by being used prematurely.

"It's about the underground."
"I was thinking about Bernardine," Jennifer said. "The life energy, the thunder is underground. It needs to be strengthened."
"Do you think she'll return?" I asked.
"Not unless she's captured." Jennifer picked up the I Ching sticks, tied them together with a piece of blue string and put them under the seat.

"People understand the pain of separation I feel about my sister," she said, "but they don't understand the need for an underground."

"This is the captain speaking." Jennifer was interrupted by a voice on the loudspeaker. "We're running into choppy air so fasten your seat belts. We hope you'll have a pleasant trip."

At six AM a stewardess woke us, we landed in Rome and took a bus to Abbie Hoffman's run-down hotel on the Via Garibaldi. Later we went out for breakfast on the Via Veneto. The empty café glittered, and the top of the counter was piled high with pastries and sweet rolls. We had cup after cup of capuccino, and Abbie practiced his Italian.

"Shall we sing *'Bandera Rosa'?"* he asked.

"Sure," I said, and we did a Yippie rendition of the old Italian Communist Party song, belting out the chorus, *"Bandera rosa triomphera, viva communismo e liberta."* The waiter smiled and applauded our act.

"Are you coming to Algiers with us?" I asked Abbie.

"No, I can't get permission," he said. "We're on appeal from the Chicago Conspiracy Trial. It's OK to go to Italy, but not to Algiers, 'cause it's a socialist government."

We spent the day sightseeing, and in the evening Abbie drove his wife, Anita, and Jennifer and me to the airport. Stew Albert met us at the gate, took a look at Anita's two large suitcases and shook his head.

"If she thinks this is going to be a holiday," he said, "she's in for a big surprise." Stew had only the clothes on his back. He hadn't even brought a toothbrush or a change of underwear, and you'd have thought he was out for a short walk rather than on an expedition to Algiers.

"Send my love to Eldridge and Tim," Abbie shouted. "Tell 'em I expect to see 'em on Saint Mark's Place by Christmas."

II. ALGIERS

On the other side of the Mediterranean, on the North Coast of Africa, Eldridge Cleaver and Timothy Leary met us at the Algiers airport. Eldridge was dressed in black—black shirt, black trousers, black shoes, and black jacket. He carried a bulging black leather case, and he quickly arranged with the puzzled Algerian officials for us to be admitted as guests of the International Section of the Black Panther Party. Leary stood behind the barrier with Rosemary, his tall, serene-looking wife. He wore a cap to cover his head because he was embarrassed by his shaved head—part of

163

the disguise he had used to escape from the United States. There was a button on his cap which said: "You can be anyone you want to be the second time around."

Stew Albert introduced us to Eldridge.

"I knew your sister," he said to Jennifer. "She's a fine woman." He turned to me: "Do I call you Jonah or Jomo?" and to Anita Hoffman he said, "So, you left your old man in Rome. How's the New York Panthers?" he asked bald-headed, nervous Marty Kenner, the official Yippie envoy to the Panthers. He sized up tall, muscular, and silent Brian Flannigan and shook his hand.

"The trial started," Marty said.

"Haven't we had enough trials?" Eldridge said. We walked past the customs barrier. There was a big smile on Leary's face. He was chuckling.

"Friends," he said, embracing Anita and Stew. "It's wonderful to see you here. I'm at peace in Algiers. It's a North African high."

"Very good Dr. Leary," Eldridge said, cutting him short.

We broke up into two separate groups. Anita, Jennifer and I went with Tim and Rosemary in their car, and Stew, Marty, and Brian went with Eldridge and DC, the field marshall of the Panthers, also a fugitive in exile. In the airport parking lot Tim turned to Anita, handed her a joint and said "Welcome to the Third World." It seemed incongruous, but Tim believed that dope was as revolutionary in Africa as it was in America. He wanted to turn all of Africa, and the whole world, on.

The air smelled sweet. The blue-black night sky arched from horizon to horizon. We got into the car. The road was black. There were no street lights.

"These Panthers are crazy drivers," Tim said, trying to follow Eldridge. Once or twice he swerved off the road, but he miraculously managed to bring us back to the hard pavement. "I've been trying to get Eldridge to do acid," he said, "but he's uptight. If we could trip together we'd be much closer." Tim dreamed about a perfect union between him and Eldridge, but it didn't look like it would ever be attained.

We soon reached our hotel, a seashore resort outside Algiers, run by a nonprofit cooperative. It was dark, but we could hear the roar of the Mediterranean, and I thought about Abbie alone in Rome, a short distance away.

164

"Boy," Leary shouted to an Arab who was sitting on the steps of the Moslem Hotel, and I thought for a moment I was in Alabama or Mississippi. "Boy, carry this luggage." Eldridge looked pained. He was trying to be hospitable, but it wasn't easy. He leaned toward Stew and spoke directly into his ear: "Algerians used to slit the throats of Frenchmen who called them 'boy.' He'd better watch out." But the Arab manager obeyed the command and carried Anita's suitcases to the second floor. We settled in our rooms, men and women separately because it was a strict Moslem custom, for married as well as unmarried guests.

"We'll call for you in the morning," Eldridge said.

"Eldridge is our genial African host," Tim said. "We ought to be up early and be ready for the tribal commands." Again, Eldridge looked pained.

In the morning we had breakfast on the patio overlooking the sea. The sky was blue, the water bluish-green, the houses white. The only other guests at the resort were members of a Russian volleyball team who always wore their red sweatsuits. I suppose that at one time I would have regarded them with awe, as the representatives of a brave, revolutionary nation, but now they looked rather ordinary and professional. Brian, the best athlete among us, introduced himself. He had attended Columbia in the late sixties, joined SDS, become a Weatherman, and during the Days of Rage he was charged with attempted murder. But at his trial Brian was acquitted. He then ran for sheriff in Chicago as "the peoples' pig." Now, along with the rest of us, he was working with the Yippies.

"You are Yippies?" the Russian captain asked. "But what is Yippie?"

"American revolutionaries," Brian said.

"Why are you in Algiers?"

"We're visiting Eldridge Cleaver and Tim Leary."

"I not know. You are friends Angela Davis?"

"No, not friends."

"She is Communist professor." The Russian smiled proudly.

"Yes, she was captured by the FBI. She's in jail."

"Is terrible. Is very repressive in your country, no?"

"Yes, but the Yippies are trying to change that."

"Very good. I like Yippies." Brian and the Russian shook hands. The Yippies had made another bizarre alliance.

"These Russian boys are very entertaining," Tim said. "But they could use some LSD."

Stew, Brian, Jennifer and I stretched out on a blanket. The sun was hot. "When I was here a month ago," Stew said, "just after Leary arrived, we tripped together on this beach. It was Tim's best acid. He smuggled in about 20,000 hits with him. Tripping in Algiers. I wrote about it in the *Tribe:* 'In Algiers the gun becomes the flower, and the flower becomes the gun.' We could trip again."

"No, I'm not ready for it," I said. "Tripping seems out of place here."

III. ACID ON LONG ISLAND

I looked at the sand, the water, the sky, and I remembered my first acid trip in 1970 on the North Shore of Long Island. I never tripped in a Weatherman collective, nor at Flint in the heyday of acid, but I tripped because Weatherman argued that acid was revolutionary. I had started my revolutionary career reading *The Daily Worker*. Ten years later I thought I was furthering my radicalism by dropping acid, but every old leftist I knew thought I was acting crazy, that drugs were counterrevolutionary.

April. It was a cold day, the sky was blue and clear, the water was rough. There were whitecaps in Long Island Sound. The red, blue, yellow and green pebbles glistened in the wet sand. I was fascinated by the sand—separate, distinct gems making up a whole, the beach. I was with Marsha and friends from Stony Brook. We had walked a long way and I was tired. I stretched out on the beach and thought that I was giant Gulliver among the Lilliputians. I had collected driftwood for a fire while Marsha collected fifty twigs for an I Ching reading. My arms ached from carrying the heavy logs. I laid them down, but Marsha gave me the twigs to hold, and they felt as heavy as the logs.

"Help me," I said. Marsha reached down and pulled me up. I dragged the logs along the beach and lifted them into the van. On the way to Marsha's house I passed out, and the next thing I knew I was in her living room. There were a dozen guests sitting on the floor smoking dope. We were the only freaks in a neighborhood of commuters, rednecks, and patriotic Americans. We were watched; we had to be careful not to smoke dope in front of the windows or outside the house and not to walk around naked or talk about politics where neighbors could hear us. Marsha was also tripping and she asked everyone to talk in a whisper. We presented a polite, conservative exterior. Marsha mixed a drink and we went upstairs to her bedroom. I was in pain. My arms and legs ached. It was a bad trip. I felt as if I had just been beaten in the 17th precinct. I was hot and cold. I was tense. I had pins and needles in my legs. I couldn't move. I was paralyzed one moment and frenetic the next.

Marsha helped me to undress. I got into bed. My right leg moved uncontrollably, round and round in a circle, and I couldn't stop it.

"I've got Jomo's mojo energy inside," I said. "But if you hold my arm down I'll push it out." I flexed my muscle and pushed and Marsha held down my right arm. I felt less tense. "Get undressed," I said. She took off her clothes, got under the blanket, and we made love. The world was a wet hinge, fluid, electric, a watery mirror, one side reflecting the other, identical side. There were no seams. The watery mirrors kissed, colors ebbed and flowed, my legs stopped moving, the pins and needles vanished, and we came together.

"You see, it wasn't in your arm but in your penis," Marsha said. We lay in bed and talked about New York subway stops: Times Square, Grand Central Station, Rockefeller Center, Grand Army Plaza, Union Square, Astor Place, Sheridan Square. The New York subway map was illuminated in my head. I saw every station, one station after the next, and the different lines—the BMT, the IRT, the IND. The subway ran in my mind, throwing off sparks, making stops, reaching the end of the line, then turned around and went back the way it had come. It returned. My mind was cleared.

I went downstairs and made a fire with the logs I had collected on the beach. We ate supper together, roast duck and rice. Late at night Marsha brought out the twigs and threw the Ching. It was "Heng/Duration." The Ching said:

In the sphere of social relations, the hexagram represents the institution of marriage as the enduring union of the sexes. In marriage the husband is the directing and moving force outside, while the wife, inside, is gentle and submissive.

Marsha put the book down.

"This is sexist crap," she said. "I bet a man wrote this," but she continued to read:

> *Duration is the self-contained and therefore self-renewing movement of an organized, firmly integrated whole, taking place in accordance with immutable laws and beginning anew at every ending.*

"I understand," I said. "The Ching is talking about our survival. The Weather people in the townhouse didn't understand duration."

"I'm all in favor of duration," Marsha said. The fire was low so I picked up a handful of twigs, threw them on the coals and watched them burst into flame.

IV. THE THIRD WORLD

Algiers, October 1970. Tim and Stew were talking about acid on the beach. I didn't want to trip because I felt that acid undermined duration. It seemed immoral to trip in Africa. LSD certainly didn't seem revolutionary in the Third World, among the wretched of the earth. It was for affluent rebels. The sky was blue, the buildings were white, and the pebbles glistened in the wet African sand. I could appreciate them without acid.

"This meeting is historical," Leary said. "Chromosome damage meets Black Panther, and that means trouble."

"Doesn't it also prevent us from making the revolution?" I asked.

"Acid is holy," Tim said. "It brings sacred life."

"Did you change in prison?" I asked. "Did the Weatherpeople affect you?"

"The best way to explain where my head's at," Leary said, "is to tell you about my reading list. I have two groups of friends: one group reads Che's *Diary*, Marx's *Communist Manifesto*, Mao's *Little Red Book;* the other group reads the I Ching, *Conversations with Don Juan,* and my *High Priest*. My reading list combines both. It's the ultimate synthesis." I was bewildered. I had taken a two-week leave of absence from Stony Brook and thought that I had escaped from the academic world, but Dr. Leary brought it all back. After acid, jail, the Weather Underground, he was still talking like a Harvard professor, and he probably would have been more comfortable in a Cambridge classroom than in the Casbah.

Late in the afternoon Dr. Leary drove us into Algiers, and we met DC in the center of town. Algiers had both French and Arabic architecture, people spoke French and Arabic, street signs were in both languages; there was a European section of the city and also the Casbah. The colonial legacy was everywhere. We stood in the center of town and watched the faces of the men.

"This is called La Place du Martyrs," DC said. "During the National Liberation Struggle the French executed hundreds of Algerians here. They captured suspected guerrillas in the Casbah" —he pointed up the hill away from the harbor to a maze of stores and houses that appeared to be built one on top of the other— "dragged them down those heavy, stone steps and shot them here. Look at this." We walked toward the water. The buildings along the harbor were built by the French and looked like medieval fortresses. The walls were thick, the windows were narrow slits. They looked as if they had been built to defend against fierce enemies. The French had departed, but their buildings still sat heavy on the coastline, looking toward France, toward home. DC pointed down to the Mediterranean from the height of the embankment overlooking the harbor.

"What color is that?" he asked.

"Reddish-blue," Jennifer said.

"The Algerians say it's their blood that gives it that color," DC said. "After the French executed members of the underground they dragged the corpses across La Place du Martyrs and threw the bodies into the harbor. The red blood of the guerrillas changed the color of the Mediterranean."

The brutality of the French imperialists came suddenly alive. In La Place du Martyrs the Yippies, Tim Leary, and even DC, an American black man, seemed like strangers. It wasn't our country, not our history or culture. We were foreigners from the most powerful imperialist country in the world, and our hippie revolution, our LSD, and our I Ching seemed inadequate, absurd in colonial, underdeveloped Algiers.

We walked down a narrow cobblestone street in the Casbah,

and I was reminded of Pontecorvo's film *The Battle of Algiers.* I half expected Ali la Point, the young thief who became a guerrilla and a terrorist, to jump into the crowded street and point a gun at a policeman. There was room for only three people to pass at the same time, and there was no space at all between the little shops. DC led us to a seafood restaurant. It was sundown, and there were almost no women in the streets—only a few late shoppers wearing veils, hurrying home. We sat down at an outside table. There were twelve of us. Eldridge sat at the head of the table. Anita, Jennifer, and Rosemary were the only women in the restaurant, and we knew that Algiers was in desperate need of a women's liberation movement, if not American, then Algerian. There was a bar in the back, a mirror behind the bar, and the bottles and the faces of drinkers were reflected in the glass. Larry and Sekou, two fugitive Panthers from New York, sat facing each other on opposite sides of the table. They had been indicted by a New York grand jury, but both had escaped the country by hijacking a plane.

"Sekou is the most amazing of all the Panthers," Marty said, and of all of us he was probably the best judge. In the winter of 1969-70 he persuaded Leonard Bernstein and his wife to give a fund-raising party for the Panthers, and in an editorial *The New York Times* attacked them for "elegant slumming." The Panther case, which had received no attention before, became front-page news, and the party was a success. Since then Marty had worked with Bobby Seale and Huey Newton and was highly respected by all the Panthers—a rare feat.

Sekou was tall and very dark, and he reminded me of Ali la Point. He was certainly as brave and daring. On April 1, 1969, when the New York City police knocked on his door to arrest him, Sekou escaped through his bathroom window. His apartment was on the fifth floor. He climbed down three flights, holding on to a water pipe, and then jumped to the sidewalk, landing on his feet. He didn't stop running until he reached Eldridge's embassy in Algiers. Sekou wanted to know about his Panther friends in New York. I had given him a copy of Michael Tabor's pamphlet "Capitalism Plus Dope Equals Genocide," a powerful description of the effect of heroin in the black community, and Brian described the Panthers' audacious actions in court before Judge John Murtagh.

"They're in control of that courtroom," Brian said. "They bop in, raise their fists, and shout 'Power to the People.' They turned that courtroom into a classroom on racism and repression."

DC ordered wine and food for everyone, and a waiter served us large pink shrimps with a cold mayonnaise sauce. We began to eat, but DC suddenly dropped his fork on the table.

"I know those two dudes," he said. We looked toward the back of the restaurant. There were two blacks—clearly Americans in their Brooks Brothers suits—drinking at the bar. "I wonder what they're doing in Algiers?"

"Check 'em out," Eldridge said, looking at them and at his own reflection in the mirror behind the bar. Then he turned back to us and asked, "What do you think about Huey Newton's rap on revolutionary suicide?" Tim and Rosemary didn't seem to hear the question; they were holding hands and kissing, oblivious of us."

"I don't like it," I said. "The idea of suicide turns me off."

"But are you willing to die for the people?" DC asked.

"What about living for the people?" Jennifer said.

"I have hang-ups about suicide myself," Eldridge said. "But revolutionary *homicide*—that's another story."

"Didn't Jonathan Jackson commit revolutionary suicide?" DC asked. But before anyone could answer him he jumped up, rushed to the back of the restaurant and darted into the men's room, to follow one of the black Americans. In a few minutes he joined us again. "Suspicious muthafucka," he said. "He told me he works for the San Francisco Department of Welfare, that he's on vacation."

"Sounds more like he works for the CIA," Eldridge said.

"They're covered," Sekou said. I looked under the table and saw that Sekou had a revolver in his hand. He kept an eye on the men standing at the bar and continued to eat with his fork.

I didn't know what to think. "Were these American black men really working for the CIA—a depressing thought itself—and spying on Eldridge Cleaver, or was Eldridge paranoid?" It was likely that the CIA was keeping a watch on Eldridge's movements, but I also had the feeling that his political perspective was somewhat distorted in Algiers, thousands of miles from home. He was more at home in Africa than Leary was, but if Leary belonged back in Cambridge, then Eldridge should have been back in Berkeley. It's true that he had set up a Panther Embassy, that he was in contact with the Chinese, the Koreans, the Vietnamese, and the representatives of African liberation movements. He communicated news of the movement in America to the Third World, and news of the Third World rebellion to America. The Eldridge Cleaver who wrote *Soul on Ice,* and ran for President on the Peace and Freedom Party ticket, combined French existentialism with the wisdom of Soledad and Folsom prisons, bridged the experience of blacks in the ghetto and white students on campus. In 1968-70 Eldridge Cleaver was my hero. I wanted to be like him, to be a revolutionary activist and intellectual. But now the Eldridge of exile, fighting for his survival and uprooted from black America, seemed confused in his political thinking. With one hand he reached for dialectical materialism, socialism, internationalism, and with the other hand he reached for Tim Leary, hippie heads, the LSD guerrillas of the Weather Underground. Something had to give. He was torn in two different directions.

When we finished the meal we walked up the cobblestone streets to La Place du Martyrs. Sekou walked behind us. DC was relaxed. He looked up into the sky at the full moon and said, "In Babylon you can't appreciate the moon's beauty, but here you have the time and space to dig on it."

"It's a far out moon," Brian said, articulating our common mood.

We drove back to Eldridge's pad to continue our celebration. In the living room there was a large marble table. Eldridge's typewriter sat in the center of the table, and there was a sheet of paper in the typewriter. On the top of the page Eldridge had written a title, "Revolutionary Integrationism," and a first sentence. The rest of the page was blank, as if he was waiting to see what would happen, then and there, before writing another word. DC pushed the typewriter aside and put down a bottle of wine, half a dozen glasses and a birthday cake. It was Tim's birthday—the very same day as Bobby Seale's birthday. Seale was in prison in Connecticut, awaiting trial on charges of kidnapping and murder. Jennifer had baked a cake and the icing—a short statement on revolutionary integrationism—read "Tim's Free, Free Bobby." We ate the cake, drank the red Algerian wine, smoked a lot of grass, listened to Otis Redding and Junior Walker records. I had given Eldridge a Leonard Cohen album—Cohen was one of his favorite poets and singers—and he put it on the turntable to hear one cut, "The Stranger." DC opened a bottle of ginseng wine Eldridge had brought back from North Korea and poured us drinks.

"It's a great party," Stew said, clinking glasses. "Maybe something big will come of it—Yippies, Panthers, the Weather Underground, Third World revolutionaries, heads—maybe we'll come together."

"Kim Il Sung drinks this shit," DC said, "and look what it did for the North Koreans." He held up the bottle to the light. There was a ginseng root inside. "If we bury this gnarled root in the earth a new plant will grow."

"Then we'll be able to make our own ginseng wine," Jennifer said.

"It'll take seven years," DC said.

"We'll come back in seven years," Jennifer said.

"I won't be alive in seven years," DC said.

"Sounds like revolutionary suicide."

Eldridge rolled one joint after another and passed them around the room. He sang the words to "The Stranger." The birthday cake, icing and all, was finished, and the ginseng wine was gone.

"Tell me," he said, "is acid really a requirement for the revolution?"

"Personally, I don't *push* acid," I said. "My first trip wasn't too good and I'm not anxious to do it again."

"It's mean," Eldridge said. "It messed up my head. Dig, I'm worried about this Leary cat. I don't know what he'll do next." Stew listened carefully and played with his beard.

"If the high priest of acid settles in Algiers and works with the Panthers it'll make freaks become political revolutionaries," Stew said.

"Leary's here," Eldridge said, "because I respect the Weather Underground, but I've got problems with the Algerian government. They're dead set against drugs, but they think that Leary is an Afro-American, another Fanon. If word gets out he's the acid king . . ."

"His rap about the unity of inner and outer revolutions sounds jive to me," I said, and the conversation disintegrated. It was late, we were tired, and we went to sleep in Eldridge's pad. When we

173

woke in the morning he was already on the phone.

"Yes, Miss Dohrn is here," I heard him say. "Very soon." He hung up and said, "The press thinks Bernardine Dohrn is here. She's the biggest thing going—Weatherwoman in Algiers." Eldridge was now playing the Yippie media game.

"I'm not sure Bernardine will like this," Jennifer said. "In the last communiqué she said that she wasn't going into exile, that she was going to stay and fight inside the United States. After all, that's the point of the underground."

"The reporters will be arriving soon," Eldridge said. "The press conference is set. They're expecting a spectacular event."

We got out of bed, had coffee and rolls and got to work. At the press conference we planned to announce that Leary was in Algiers with the Panthers, that the Weather Underground had helped him escape from prison and leave the country, and that the old Yippies were reconstituting themselves as the new Youth International Party. As minister of education I was going to help draft the statement and prepare the press conference. But as we began to work on the press release our differences became clearer. Eldridge wanted a statement which would make sense to the Algerians, North Koreans, and the African liberation groups which had their headquarters in Algiers. Leary wanted a statement for freaks in the U.S.A. and Europe. He wanted to address his statement to the "brothers and sisters in the psychedelic underground." Eldridge wanted the statement to be directed to "the progressive and peace-loving anti-imperialist peoples of the world." We tried to write a statement, but at every step differences prevented us from going ahead. Leary's first world and Eldridge's Third World didn't make one world.

All day long the phone rang and reporters asked for Bernardine Dohrn. Then Huey Newton phoned from California wanting to know what was happening, and, as best he could, Marty Kenner explained. There was even a gap between the Panthers themselves. Each day we could see the split grow larger. In Oakland the Panthers talked about voting at the polls, going to church, black economic development, and in Algiers they talked about killing cops, North Korea, and African socialism.

In the afternoon DC returned to the pad with a copy of the international edition of the *Herald Tribune*. There was an Associated Press story about Bernardine Dohrn and a photograph which we cut out and taped to the wall. He also brought his own hot news item. "The Algerian government has just found out that Leary's not black, that he's the acid king. In New York their representative to the UN is a laughing stock. And there are a hundred reporters at the Algiers airport waiting to see Miss Dohrn and Dr. Leary. The Algerian government hasn't seen so many reporters since the last coup d'état."

We sat quietly all day, watched the Algerian kids in the street, smoked dope, read the *Herald Tribune* again. Stew talked to Marty about Albert Camus, Brian shadowboxed, Jennifer listened to records. At suppertime Eldridge came back. "The press conference has been canceled," he said. "They don't want publicity about the King of Acid." Eldridge had tried his best, but the Algerian government wouldn't let him be a friend to both the psychedelic and the Third World revolutions. They chose for him. They had cleaned up the drug trade when they expelled the French, and now they didn't want it to return in the guise of a revolutionary blessing from America.

"But there's a new scenario," Eldridge said. "DC, Dr. Leary, Miss Dohrn, and Marty Kenner will go to the Middle East to meet with the Palestinian guerrillas. You've got to be ready to go at any time. Meanwhile, tomorrow you meet with the representatives of the Provisional Revolutionary Government of South Vietnam."

"I guess if Leary can show he's a friend to the Palestinians," Stew hypothesized, "it'll help his chances with the Algerian government. Leary'll become an Arab. How did New York Jews like us get mixed up with this?"

The next day DC drove us and Kathleen Cleaver to the embassy of the Provisional Revolutionary Government of South Vietnam. It was an occasion of friendship, dignity and sanity, and reminded us that representatives of the first world and the Third World could work together as brothers and sisters to end the War in Vietnam. Kathleen spoke excellent French and was our translator. At first the Vietnamese took us for liberal, peace-loving students, and accordingly they served us Coca-Cola. They talked about the invasion of Cambodia, the political prisoners in Saigon's jails, Thieu's dictatorship. We talked about the protests against the invasion of Cambodia, Kent State, the burning of the Bank of America in Isla Vista, and the fall offensive of the

Weather Underground. The ambassador smiled. He spoke in Vietnamese and his assistant brought out a bottle of scotch and gave us drinks.

"You are American revolutionaries, then. Right on! We drink to the armed struggle." We raised our glasses and downed the scotch. Then the Vietnamese gave us rings made from the scrap metal from U.S. planes shot down over the South. "You must come to liberated Saigon," the ambassador said.

"And you must visit us in liberated New York," Jennifer said. The ambassador laughed, and we said goodbye, formally. Then we drove to the airport. Anita Hoffman flew to Paris to meet Abbie. DC, Leary, Marty, and Jennifer went to the Middle East to see the Arabs.

For two days Brian, Stew, and I stayed with Eldridge and Sekou, smoked dope, wandered in the Casbah, and grew bored. We wanted to be back in New York.

"Aren't you planning to go to Paris?" Eldridge said one morning. We had wanted to go for days, but Eldridge had always insisted that we stay another day. We packed our bags, looked out the window for the last time, and said goodbye.

"I'll see you in Babylon," Eldridge said. "I'm gonna return." He opened the top drawer of his desk, took out two revolvers and stuck them inside his trousers. "Let's go," he said. I looked around the room. Bernardine Dohrn's photo was pasted on the wall, Leonard Cohen's album was on the turntable, and Eldridge's typewriter was sitting in the center of the marble table. There was the same sheet of paper in the roller.

V. PARIS

Brian, Stew and I flew to Paris to meet with Jerry Rubin, Abbie Hoffman, and the French bureau of the Yippies—Paris lycée students who had corresponded with us and had started their own chapter of the Youth International Party. Stew breathed a sigh of relief when we reached the Left Bank. "That was one of the heaviest trips of my life," he said. "We've been dealing with two egomaniacs." It was late October, Paris was cool, the leaves had turned color, the trees in the Luxembourg Garden were in long, straight rows. We were no longer in the colony. This was the capital. Abbie reminded us that all telephone calls from Algiers to

Europe, America, or Asia, still went through Paris. It was another legacy of colonialism. We stayed at Victor Herbert's apartment—a crash pad large enough to house twenty-five people comfortably. There were nearly a dozen bedrooms, one enormous living room, thirty feet high, a window extending the full length from the floor to the ceiling, and a kitchen where Steve Ben-Israel cooked gourmet vegetarian meals, and Phil Ochs, wearing a black leather jacket and greased hair, played fifties Elvis Presley songs.

All shapes and varieties of Frenchmen and Frenchwomen came to see the American Yippies on exhibit at Victor Herbert's Dada apartment and to ask questions about cultural revolution ("Does the cultural revolution precede the political and economic revolution?"), smoking dope ("Is marijuana revolutionary?"), and the Weather Underground ("Do bombs transform consciousness?"). In Paris the Yippies weren't essential, but they were nice to have around. They could shake up the moribund old French left and show French radicals the necessity of cultural upheaval.

One afternoon we went into the streets to demonstrate. Alain Geismar, one of the leaders of the May 1968 rebellion, had been sentenced to prison. Several hundred other Maoists were already serving prison terms. Students fought with Parisian gendarmes; when the police caught demonstrators they lifted them off the ground, turned them over and spanked them on their behinds. Jean-Jacques Lebell, an anarchist and a writer who spoke English as if he had always lived on the Lower East Side, escorted us around Paris.

A police station in the sixth arrondissement had been fire-bombed and Jean-Jacques liked to believe that the police were looking for him. So we were always on the move, taking the long way around to reach our destinations. Occasionally Jean-Jacques would disappear in the middle of a conversation, or as we were walking down the street, but he'd reappear miraculously around the corner. In Algiers these games would have led to trouble. In Paris they were relatively harmless.

"Anita tells me that Algiers was weird," Abbie said. We were walking along the Seine toward Notre Dame to see the gargoyles.

"It was," I said. "Put Tim and Eldridge in the same room and there's bound to be an explosion."

"What would you choose? Exile or the underground?"

"I'd probably go to jail," I said. "That probably sounds absurd to you, especially since I was tortured in prison, but the underground seems remote to me, and Eldridge's exile looks lonely and depressing. At least in jail there's a community of brothers. You can be part of a political group."

"I'd go to Sweden," Abbie said. "But each to his own."

The next day Jerry Rubin, Stew, and I went to visit Ellen Wright, Richard Wright's widow, Eldridge's European literary agent, and also an exile, though the conditions of her exile were very different from Tim's or Eldridge's. Mrs. Wright was a fugitive from American racism, not from jail or the police. She was born in Brooklyn, was Jewish, an old leftist, but she seemed at home in Paris. On the bookshelves were editions of Wright's *Native Son, Uncle Tom's Children, The Outsider, White Man, Listen!,* and *Eight Men,* and I remembered that, long before us, Richard Wright had been preoccupied with black fugitives and exiles, black strangers in a white world. Eldridge Cleaver seemed to be like a character in a Wright novel. I wondered whether he would die in prison like a native son or in Paris like the exiled Richard Wright himself.

One evening when we were eating at Victor Herbert's, Marty Kenner phoned long distance from Cairo. The trip to the Middle East had been a catastrophe; they had been to see the pyramids and were caught in a dust storm; Jennifer was attacked by Arab men; DC had phoned the Korean embassy to ask for help, but it turned out to be the hostile South Koreans, not the friendly North Koreans; and Leary himself was hunted down by reporters until they trapped him in a bathroom.

"It's a Marx Brothers movie," Stew said.

In Paris we made friends and had fun. One group of the French Yippies met regularly at Chou Chou's home on the right bank near L'Opera. Chou Chou was a French student preoccupied with America. He lived with his mother in an old, but tidy apartment house. Abbie and I climbed the stairs and rang the bell. A woman wearing an apron opened the door, smiled and led us down a long hallway. I looked into the kitchen. Onions were hanging from the ceiling, and big copper pots were on the wall. There was a grand piano in the living room, and the bookcases were filled with rare editions of the collected works of Balzac and

Victor Hugo. There were doyle cloths on the backs of the chairs and sofas, an old Aubusson carpet on the floor, and beautifully framed Daumier prints. The woman adjusted her glasses, knocked on Chou Chou's door and turned the knob. We walked into the small, smoky room. Thirty French kids were sitting on the floor. There were posters of Weather fugitives, Rap Brown, and Angela Davis, and a map of the U.S.A. with pins indicating where Bobby Seale was in jail, where the Conspiracy trial had taken place, where the Bank of America had been destroyed. In the United States I knew radicals who were preoccupied with events in Cuba, Vietnam, and China. Here were French radicals absorbed by America. They were encouraged by our revolutionary surge. It made me feel that American leftists could contribute to the international revolutionary movement.

Chou Chou and his friends were smoking dope, listening to the Grateful Dead, and talking about their latest action—the disruption of a speech by an American general. Abbie said a few words in French. "One day," he said, "there will be one world. No boundaries. It'll be a planet without empires or colonizers. Liberty, Equality, Fraternity. Down with the Bastille." The French Yippies broke into a round of applause, whoops, and hollers.

The next day I flew back to New York. Brian, Stew and Jerry went to Germany, then London, where they disrupted the David Frost TV show, and then to Ireland. I returned home, as I had left, an internationalist. But at the same time I was more aware than ever before how uniquely American I was, and I didn't feel apologetic. I was an American radical and that was as good as any other kind of radical. I didn't want to be a member of the Viet Cong or the Red Guards, and I knew that no one, not the Chinese nor the Russians, would make our revolution for us. And by the same token it wasn't the job of the Yippies to make the revolution for the Algerians or the French. The Yippie revolution was an American revolution and I was glad to be at home, on native soil, to dive back into the sea of hippies and students at Stony Brook.

CHAPTER
TEN
TEACHING

I sat in my office and waited for the meeting to end. The bookcases were filled, the desk was piled high with papers. At a closed meeting my colleagues in the Stony Brook English Department were discussing whether or not to give me tenure. I had been teaching at the university since September 1967. Through all the changes in the late 1960's and in my life, teaching had been a constant. But what I taught and how I taught had changed and the changes were the topic of discussion at the tenure meeting. While they reviewed my academic career I evaluated my own development.

I. 1967

I came to Stony Brook from the University of Manchester, a red brick university, in England. I had gone to Manchester because I wanted to get away from Columbia and Lionel Trilling and because I wanted to study with Frank Kermode, author of *Romantic Image,* and a darling of the New York literary crowd. He was a regular contributor to *The New York Review of Books* and one of the editors of *Encounter* magazine when it was revealed that the magazine was funded by the CIA. Kermode was less of a snob than Trilling, less of an elitist. He shared the ideas for his book, *The Sense of an Ending,* with us. He was informal, friendly, and talked for hours with students in our small graduate seminars. Kermode was deceptive; he was Trilling's British counterpart, and it's not surprising that they became friends. Beneath his aesthetic exterior Kermode was a liberal anti-Communist. He claimed that he knew nothing about the CIA connections with *Encounter;* but I suspect that he did.

Manchester offered me more academic freedom than Columbia. It was a provincial university, not a seat of power like Oxford or Columbia, and there was less pressure to belong to a school of thought. I was *the* American abroad, people expected me to be odd and eccentric, and they let me follow my own inclinations. But fundamentally, Manchester wasn't very different from Columbia. The same attitudes toward literature were shared by both English departments.

Stony Brook was a new university, officially a branch of the State University of New York, but academically a satellite of Columbia. My English degree was like a holy parchment in this new American red brick university, simply because it was "English." The chairman of the English Department was an old leftist who rambled on about Marxism and the dialectic, but he was concerned about his own status and power. He was wealthy; he drove a pink Cadillac, and the graduate students called him the "Cadillac Marxist." He hired me because he knew that I was a radical who played by the rules of the game. I published in the scholarly journals and thought of myself as a professor first, a Marxist second, and a radical third. I was hired to be the house Marxist. There were professors who related literature to theology, literature to myth, literature to philosophy, now there would be a Marxist professor who would analyze literature and society. Each professor tilled his own plot and didn't trespass on anyone else's plot. Stick to your area of specialization, attend department meetings and cocktail parties, do the bidding of the chairman, and tenure was assured. The chairman was also building his own power base, and since he hired me I owed him an obligation. He wanted to institute a tutorial program. Faculty members were opposed to the plan because it would mean more work for the same pay. Also, it was an innovative program and they didn't want to change their set ways. The chairman believed that the tutorial program would improve the quality of education. He also wanted to be known as the man who had introduced the tutorial system to Stony Brook.

One day he called me into his office. He filled his pipe, lit it, and sucked at the stem. He was soft-spoken and genial.

"Jonah," he said, "I'd like you to report on the tutorial system in England. You're the specialist in British education." A week later at the department meeting I painted a glowing picture of my tutor and Manchester. I wanted a tutorial system at Stony Brook for academic reasons, but I also wanted to go with, not against, the power.

I was disappointed with the chairman. I knew that I'd have to be cagey with him. At my interview he had made snide comments about F. O. Matthiessen's homosexuality. In 1967 I wasn't prepared to defend homosexuality, but I resented his wisecracks about my favorite literary critic, and the author of *American Renaissance*, a radical, a Harvard professor who committed suicide. The chairman also suggested that "my wife" drop out of law school and help me in the early stages of my career.

"It's your profession or hers," he said. "Why not inspect a model home, make a down payment and move to Stony Brook?" I went to Storey Book Homes. The neighborhood was barren. No one was in the streets or the front yards. No kids played outside. Everyone was behind fences or indoors. When "my wife" and I didn't move from New York to Stony Brook the chairman sent me a letter of censure.

"I no longer have implicit faith in you," he said. He was a hawk watching each move of every teacher in the department.

I went to all the faculty meetings, assigned term papers, gave final exams, midterms, and was a strict marker and severe disciplinarian. I knew almost no students, and I had few friends on the faculty. Most of the teachers followed a traditional approach to education. They had formal relations with their students. Some of the faculty members were excellent teachers and solid researchers. Some were warm people, but there was always a firm line of demarcation between the teacher and the taught.

Most of the professors thought that Shakespeare's heroes were more alive than Ho Chi Minh or Eldridge Cleaver. Students had almost no rights, no control over the courses offered, grades, methodology. The teachers I knew best were cynical about the university. They called Stony Brook "the whorehouse" and their colleagues "prostitutes." They detested the professors who wrote articles for scholarly journals, as well as the bureaucrats who sent out memos, demanded reports, and evaluations. My friends wrote poetry and fiction; at lunchtime they drank with the construction workers in the neighborhood working class bars. When classes were over in the afternoon they returned to the bars. From three to six they drank, ate pizza and hero sandwiches, played the jukebox, and tried to pick up secretaries. Two professors were from Michigan. They were both 6'5" tall and weighed over 250 pounds. They thought that they were the sons of Papa Hemingway. They loved to fish and hunt. They had worked in

lumber camps and they used the lumberjacks' term for women—
"flat cocks." They were all married but had contempt for their
wives, who stayed at home taking care of the kids, cooking,
dusting, and cleaning. They were cynical about political activity;
when I asked them to come to a demonstration they made jokes
about Jews, blacks, women, radicals, fags. They also hated
American society, technology, the Pentagon, commercialism, the
war, money. They wanted to go back to the frontier before the
era of the highway, the billboard, the motel.

Teaching my first year made me feel I was forcing myself to
become someone I wasn't. I talked, dressed, smiled, carried
myself like a professor. It was a performance. Every day I sensed
that I was doing violence to myself. For the first term I didn't
once consider making friends with students. In the fall of 1967
Stony Brook students were still straight, apolitical. They came
from lower- and middle-class Italian and Jewish families and were
on the make. The men looked like me in 1959 when I was on the
high school football team, and the women looked like cheerleaders. I gave them up for lost without even giving them a
chance. And I gave myself up, too. I worked in the system but
thought it was a farce. I was bitter. Being an academic was like
being a con-man. You specialized in forgeries—M.A.'s and
Ph.D.'s—and counterfeiting—lectures—and rose to the top. I
worked within a system I regarded with contempt and did
nothing to change. I was dissatisfied with myself.

II. 1968-1969

The Columbia uprising of April 1968 and the Columbia Liberation School of July and August 1968 changed my attitude toward
teaching, students, my colleagues, and the university. After I was
arrested at Columbia I became politically active on the Stony
Brook campus. I was no longer the house Marxist but the field
radical. In the fall of 1968 I taught a course entitled "Literature
and Revolution," inspired by a course I helped prepare at the
Columbia Liberation School. I also envisioned it as a response to
Daniel Bell's course on "Literature and Revolution" given at
Columbia when I was an undergraduate. The course began with
Paine and Burke and the French Revolution and ended with
Lenin and Trotsky and the Russian Revolution. We read history

184

and literature, traced the image of revolution in literature, the impact of revolution on culture. Fifty students enrolled, but only a half a dozen were interested in the theme. Most of the students were indifferent.

"Literature and revolution is your area of specialization," one student said. "Other professors have their own areas of specialization, Blake or Milton, or the sonnet." The students were uncomfortable in class because there was an articulated political perspective and a social context; they were asked to express their own views on revolution. All their school lives they had been taught that literature and life were separate, that a poem doesn't mean but is, that books don't express ideas, that poems are about eternal feelings. Rooting literature in a historical context seemed to be soiling it. The most articulate student in the class was also the most conservative. He argued that conservatives were better writers than revolutionaries because they had leisure, money, a stable social environment.

"Everyone knows," one student said, "that you can't write during a revolution. There's no such thing as a revolutionary culture. Culture takes time, decades of accumulated wealth. Revolutions destroy culture." I wanted to use my authority as the teacher to combat him, but I felt that I'd be playing the conservative, not the revolutionary. So I gave him the floor and felt uneasy allowing him to propagandize. The topic of revolution was new, but my approach was traditional. I was the teacher, they were the students. I lectured, corrected papers, evaluated their oral reports, and gave the grades. And the political dynamic of the classroom, the student-teacher conflict, was more immediate, more real, than the politics of Burke, Paine, Lenin, Trotsky.

In the fall of 1968 I was active at Columbia. Gus Reichbach, a law student, was put on trial by the Columbia student-faculty judiciary for his part in SDS demonstrations. I disrupted the hearing by leaping onto the table, trying to wrest the gavel from the hands of the chairman. I danced on the bench, kicked the briefs to the floor. The Columbia *Spectator* reported it as guerrilla theater: "Jonah, the prophet of disorder, brings justice to the law school." But the Columbia administrators and teachers weren't amused. My colleagues at Stony Brook wanted me to apologize. My former Columbia professors said that since I was "a scholar and a gentleman" it was morally incumbent on me to apologize. When I didn't apologize, I was arrested in February 1969. Columbia University was the complainant. My former teachers were responsible for having me arrested and sent to jail, for they now regarded me as the enemy. I was charged with attempted petty larceny and disorderly conduct. At the trial Gerald Lefcourt, my lawyer, later a lawyer for the New York Panthers, said "Your honor, we are not dealing with a common criminal. My client is a graduate of Columbia College, he has a Ph.D. from the University of Manchester in England, he is a married man, has published articles in scholarly journals."

"If he's so smart," the judge said, "he should have known better. Thirty days or a $250 fine." He pounded the gavel and I paid the fine.

In the fall and winter of 1968-69 I had another kind of education outside the classroom. I spent most of my time in the Ocean Hill-Brownsville section of Brooklyn working on a book with Richie Kalvar, a photographer. The book was about the movement for community control of schools. I was a tape recorder and Richie was a camera. We felt like invaders in an all-black neighborhood. I would preserve on tape the words of the black world. Ocean Hill-Brownsville would tell its story through me. Richie would preserve the faces of the community on film. For months we roamed the streets, drank in bars, played pool, talked to winos, junkies, thieves, kids who rarely went to school, men with part-time jobs. They had the wisdom of the street. At first we were afraid of the young blacks but soon we sat together with them on wooden orange crates under the awning of Rodriguez Bodega, drank "Twister" wine, and talked.

Since our book was also about the public school system we knew that we had to leave the school of the streets for PS 55 and IS 271. But I didn't want to go to school; I was afraid that I'd find the classroom deadly after the joy of the street. The black kids in the street had energy, street lore, and I was afraid that in school they would be ordered to behave. For me schools had always been repressive institutions. But the grade schools and the junior high schools in Ocean Hill weren't as disappointing as I had expected. In the Afro-American history classes kids read Malcolm X's *Autobiography* and Langston Hughes's poems. The schools were necessary, the teachers were often warm, dedicated people, but I felt emotionally tied to the men on the street. I had lived in schools for over twenty years, had spent much of my time with teachers and students, and I wanted to escape from classrooms, seminars, chalk, lectures, colleagues.

In the spring of 1969 I taught English 509, a graduate course on women's liberation, pornography and literature. We read the Marquis de Sade, *Anna Karenina, Madame Bovary, Middlemarch, The Story of O, Zap Comix.* Jack Thompson, an associate professor, a writer for *The New York Review of Books* and *Commentary,* carried on a campaign against me. He called the course "dirty books 69."

"Raskin's a sex pervert," he said. Curiously enough, he was also carrying on a campaign to have the National Guard patrol the streets of New York and protect whites against black muggers.

The chairman shoved a copy of R. Crumb's comix into my face. "Is this what you're teaching?" he shouted. "You're corrupting the morals of minors."

"The students brought that to class," I said. "They introduced me to Crumb. If anyone's being corrupted it's me."

English 509 traced the image of women in literature from the French Revolution to the present; the class was run by women, but most of my colleagues assumed that it was a scandal and an outrage. The department enacted a special rule: no assistant professor (I was an assistant professor) could teach graduate courses except by special permission of the chairman. And of course I was denied permission.

III. 1970-1972

In 1970-71 I taught English 226, a course on contemporary American culture. This time the subject matter and the format were both revolutionary. It was an experimental course. There were 1,200 students. Participation in guerrilla theater actions transformed my view of the classroom. Since courtrooms, the streets, the Broadway theaters themselves offered a stage, why not a classroom? English 226 was an event, a spectacle. I wanted to break down the barriers between the classroom and the world. We didn't leave the classroom, and we didn't literally tear down the walls. Instead we brought the world into the class. People from the community spoke to the students, and we also created a community in the classroom—a small town of 1,200. I wanted to have an impact on the whole university, and I knew that 1,200 students would quickly transmit their experience to the rest of the university. There were no requirements in English 226. Everyone who enrolled was automatically given a B. If the student did exemplary creative work he or she received an A. Attendance, exams, and papers were not required.

My experience at Stony Brook had taught me that students would do anything for a grade—they would go to bed with their professor, they would even tell me they were Marxists. My students were cynical about grades. They felt that grades didn't reflect ability or intelligence, that grading systems were arbitrary. In the sciences teachers failed a percentage of students each year to keep down the number of pre-med students, to restrict the flow of students to medical schools—at a time when we needed more doctors. Grading was the key to power. Since teachers gave grades they could determine a student's future life and career. When I gave 800 A's and 400 B's the grading system of the university was disrupted. The grade-point average of the school rose, and the administration felt that the standards of the university were being undermined.

I wanted to end competition and individualism. I didn't want students to feel the enemy was the student sitting in the next seat. In 1967-68 I found that competition was so fierce that students cheated, paid graduate students to write papers, or handed in papers written years before by older friends who had graduated. Punishing students who cheated or plagiarized didn't prevent cheating or plagiarizing. Students knew that most professors plagiarized their lectures from books by other scholars. A professor in the psychology department gave A's to the women he slept with. Under these circumstances students didn't respect their teachers. But they behaved, because the grading system was like a loaded gun pointed in their direction. If they protested the grade could go off and they'd be injured. I encouraged students to cooperate, to share and not hoard their knowledge, and there was often a genuine sense of a family in English 226.

The class was divided into groups, or collectives. In most classes students avoided disagreements. I wanted debate and argument to be the core of this class. I wanted people to articulate their feelings rather than conceal them. The radical white students, the black students, the feminists, formed groups and

188

presented their collective projects to the class: mobiles, posters, poetry, rock. People cooked food; at the start of each class we ate together. Then the fights began. When a member of the group spoke, he or she articulated a collective rather than an individual view. Candidates for student council debated one another about local, national and international issues. Students organizing anti-war rallies, rallies for the Panthers, or poetry or rock festivals came to class to talk about their projects.

The main problem with the class was that a large chunk of the students were passive spectators; they sat and silently watched the blacks, the feminists, the professor perform. I tried to break down the distinction between me and the students: I slept in the dorms, ate, smoked dope, went to the movies, and to rock concerts with students. I flaunted my friendship with students before the colleagues who had rejected me, and they resented my popularity. Some students also thought that I was crazy, that I ought to be called Professor Raskin, and not Jomo. They were annoyed that I lived in the dorms and smoked dope. Because I didn't act like the other professors they were unsure how to relate to me.

By the end of my fourth year I was the hippie, radical professor. I became a stereotype on campus. I had an initial impact. People discussed the class, the approach to education, tried experimental projects, and found that a lot of creative energy was released. But English 226 was treated as a one-man show. Most students thought that I'd be fired for teaching the course and that this was my parting shot. Being the Yippie professor was complex. Students expected me to offer more audacious, more shocking performances with each class. And to have one Yippie class in the midst of the university was unreal. Students went from my classroom to a chemistry exam, or from a formal lecture on European history to English 226 and the shift was often disturbing, confusing. English 226 was a Utopian experiment.

Some students liked my class because it was anti-authoritarian. Others registered for English 226 because they received an automatic B and because they were entertained. "Let's check out Jomo today and see what gig he's doing," I heard a student say. The class encouraged their rebelliousness, but often they were rebellious only within the legitimate confines of my class and not elsewhere. It provided a place within the university for students

189

who would normally have dropped out. I talked about my drug experiences, my marriage, the 1950's, my parents, Columbia, Algiers, and students found it fascinating. "But is it education?" one student asked. I also became a teacher/moralist. I demanded that students live differently because they had the experience of reading a Kurt Vonnegut or a Doris Lessing novel. I wanted immediate change. When it didn't occur I was disappointed.

Most faculty members regarded the class as an attempt to undermine the university. They saw it as pure anarchy, and they were petrified by it. They claimed they accepted the reading list—the books by George Jackson, Eldridge Cleaver, Gary Snyder, Abbie Hoffman, Marge Piercy—but privately they sneered at this literature. In 1968-69 they had attacked the content of my courses. By 1970-71 they knew they had to attack the form, the style. They had to declare that I was a nonteacher, involved in noneducational work. The rule that each professor could till his own soil no longer applied. They were so threatened by the community of 1,200, the commune which met on Tuesdays and Thursdays for seventy-five minutes, that they allowed only thirty-five students to enroll in my classes for the 1971-72 semester. There was a sit-in in the chairman's office, letters of protest, a petition, but he wouldn't change his mind. I didn't appeal to the president of the university because I thought that if I behaved myself, if I wasn't openly antagonistic, the department might give me tenure. But I didn't go backwards either. In 1971-72 students planned the courses with me, and they evaluated and graded their own work. I no longer submitted grades to the registrar. It was too late to start behaving.

After the Attica rebellion I designed a black and white poster and tacked it to the door of my office. It said:

Sam Melville

Killed Attica

September 13, 1971

Soon I received letters of protest from faculty members who said that I was once again egotistical. The simple statement of Sam Melville's death aroused their anger. It was rhetorical and bombastic to them. If I said hello they thought I was assaulting them.

I found that my colleagues would sign almost anything. They wrote a letter to Mayor Lindsay after I was beaten in the 17th precinct calling for an investigation. It was a decent act. But

190

teachers would do nothing to disrupt their teaching and research schedules. They'd sign a petition demanding U.S. withdrawal from Cambodia, but they didn't encourage students to demonstrate, and they felt that they had done enough by *saying* they wanted peace.

Many of them were afraid that they would lose their jobs. They saw the new repression coming, and they anticipated it. To express their loyalty and trustworthiness they began to purge radicals from the department. From 1968 to 1972 many teachers were forced to leave because of the blatant hostility toward them or because they were fired or denied tenure. At the same time new radicals were hired at the bottom of the ladder so that it didn't look like an official policy of repression.

I hoped that my book, *The Mythology of Imperialism*, published by Random House in 1971, would strengthen my chances of getting tenure. In the winter of 1968-69 I finished the first part of the book, but by the summer I decided to discontinue the work. It seemed irrelevant to write a book about British writers when there were demonstrations to organize, leaflets to write, friends in jail and on trial. It wasn't until the winter of 1969-70, when I was recovering from the beating in the 17th precinct, that I decided to take up the work again. I reviewed my life and realized that literature was important to me. Maxwell Geismar, one of the editors of *Ramparts,* author of *Henry James and the Jacobites,* encouraged me to write the book, and because he thought that it was important I gave it serious thought. With nothing else to do but recuperate, read and write, I returned to Joseph Conrad, to *Heart of Darkness, Lord Jim, The Secret Agent, Under Western Eyes, Nostromo.* Conrad, the exile, the Pole living in England, had at least two warring selves. He was torn by the contradictions in his experience, and from them he forged his art. He was a fascinating figure to me. I could see some of my own conflicts reflected in his life and art. Then in the spring of 1970 I read widely in E. M. Forster, D. H. Lawrence, and Joyce Cary, and when I wasn't demonstrating or organizing a demonstration I wrote the last part of the book. In Algiers I finished it. *The Mythology of Imperialism* offers a view of Conrad, Kipling, Lawrence, Forster, Cary, and Eliot as seen through the eyes of an American radical living the crisis of the late 1960's. I thought that by looking at five British authors living in a disintegrating empire we could learn about the collapse of imperial America. Shortly after the book was published it was attacked as "Maoist literary criticism" in *The New York Times* and *The New York Review of Books.*

In the first chapter, "Bombard the Critics" (a pun on Mao Tse-tung's big character poster in the Cultural Revolution, "Bombard the Headquarters") I stated that there were "wanted posters" for T. S. Eliot, E. M. Forster, F. R. Leavis, and Lionel Trilling. They were establishment critics who preached the necessity of order, myth, stability, a conservative tradition. What we need, I said, is to emphasize revolution, antagonism, transformation, synthesis, the process of conflict and change. The "wanted posters" image was both humorous and deadly serious. The FBI had issued wanted posters for Eldridge Cleaver, Jane Alpert, Mark Rudd. I didn't think that they were the enemy. I didn't want them apprehended. But I did want students to see that Trilling and Eliot were guilty of creating a conservative, anti-Communist, and often racist literary perspective. Trilling had been against the student rebellion at Columbia. He denied the existence of black culture and scorned Langston Hughes, a "neighborhood writer," and one of our best poets and short story writers. Trilling was opposed to a gay lounge at Columbia because he thought that repressed homosexuals were more neurotic and therefore more creative than gay people who were open about their sexuality.

A few days before the tenure meeting Alfred Kazin walked into my office and asked, "Is there really a wanted poster for Lionel Trilling?"

"No, it's a joke." Kazin and I had talked on and off for five years. He had been a radical in the 1930's, had written autobiographical reminiscences about his early years in New York, and he wrote extensively about the American novel. His son had been in SDS; Kazin scorned the new left. He had read the manuscript version of *The Mythology of Imperialism* and told me I was a "Bolshevik Leavis." Whenever I spoke of the war in Vietnam, Kazin talked about Israel and the fate of the Jews. Whenever I talked about racism in the United States, he turned the topic of conversation to the Soviet Union and Stalin. He continually criticized the new left because in his view it had created no culture, unlike the left in the 1930's. When I suggested that George Jackson was a fine writer he called him "a professional black man."

"You're acting like a little Beria," Kazin said. "By issuing a wanted poster you're inviting cultural terrorism. I'd rather be with Trilling in a Siberian prison camp than with you in the Kremlin. You're a Stalinist." He walked out of my office.

That was my Stony Brook life. What would the department decide? I sat and waited, wrote a few letters. Gerry Nelson, an associate professor, author of *Ten Versions of America*, a friend, walked into my office and sat down.

"It's over," he said.

"And?"

"It's negative. You didn't get it."

"Why? What happened?"

"You called him Irving."

"Was that the reason?" I asked Gerry. In a review of Irving Howe's book, *Decline of the New*, published in *Scanlan's*, I had referred to Professor Howe, the editor of *Dissent*, a professor at Hunter College, as "Irving."

"Jomo, your colleagues were shocked that you called the great professor by his first name," Gerry Nelson said. "I tried. They hated English 226. They thought that you were trying to destroy the university."

"Maybe I was. At least this one."

"They should have given it to you. You wrote a good book, the students like you. They're just threatened by you."

"You did everything you could Gerry." I looked down the corridor. I saw my friends (eleven professors voted for me) walking with the professors who were opposed to giving me tenure. They shook hands, talked quietly. They had not agreed about my specific case, but now they had to continue living and working with each other day after day in the same department. I felt as if I had been the topic at a debating match, and now that the match was over I was forgotten and the two teams praised each other for their arguments. It was all the game of English Department politics. The leader of the faction who was opposed to giving me tenure explained, "I didn't think you wanted tenure. After all you're a radical and tenure is a conservative thing."

"Let me decide that," I said.

A month after the meeting I issued a manifesto I had written as the minister of education of the Youth International Party. The manifesto was based on my Stony Brook experience.

Yippie Manifesto on Education

1. American education is a shuck. Students should be cultural revolutionaries. Disrupt classes; don't sit and behave. Challenge your professors; resist brainwashing.

2. Call your professor by his or her first name. Try treating him or her like a human being and maybe he'll stop treating you like an animal. Students should have the power to decide who gets and who doesn't get tenure.

3. We are a people. We gather together at rock concerts, smoke-ins, demonstrations, on communes. We must gather together as a people in the classroom to break the alienation and isolation of University life.

4. Grades are repressive. They sustain the death culture. They determine who succeeds and who fails. They encourage individualism, egotism, and competition. Abolish grades. No exams. Moratorium on term papers. Be creative.

5. Resist the Death Culture in Education. Build the Life Culture. Schools are for the people, not for the tenured professors, for joy not for despair. Liberate the universities.

Like all Yippie documents it was both satirical and serious. John P. Roche, President LBJ's cultural advisor in the mid-1960's, saw none of the humor or the satire. In his syndicated nationwide column he called English 226 a "sandbox" and asserted that it was right that I didn't get tenure because I was destroying the fabric of American education. He was terrified by the idea that students would call him by his first name.

I also issued a wanted poster for Lionel Trilling. I identified my old professor as a "cultural imperialist," "a literary cricket," a member of the *"Partisan Review* mob." His crime was "brainwashing." There were two photographs, fingerprints, and his signature. It looked like an official FBI poster. I sent it to college English departments around the country.

By 1970 I had found that it was difficult to teach and be politically active. In the classroom I wanted to be in the street, in court, on a commune, and my life on the street and in communes made me suspect for the classroom in the eyes of my colleagues. In 1971-72 I tried to be respectable. I wanted tenure, but my idea of respectability wasn't their idea of respectability. And in 1972 my idea of respectability wasn't what it had been in 1967.

Gerry Nelson and I walked down the corridor of the English Department. Except for the secretary everyone had gone home. Office doors were locked. The janitor was sweeping the floor. I felt that the university was still what we had said it was in the 1960's—alienating and dehumanizing. I no longer thought of myself as an intellectual, an academic, a professor, and I didn't think that I had *failed* because I didn't have tenure. In 1968, before the Columbia rebellion, I would have felt crushed if I had been denied tenure, because I identified myself with the university and the life of the professor.

I remembered a conversation I had at Flint with a Weatherman a few months before he became a fugitive. In some ways it was out of keeping with the overall tone of the meeting, but it reflected a deep, genuine feeling.

"If you can teach and not let them control you," he said, "then you're liberated inside the system. You don't have to drop out." At the end I didn't think of myself as Professor Raskin, but as Jonah. In 1968 leaving would have been painful. But in 1972 leaving felt like liberation. It was good to be going. I took a handful of books from the shelf, a few pencils, and a pad of yellow paper, and I closed the door and gave the key to the English Department secretary. Gerry put his arm around my shoulder and we walked outside.

"Good riddance to Stony Brook," he said.

I drove to Huntington and stopped off to see my parents. To her friends, my mother jokingly referred to me as "my son the professor." My father had wanted me to get tenure, to continue to teach. He thought that I had a "good job," that I could have a "good political influence" on young people. But my parents weren't angry at me now that I didn't have tenure. They thought that it was a "good change."

"Stony Brook doesn't know a good teacher when they see one," my father said.

"He was too revolutionary," my mother said.

"Listen, he wasn't going to compromise his values," my father said. They talked to each other as if I wasn't in the room.

"How is he going to support himself?" she asked.

"I won't starve," I said, interrupting their dialogue, "Don't worry about me."

"Starve you won't. But how are you going to support us in our old age?" my mother asked. For my father there was nothing more to discuss. He was already at the front door in his coat and hat.

"How about some Chinese food?" he asked. "My treat." The three of us were out the front door in a few seconds, and it seemed as if I had never, ever left home.

CHAPTER
ELEVEN
OUT OF THE WHALE

When I meet people for the first time they usually ask me who I am and what I do. Over the past two years I've told them about this book. Mostly they're shocked and exclaim, "How old are you?" as if to say that one has to be ancient and formidable before one is entitled to write one's autobiography. "What have you done?" others ask aggressively on the assumption that no one my age could have done anything worth writing about. I had encouragement from close friends but there were critics who informed me that sixties radicals like me were equipped to write history or sociology but incapable of writing autobiography because we had no inner life, no emotions or feelings. To me that was like saying we're just cardboard replicas of real men and women, that we don't exist.

This autobiography is a proclamation of our collective existence. Alone I haven't done anything very significant (and I'm not offering false modesty) but together with other people I've helped in a small way to change this country. I haven't written this book to say "look how important *I* am," or "everybody look at me." I don't think that what I've done is unique or peculiar, and I don't think that I'm weird. It seems to me that a lot of people have had experiences very similar to mine. Maybe we didn't recognize one another then and there, but we've been together in the same place at the same time; I hope we'll recognize one another now.

I've written about myself to describe the times we've lived through, to offer a record of growing up in an old left family and becoming a member of the new left family of radicals. And that means including dreams and feelings, descriptions of friends and lovers, as well as important ideas and historical events. This book is a social document, but it's also a personal statement. Some of the incidents I've described here were in the newspapers and on television, but other things were lodged privately inside until I lifted them up and set them down on paper. Writing this book has been for me a "coming out" and a "surfacing." From my own experience I know that you don't have to be gay, a woman, or a fugitive to come "out from under," to come "out of the closets," to surface.

Sometimes, because I'm a white, North American, college-educated, heterosexual male, I've been labeled as, and made to feel like, I'm the enemy. I've learned a lot about my own oppression from black people, women and gay men, but I also know that you don't have to be black, female, or gay to feel the weight of oppression, or simultaneously the joy of liberation. Sure there are white, North American males who are the enemies of the people of the world, but there are also a lot of them who are, and who can be, friends to the peoples of the world. I don't think that any of us will be free until we learn to recognize our true friends and enemies, to understand that none of us will be free until all of us are free, that the chains which fetter the slave fetter me and you, that the slave's escape route will show us the path to our freedom too. One day soon we'll all live outside the whale.

I feel like I've dug down into my secret underground self and brought it to the surface. I've mined my soul. Sometimes it was painful or embarrassing; what I found was ugly or disappointing, and I didn't want to dig too deeply. Still, I'd force myself to go ahead because I decided that if you're writing your autobiography you might as well not repeat any untruths to yourself.

I started to write this book in the winter of 1972 at about the time of my thirtieth birthday. Turning thirty *wasn't* a traumatic event, but it was a catalyst forcing me to gather up and sort out my experiences. I also had a sense that it was the right time for us as a people to look back, to preserve and evaluate the past. In the sixties the future seemed all-important. We worried about tomorrow and didn't think much about yesterday because history looked like a ball and chain, and we wanted to reach the future at the next instant. When I started to write my autobiography I was more and more preoccupied with the past. Some friends who had misgivings about this enterprise were afraid that I was escaping from present dilemmas into a comfortable past, but that wasn't my intention, and I don't think I've recreated a romantic or idyllic past.

The past, as I see it, is neither exotic nor grotesque, but complex and changing. It isn't static but shifts like the times we live in. I hope that by looking at the past we can see the cycles of our lives, the repeated patterns, and can escape from them into something new and different. The denial of our heritage doesn't free us from time but only traps us deeper and deeper in the same place; then we don't go anywhere. That's why it's vital to compare our lives with the lives of our parents and their parents, to watch the dance of the generations, to know how our fathers and mothers were different from, and also the same as us.

We need continuity; we need to be a people who embody our own history. So, I want to harvest the fruit of my grandparents' and my parents' experience, devour it, and make it a part of my own experience. I want to feel the seeds of the thirties, forties, fifties and sixties inside me, coming together into the fiber of the seventies. I want to fuse it and make it into something strange and familiar, bitter and sweet. And I want to do this with you, to make it a communal process.

I've tried to remember and record a lot of things I think I'm not supposed to remember and record. Not that they're psychologically forbidden, but there's a social taboo. We're not supposed to remember historic rebellions or past injustices. In school we were taught that the darkies loved their kind, white masters on the plantations, and that when they were freed they acted like animals driven by instinct and never by reason. Today, we're offered myths about the fifties and sixties, or else we're given a complete whitewash.

For example, early in 1974 there was an informal, unofficial movement reunion on the Dick Cavett show in an ABC-TV studio. Tom Hayden, Abbie Hoffman, Rennie Davis and Jerry Rubin were on stage with Cavett and about a hundred radicals, including myself, were in the audience. It was a funny, dignified, and annoying program; it was taped but broadcast was delayed because ABC's executives found it too controversial and refused to televise it. In question after question, Cavett tried to force Rubin, Hoffman, Hayden and Davis to renounce the decade of rebellion, apologize, admit they were wrong, and present themselves as quiet, middle-aged conformists. But Tom, Rennie, Jerry and Abbie celebrated the antiwar movement, the cultural rebellion of the sixties, called upon people to engage in political activity now, and described the seventies as an upcoming decade of upheaval and rebellion. The studio audience applauded, but it wasn't what Cavett wanted. When we hear the word censorship we tend to think of Russia and Solzhenitsyn. But it happens here too. The television networks present only those edited portions of the past, and the present, that they want us to see. When we want more than that, we've got to fight for it.

I. WHERE ARE THEY NOW?

I'm going to follow a tradition of the nineteenth-century English novelists and tell you what some of my friends and family are doing, bring you up to date, and show you the arc of their lives thus far.

In the fall of 1972 my parents sold most of their possessions, accumulated over thirty-five years, including the house we had lived in since 1945. My father retired from his legal practice—he had started working as a lawyer in Huntington in 1938—and was no longer a prisoner of the law which had delivered him from the poverty of the thirties. Thanksgiving Day was the last time the Raskin family was together. We gathered for a feast in New York because the Rogues Path house was cold and empty and waiting for the new occupants. We were sad, but my brothers and I were proud of our roving parents. My father was now sixty-two, my mother fifty-six, but they were as adventurous as they'd ever been. In the sixties they had been first, out of curiosity, to Russia (they were disappointed), then to Cuba (they were ecstatic), and finally to Chile (they were apprehensive). Now they were vagabonds in America looking for a new home. They bought a VW bus, headed west, camping out in parks and along the road, visiting old friends, and unwinding after years of work, raising a family, keeping a house going. They went south to Mexico, north to Montana, and now they're living in northern California in a new, small house on a plot of land covered with redwood trees, and thick blackberry bushes. They're hard-working, middle-class hippies. They live close to the earth, planting and harvesting their own fruits and vegetables. Sometimes they're lonely for New York, but they're not coming back after starting anew on the West Coast.

My parents had left Manhattan in the late thirties and settled in Huntington, then a small rural town surrounded by potato farms and large tracts of wood and pasture. I have the feeling that

200

moving from the city to the country then wasn't very different from leaving cities for rural areas as young people did at the end of the sixties. When my parents came to Huntington, they didn't drop out—they continued to be Long Island radicals—but they did leave behind them the urban Depression, the trade union movement, and intellectual, radical circles to live in simpler, quieter surroundings. They started a family. Back in the forties they raised chickens, planted a garden, did a lot of their own carpentry. My mother was a natural food fanatic and raised us on wheat germ, molasses, yogurt (there was meat and potatoes too), and never allowed packaged white bread in the house. She started a cooperative nursery for prekindergarten kids—a kind of free school where children weren't strictly regimented and originality and creativity were encouraged. But as my father became a more affluent lawyer, as my parents accumulated more possessions, as we got older, our lives got more complicated. By the mid-fifties Huntington was a small city. My parents stopped raising chickens, neglected their garden, were more removed from the land.

Leaving Huntington and moving to California means going back to their funky roots. My father works with his hands five or six hours a day, enjoying manual labor on the land, after so many deadening years of mental labor in a law office. My mother does a lot of cooking and sewing and still has time for her sculpture and painting. They're at home among the Sonoma County hippies, and they've also met older folks like themselves, including lefties who were booted out of Hollywood twenty years ago because of their radicalism, moved north, and started their own orchards and vineyards. My parents' experience makes me feel that the city-country, country-city phenomenon is, like so many other things, a cyclical process. It goes in waves, it's generational.

Of course, not everyone gets caught up in that cycle. Emma for example, has never lived outside of a city. But in the summer of 1972 she went to China for a month, traveled thousands of miles, visited communes, work brigades, schools, homes, and returned to New York with renewed revolutionary fervor and optimism, as well as Red Army caps, Mao jackets and copies of *The Little Red Book.* A good many of our movement friends viewed the U.S. recognition of China as a sign of the failure of the Chinese revolution, but Emma regarded it as a political triumph for China and a sign of the failure of U.S. imperialism. For

Emma, China was an overwhelming emotional experience. She was profoundly moved by the material development of a once-underdeveloped country and equally moved by the abundance of human kindness, generosity, and "goodness." When I first met her she was defending the Soviet Union along the line. Now she sees the Russians through Chinese eyes and defends China against all critics.

I've learned a lot from her about both Russia and China, but I'm also irritated by her blanket support of whatever country she regards as *the* revolutionary vanguard nation. If one criticizes China she takes it as a sign of one's lack of radical faith and one's need of a sermon. The Chinese revolutionary experience is surely extraordinary. As the Russian Revolution was the critical historical event for my parents' generation, the Chinese Revolution had a decisive impact on most radicals of my generation. We all read Bill Hinton's *Fanshen,* Edgar Snow's *Red Star over China,* Mao's *Little Red Book,* and sometimes we imagined that we were Red Guards bringing a Cultural Revolution to the U.S.A. Most of us, at least at some times, liked to think of ourselves as Maoists of one stripe or another, and China did inspire us at Columbia, Chicago, on communes and in collectives. But we've learned that we have to make our own revolution on American soil, that the Chinese won't make it for us, and while we can learn from them it's dangerous and silly to imitate them.

When Emma came back from China she announced that there were no jails in the entire country. I was skeptical. Another friend, a nurse in her mid-twenties, also traveled to China at about the same time and visited a prison. She described it to me, and we agreed that we'd like to see a China, an America, a world, for that matter, where there are no prisons, but the existence of prisons in China doesn't mean, for me or for my friend who visited them, that China is just like America, that nothing has changed there, that the revolution was betrayed. The intellectuals (like most of my Columbia professors, who make a tidy income teaching courses and writing books about the betrayal of the revolution in Russia, China, Cuba, and Vietnam) don't offer us much help. They taught us the immorality and the unaesthetic nature of revolution, and when she's compared with them, I'll take Emma and her joyful optimism about the revolution most any day. But the fact that the Chinese aren't afraid to show (some) Americans their prisons makes me appreciate them more, because they aren't hiding the limitations of their revolution, and because they're asking for and accepting criticism. The fact that young Americans aren't disillusioned with the Chinese Revolution, or revolution in general, knowing that China isn't a Utopia, makes me feel we're apt to be more thoroughgoing and consistent radicals than the thirties Communists who thought that Russia was a paradise and then, after the trial of the Trotskyites and the Hitler-Stalin pact, did an abrupt aboutface and decided that Russia was *the* modern hell, that therefore all revolutions were obscene. I think that my generation of radicals feels that no matter what happens to the Chinese Revolution there ought to be, and in all likelihood will be, an American Revolution. Since it's a small world we're all connected, but we don't win or lose here because of what happens in Peking.

What of the other old lefties portrayed here? The Gordon twins, after being blacklisted and exiled from academia, are writing now about the history of the trade union movement, black resistance to slavery and Jim Crow, and the nineteenth-century origins of U.S. imperialism. Their work, eclipsed in the fifties and early sixties by the consensus schoolbooks of the liberal anti-Communists, has been resurrected and is widely read. That makes me think that in America radicals often have to be old and long past their prime days of political activity before they're appreciated. And only when they're dead do they stand a chance of becoming heroes.

Peter Gordon is thirty and teaching history at City College, where his father and uncle were fired in 1940. He's published a few books but hasn't yet received tenure, because of his radicalism and also because not many young college teachers are getting tenure these days. The old professors tell them they're lucky to have a job at all. Peter's wife, Stella, works for a television network, studies yoga, and, while she isn't involved with a women's liberation group, is actively involved at home and at work in the cause of women's liberation.

I've lost touch with most of my college friends, but I still see Kurt Thomas and Tony Meyers, who've both come out and are active in the gay liberation movement. They're both still radicals and they write often for left-wing publications. Alan Singer is a psychiatrist and has served his time in the U.S. Army; Steve Raab is a professor, Hal is a successful lawyer, Marsha went back to college for her degree. I haven't seen or heard from Sheila for years and wonder where she is. There are still court charges pending against her in Pittsburgh for her part in a Weatherwomen's demonstration in September 1969. She was arrested but never brought to trial and technically she's a fugitive from the State of Pennsylvania. My brother Adam, after roaming the U.S.A. and Canada, has settled down in San Francisco with a group of friends and gets by working a few days a week. He's one of the last original hippies, having a harder time in these much less prosperous, more cynical days. But he's surviving and trying to live the life of the new Communist man. My brother Dan, after living in the country for two years, has returned to New York with his wife. He gave up working on his Ph.D., for the time being at least, and he has a job outdoors in the open air as a surveyor. The movement brought us close together, and now that we live in the same apartment house we see a lot of one another.

I've been living and working in New York, though I've spent large chunks of time on Cape Cod, in the Catskills, and in New Hampshire. I've been back to England a couple of times. In December 1972 when the U.S. was bombing Hanoi I visited with the North Vietnamese in London and heard a firsthand account of the destruction and their resolve to continue the struggle until peace was achieved, and all U.S. troops had left Vietnam.

I've spent a lot of time thinking about my personal relationships. For a long time I had a series of *ménages à trois,* which were all very different, difficult, and disappointing, and I don't want to try again. For half a year I lived in Midtown Manhattan, near Times Square, with a collective of artists who were all in Sullivanian analysis, but that was too disembodied an existence for me. There were a few brief affairs, some mean and ugly, some tender and gentle, and some short spells of celibacy and isolation. I've participated in several men's liberation groups, have reevaluated my marriage and my relationships with women, and I've been trying to escape the old patterns of sexism, of oppressor and oppressed. It isn't easy, and it takes work, but I've been doing it with other men in a constructive way and we've found that it's worth it. It's liberating to discard the stereotyped male roles.

Now I'm living with Maisie, and the two of us share a small

apartment with another couple. Maisie's in her mid-twenties; she has long red hair and freckles and, probably because she used to be a dancer, is graceful. But she's tough, too. Her family is proper, kind, Bostonian. WASP's. Her mother's ancestors came over on the Mayflower, and until she protested she was listed in the New York and Boston social registers. Maisie's the closest friend I've ever had who's so unlike me in background and experience. That makes me feel that I'm more accepting and less a prisoner of my radical heritage. There isn't a trace of the old left in Maisie, but at Madison and Columbia she became active in the antiwar and women's movements and her anger at injustice and her compassion for the oppressed is as deep as that of anyone who grew up in an old left family.

We don't psychoanalyze each other endlessly, but we take time to talk over problems, share insights, and try to learn and grow together. It's a challenging relationship, deep and solid, and it renews my belief in love and friendship. I haven't gotten a divorce from Sheila; Maisie and I aren't considering marriage, so we'll go on living together as we have been. We're a couple. There's mutual responsibility, but we're also separate individuals with our own lives, and so far that's made for a relationship that hasn't been oppressive for either one of us. There's tension, but not real antagonism, and we've been learning how to resolve conflicts so that neither one is, or feels, he or she is the winner or the loser.

II. *UNIVERSITY REVIEW*

When I left Stony Brook in June 1972 I started to work full time for *University Review*. I had been writing for the paper since the spring of 1971, but I wasn't on the staff and was regarded as an outsider. In those days *UR* was a business enterprise which called itself a collective. But it was a phony collective, a collective only in name. Initially *UR* celebrated rock and film stars and promoted European scholars like Lévi-Strauss and Lucien Goldmann. It wasn't a left-wing or an underground paper like the Berkeley *Tribe* or the *Rat,* because it didn't offer movement news and also because it sold large tracts of space to advertisers. *UR* was a hip capitalist paper sustained by the rock, book and movie industries, but inevitably, because of the times, it reflected the radicalism of students and freaks.

There were two rival camps at *UR:* the radicals and the swinging businessmen. Beginning in the summer of 1971 there were skirmishes and then battles between them. The radicals took the offensive and in the fall of 1971 published the first sustained political pieces in *UR:* an article about the Pentagon Papers, another on George Jackson, and an editorial about Attica. We portrayed Dan Ellsberg as *our* revolutionary hero, a white-collar guerrilla. Publication of the Papers was the agent, we argued, which would spur us on to greater antiwar activity. So far as we were concerned, the handwriting was on the wall: the war would soon end. Publication of the papers was a sign that the whole country was opposed to the war. When loyal men like Ellsberg disaffect and when establishment papers like *The New York Times* challenge the government, you know that the warmakers must be in retreat. And they were. It took another two years to sign a ceasefire agreement, but from the time the Pentagon Papers were published a ceasefire was inevitable.

Looking back now, the period when Ellsberg released the Papers seems extraordinary. Spring came early in 1971. In February the Weather Underground bombed the U.S. Capitol to protest the invasion of Laos. In April radical feminists marched on the Pentagon carrying red, blue, and yellow Viet Cong flags. On April 28th hundreds of thousands of people flooded the streets of Washington, swept round the historic monuments of Jefferson, Washington, and Lincoln, peered through the fence at the White House, and demanded immediate withdrawal. The soldiers themselves, the young, bearded, freaky-looking Viet Nam Veterans, staged Dewey Canyon III in the District of Columbia, denounced the war, enacted their guerrilla theater "search and destroy missions," and tossed away their medals.

Then came Mayday: students and freaks camped in the parks, blocked traffic in the streets, were arrested, detained, released, and then circled the Justice Department to protest Attorney General John Mitchell's illegal round-up. There was no way for ordinary Washingtonians to avoid us, to close their ears and eyes and block out the news of B-52s, napalm, strategic hamlets, tiger cages. We were riding high on a crest of energy, and then we heard Rennie Davis on TV call Mayday a failure. "If the Government doesn't stop the War," Rennie said, "we'll stop the government." I was with a group of Mayday organizers and we were stunned. We admired Rennie's persistent antiwar activity, his organizational ability, but we didn't share his apocalyptic, messianic vision. "Stopping the Government" meant making a revolution, and by the spring of 1971—after the Days of Rage, the townhouse explosion, the splits in the Panther Party—we knew that the revolution wasn't imminent. Ending the war was feasible, but ending the government was an illusion.

Mayday was a success. We sensed it, and then publication of the Pentagon Papers verified that feeling. What happened in Vietnam was decisive, but our demonstrations created an atmosphere which made it possible to publish the Papers. We had ripened time, and Ellsberg and the *Times* seized it.

We were optimistic. Even the Justice Department's nationwide grand jury investigations of Mayday and the Weather Underground didn't daunt us. In New York the Yippies revived their old jokes and scripts and made the grand jury look like a farce. The hearings were closed down, and movement paranoia was held in check.

But the euphoria was soon punctured. I remember sitting around the *UR* office. The paper was ready to go to press with the Pentagon Papers article as a feature, but the issue was soon changed, the cover shelved and our feelings blasted away. The radio was on, and the news broadcaster announced that George Jackson, Soledad Brother, serving a one-year-to-life sentence, and in his tenth year behind bars, was shot and killed by California prison guards. We sat there stunned and in silence.

A few short weeks later, before we had time to recover, we heard that at Attica prison forty-two inmates and guards were slaughtered by Nelson Rockefeller's New York state troopers. Vietnam seemed far away; Ellsberg's triumph receded, and it looked to us as if the edge of racism hadn't been blunted at all but was sharper than ever. We had seen it before—the murder of Southern black students, Harlem, Watts, and Detroit men, women, children, the murders of Malcolm X, Martin Luther King, and Fred Hampton. Genocide was still a shock. At least our capacity to be outraged hadn't been diminished. But that was small consolation. There were meetings, demonstrations, rallies. Radicals who were tired of marching, who complained that demonstrations were obsolete, went into the streets once more.

UR, like the movement as a whole, responded to the massacres. In the September issue there was an article about George Jackson, and on the cover was a photograph of three Attica brothers. The caption read, "Where were we?" The editorial was an angry, self-critical attack on the citizens of Woodstock Nation because they had not camped beside the walls of Attica to demand the Age of Aquarius for prisoners as well as hippies.

The new *UR* was born. It was the first issue that didn't emphasize the chic world of rock. Neither Mick Jagger nor Joe Cocker was on the cover. Vietnam and George Jackson took the place usually devoted to Grand Funk Railroad and European structuralism. But the future of this new paper was in doubt. The publisher and several members of the business staff were apprehensive. The cover photo of the Attica Brothers and the condemnation of Woodstock Nation were "too heavy" they said and "would turn off hippies and advertisers." The radical camp retreated temporarily; the pendulum swung in the other direction, and the business wing was briefly ascendant again. On the cover of the next issue of *UR* was a nineteenth-century photo of the German royal family with the caption "We are advertised by our loving friends." It was the biggest, most profitable issue ever, and far less political than the issue with the Attica Brothers on the cover and Dan Ellsberg and George Jackson on the inside. But there was no going back. It was too late for *UR* to remain an appendage of the rock industry. Our readers and our writers too were tired of glib articles about glamorous singers and musicians. Some people resigned, and the founding editor and publisher began to pull out and relinquish the paper to the new, more radical staff members and writers.

The conflicts about youth culture, the revolution, and hip capitalism which took place, not only at *UR* but in the movement at large, forced me to examine my own ideas. I discovered that I had mixed feelings. In hippie territory I rejected my straight identity, dropped the name Jonah, became a freak, and called myself Jomo. But Jomo is an African, not an idyllic hippie, name, and Jomo is a hippie rebel, Mao Mao/Mau Mau Jomo, the mojo man. I have long hair, a pierced ear, smoke dope, dig Mick Jagger, but I'm not a mellow-yellow drop-out, and I don't dig the Jesus freaks or the Hari Krishna. I look to the East, but not to sacred temples or lofty gurus. I suppose I believe in magic, but I'm not a mystic. My magical amulet is a Vietnamese ring given to me by a representative of the Hanoi government, the ring with a voice, the ring which says, "I am a sphere of peace and friendship. I am a circle of hope. I am more potent than high school, fraternity or marriage rings. I decide the fate of nations, the course of war and peace, life and death. I transcend time, space, power and wealth, I bring Vietnam to America, and I transform you."

When I thought through my ideas, I put them down on paper in an article entitled "Children of Imperialism." I criticized hippies who are enamored of Buddhist rituals and idealize black junkies but know nothing of Ho Chi Minh and aren't saddened or angered by the deaths of the Attica inmates. These children of imperialism are like their parents, the "grown-up" Americans who want to sell *their* culture and moral values to the rest of the world. The young hippies and the old honkies—whatever their considerable differences—are both Americans to poor Asians, Africans, and Latin Americans. Young white people, I argued, ought not to be children of imperialism but hippie rebels in the heart of the empire. Furthermore, we wanted *UR* to be a paper by and for young radicals.

In time we became a family. There was Adam, Louise, Gumbo, Myrna, Minton, Maisie, John, Jim, Jackie, Josh, Debby, Sara. There was Stew Albert, my friend from Algiers and Paris, Berkeley sage and street fighter, a Yippie co-conspirator at the Chicago Conspiracy Trial. Stew was a walking, talking newsreel of the sixties. He'd reminisce for hours about the glorious days of yesteryear on Telegraph Avenue, in Eldridge Cleaver's pad, or in Brooklyn reading Trotsky and lifting weights. In 1973 he moved to the country and lived with Judy Gumbo in a cabin on top of a mountain. There was Robert Friedman, the editor of *Spectator* during the Columbia Insurrection of 1968 and a newspaperman to his bones. All day and most of the night, month after month, he sat at his desk writing, talking on the phone, chuckling to himself. There was Lewis Cole, one of the leaders of the 1968 Columbia Insurrection, an SDS spokesman, and an ideologue. Tall, lanky Lewis was a novelist, taught English at both a community college and inside a jail.

We didn't live together communally, but we worked collectively and shared responsibilities. We had no official statement of principles, but we were self-conscious about our values and our stance. We wanted to be undogmatic and to avoid cliquishness; we wanted to talk to a wide audience rather than speak for a coterie or the cadre, to write clearly and straightforwardly, rather than dazzle or pose as the avant-garde. We were determined to participate in campaigns and causes and didn't want to be sideline journalists. We didn't always succeed; sometimes we failed. But we assumed that failure wasn't inevitable, that we could outsmart or outdistance it.

At first our offices were on Broadway, across the street from Columbia. We looked out the windows at the campus and watched the changing scene. For the first time in five years, Columbia was quiet in the spring of 1973. There were no barricades, no seized buildings, no smell of grass, no sound of the Grateful Dead. The movement was fragmented, the culture copyrighted, the old professors were as entrenched as ever, the old rules and regulations in effect, the atmosphere cynical and despairing. Some of us were sad, others angry. There was a vague sense that history had betrayed the left. The new generation acted less anti-authoritarian and more respectable than the undergraduates of the sixties. The freshman class drank beer, watched topless go-go dancers, talked about Mark Rudd as if he were a mythical figure from the remote past. There were upperclassmen who had returned to college convinced that the revolution was an illusion, that communes could never work, that Utopia was a sick joke. They were headed for law school, marriage and straight jobs.

But the Columbia students of the seventies—though they didn't sit in, march, or drop out—weren't civilized conformists. Students were concerned about Wounded Knee, Watergate, Chile, and sympathetic to radical views.

Furthermore, movement brothers and sisters hadn't sold out. They weren't depraved, decadent, counterrevolutionary. There were a few casualties, and there were some hustlers, salesmen, conservatives, but most of our old new-left friends had ordinary jobs and worked on small, undramatic, but significant, political projects.

In the forties and fifties business tycoons, rats and informers emerged from the ranks of the unsuccessful thirties revolution. But they were the exceptions. Mostly there were radicals like Sam and Millie Raskin, Peter Gordon's parents, Sheila's mother, Emma, Josepha's father. They maintained their honesty, were courageous, unbroken, dignified. So, too, the Fall didn't begin when the sixties turned into the seventies. Freaks weren't corrupted and the family of sixties rebels has, so far, maintained its integrity.

The extended movement family I know and belong to doesn't want to forget or reject the sixties. We want to preserve that which had been a fight to win: our rights, our freedom, our place in history, in the streets of Chicago, in the liberated buildings at Columbia, in the communes of Vermont and Colorado, in Judge Julius Hoffman's and Judge John Murtagh's courtrooms, at Woodstock, Peoples' Park, in the offices of *The Rat,* at Kent State and Isla Vista.

We want to celebrate the peoples' achievements. It wasn't Nixon's secret strategy or Kissinger's diplomacy, but the protests of students, writers, teachers, hippies, radicals, like ourselves, which led to the signing of the Paris Accords. We, not the presidents, senators, advertising executives and news broadcasters, created and are still creating history. The sixties is *our* past, not theirs, and we're proud of it. We're not a lost, damned, corrupt generation. We're the future, we've got hope, discipline, dedication. We're a tribe and a family. We're not cynics, victims or schizophrenics. We don't expect Utopia but we're not disenchanted. We don't anticipate the Millennium or the Apocalypse, but we're not pessimists.

In the late sixties I was embarrassed by and anxious to reject my own intellectual and old left past. The old left of my mother and father emphasized organization, ideology, party, history, economics, work, the factory, unions, class struggle, marriage, and stressed Europe and the Western world, especially the Soviet Union. The new left of my sisters and brothers emphasized action, anarchy, spontaneity, sex, grass, consciousness, the street, the gun, and stressed the Third World (especially Cuba and Vietnam), and race. I wanted to prove to myself and my contemporaries that I wasn't a "red diaper baby" frozen in the petrified forest of the fifties, that I wasn't Professor Raskin, A.B., M.A., Ph.D., the intellectual, the scholar and literary critic. I discarded my tweed suit, my horn-rimmed glasses, my pipe and tobacco pouch, put on dungarees and boots and took to the streets to prove that I was a fighter and a brother to the wretched of the earth. I buried my father's old left history, discarded the fifties and started anew.

Everything seemed melodramatic, surreal, and I didn't think that anyone else before in history had lived or thought as we were living and thinking. Sometimes I literally lost my sense of balance. I leapt into space, crashing through to the other side.

My life looked, not like

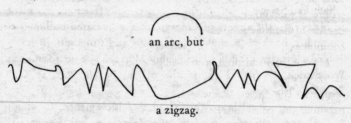

I went from the old left to the new left, from Columbia's liberated buildings to Stony Brook's quiet classrooms, from the Yippie underground to the academic overground, from rebellion to liberal caution, from Black Panthers to white middle-class students, from colonial Algiers and underdeveloped Africa to cosmopolitan Paris and affluent New York, from the prison to the street, from collectivity to loneliness.

But there were times when it did come together. The extremes formed a whole. Writing *The Mythology of Imperialism* and teaching at Stony Brook from 1971 to 1972 I felt that I had synthesized diverse elements. When I did antiwar activity I focused my old left experience with my new left energy. Reporting on the trial of the New York Panther 21, I was a journalist and also a political organizer. And writing my autobiography and working for *UR* is an opportunity to fuse past, present, future, writing, thinking, organizing, mind and body, old and new. Maybe that's too much to hope for, to expect, but I'm not compromising now.

In the sixties we came of age. We expanded, explored, exploded, rebelled, resisted, reformed. And now they want to rob us of *our* sixties, make us adolescents again and substitute old, old lies—individualism, consumerism, alienation, authority. Well, we won't let them; we'll resist, sabotage, and maybe, just maybe, we'll win.

III. THE ROSENBERGS, AGAIN

Not by accident, but by design, the vendetta against the radical sixties coincided with the revival of the apolitical fifties. On the agenda for the counterrevolution was the abolition of today's radicalism and the revival of yesterday's conservatism. So, movies, television, books and records offer us the funny fifties, the decade of double dates, drive-ins, rock 'n' roll, family comedy, soda pop, cheerleaders, high school jocks, the senior prom, going steady. I remember it, and it's certainly very different from the decade of demonstrations, defiance, be-ins, sit-ins, marijuana and communes.

My football uniform, my high school ring, my flat top were very, very real. But I don't want them now. I don't want to return to the fifties. They weren't a gas. To revive fifties cool, paranoia and conformity is madness. It's not the sixties radicals, but the fifties faddists, who are suicidal. Returning to the fifties is retreating into a glacier, back into the Ice Age, and I'm not going.

Most of the radicals of the sixties who joined SDS, called themselves Yippies, marched for peace, supported the Panthers, didn't live through the repressive fifties, didn't come from old left families. They became political in the Kennedy era, turned to resistance under Johnson and rebellion under Nixon. With the decline of the movement they became increasingly interested in their roots, in the history of the American left. At *UR* we looked out the window of our new office at historic Union Square, imagined the days of soap box orators, the Depression, Joe McCarthy, and wondered, "Will the seventies be like the fifties? Does history go in cycles?"

In the summer of 1973 I decided to try to answer those questions. I wanted to excavate the past, but I didn't dig in Union Square. I traveled to Springfield, Massachusetts, to interview Michael and Robby Meeropol, the sons of Ethel and Julius Rosenberg. I hadn't seen Michael for several years. He looked more or less the same: light hair, moustache, glasses, and a playful smile. When I was at the University of Manchester and Michael was at Cambridge, we were close friends. When we returned to the states we kept up our friendship, but then drifted apart. Michael was at Madison, then in Chile, doing research and teaching, with a wife and kids. In 1969 I felt politically distant from him. I was closer to the Yippies and Weatherman, and Michael wanted to form a more traditional third party and go to the polls. I thought that electoral politics was dead-end liberalism. But by the summer of 1973, the year of the Vietnamese ceasefire, Watergate, and the twentieth anniversary of his parents' execution, the differences of 1969 seemed insignificant. Michael and his younger brother Robby had just surfaced, had acknowledged their parents publicly for the first time, and it was front-page news. For the first time in our relationship we talked openly about Julius and Ethel, the execution, growing up in the repressive fifties.

The days we spent together, the writing which sprang from our meeting, made me feel that though Michael Meeropol Rosenberg is unlike anyone else, we share a common historical experience. As Michael talked about himself, his parents, his brother, my own past came into focus. We sat in the back yard. Michael was wearing shorts. His daughter Veronica Ethel and Gregory Julian, an adopted black son, were playing, and the dog was barking. The afternoon sun was warm. Michael took me back.

In the early fifties, before and immediately after Julius and Ethel were executed, Michael defended their innocence. He wanted to free his parents, but he was soon frightened. Teachers and parents of school friends intimidated him. He was a Red, his parents were spies, they said, and they didn't want him to subvert their All-American children. He had shouted and protested, now he would behave. That was in the mid-fifties. I remembered those days too. Michael conformed as I had conformed. He learned, as I learned, to be silent, to adjust. In school Michael defended America, the church, patriotism. He was afraid to be known by the name Rosenberg. He even denied his parents. When he was adopted by the Meeropols—an old left couple who worked in the theater—he thought that he was safe. His new name was a disguise and gave him protection.

But in the sixties it wasn't protection we wanted. Our courses weren't identical, but they were similar. Michael belonged to the Committee for a Sane Nuclear Policy, marched for integration and civil rights, protested the CIA-backed invasion of the Bay of Pigs, opposed the war in Vietnam, supported the Panthers, joined SDS, brought radicalism to the classroom. Our paths crossed, then, and now they've crossed

214

again. The contours of our lives correspond.

Thus, there have been three Jonahs: Jonah the professor, Joe the jock, Jomo the radical. And there were at least three Michaels: Michael the fifties All-American kid, Michael Meeropol the college radical and Marxist intellectual, and Michael Rosenberg the son of radicals executed as atom bomb spies for the Russians. The Rosenberg Michael was hidden deep beneath the surface; before 1973 he revealed his secret identity only to a few friends.

Michael and Robby are extraordinary because Ethel and Julius are their parents. But they are like the sons and the daughters of many other thirties radicals who were investigated, exiled, fired, and jailed. Like Michael and Robby, the children were frightened by McCarthyism and the FBI and conformed, but in the thaw of the sixties they surfaced and rebelled. They joined the movement, the crowd in the streets, looked like freaks and hippies, lived in communes, dropped out. They connected the old left with the new left, they linked the thirties with the sixties.

In the sixties the children of thirties radicals pushed their middle-aged parents into politics again. Maybe the parents were at first unwilling to march or protest again after so many years. But by demanding that their parents demonstrate, the children were applying their parents' own original values. In a true, historical sense they were thanking the old leftists who kept alive the sparks of the thirties in the cold, cold fifties. Despite their differences in life-style, young and old marched side by side. Jonah, Dan and Adam and their father and mother, Josepha and her father, Konstantin Spiegel, Peter Gordon and his parents, Sheila and her mother, Emma—these two generations of radicals were on the same family tree. On the limbs of this tree are Sacco and Vanzetti, Bill Haywood, Mother Bloor, John Reed, Eugene V. Debs, Paul Robeson, Agnes Smedley, W. E. B. Du Bois, Ethel and Julius Rosenberg, the Scottsboro Boys, Fred Hampton, Elizabeth Gurley Flynn, the veterans of the Abraham Lincoln Brigade, CIO organizers, civil rights demonstrators, antiwar protesters. It's a living tree, a tree of liberty; its roots extend deep down in the earth, its branches reach into the sky.

Jonah, the writer of this book, stands in the shade of this tree. Jonah's book is almost ended, but Jonah's life, he hopes, is far from finished. Under the tree Jonah discovers himself, returns to the surface of the earth, and gazes up at the stars. Jonah is Jonah. He isn't *the* professor, *the* jock, Jomo, *the* husband anymore. He's just Jonah, outside the whale, no longer a prisoner or a fugitive. He's neither running nor hiding. He feels at one with himself, with his parents, the past, his peers, and the present. Jonah hasn't become well-adjusted, hasn't compromised or settled for less. He has been tested in the whale, and he knows his strengths and weaknesses. He won't retreat by crawling back into the whale. He knows what it means to be Jonah.

He lives in the city. It's not ancient Nineveh, but like the Biblical city it's violent and corrupt, the Empire State's imperial city. Jonah isn't alone or friendless in the city. It's his home. He's not an outsider or an alien. He doesn't preach doom and destruction, doesn't prophesy the end of the world, but he believes in the slow and steady revolution of everyday life. The city will be reformed, he hopes, and will become a home for lovers, workers, poets, philosophers, fishermen, farmers, wild dogs, and stray cats. And when that day comes this Jonah, unlike old Jonah, won't be alone outside the walls of the city talking to God. He'll be standing in the shade of the tree, the tree of life and liberty, with friends, relations, mothers, children, lovers, brothers on the earth, on this land, that's our own.